T0301495

STUDIES ON ETHNIC GROUPS IN CHINA

Stevan Harrell, Editor

STUDIES ON ETHNIC GROUPS IN CHINA

Cultural Encounters on China's Ethnic Frontiers,
edited by Stevan Harrell

Guest People: Hakka Identity in China and Abroad,
edited by Nicole Constable

Familiar Strangers: A History of Muslims in Northwest China,
by Jonathan N. Lipman

Lessons in Being Chinese:
Minority Education and Ethnic Identity in Southwest China,
by Mette Halskov Hansen

Manchus and Han: Ethnic Relations and Political Power
in Late Qing and Early Republican China, 1861–1928,
by Edward J. M. Rhoads

Ways of Being Ethnic in Southwest China, by Stevan Harrell

Governing China's Multiethnic Frontiers, edited by Morris Rossabi

On the Margins of Tibet: Cultural Survival on the Sino-Tibetan Frontier,
by Åshild Kolås and Monika P. Thowsen

The Art of Ethnography: A Chinese "Miao Album,"
translation by David M. Deal and Laura Hostetler

Doing Business in Rural China: Liangshan's New Ethnic Entrepreneurs,
by Thomas Heberer

Communist Multiculturalism: Ethnic Revival in Southwest China,
by Susan K. McCarthy

Religious Revival in the Tibetan Borderlands:
The Premi of Southwest China, by Koen Wellens

In the Land of the Eastern Queendom:
The Politics of Gender and Ethnicity on the Sino-Tibetan Border,
by Tenzin Jinba

Empire and Identity in Guizhou: Local Resistance to Qing Expansion,
by Jodi L. Weinstein

China's New Socialist Countryside: Modernity Arrives in the Nu River Valley,
by Russell Harwood

CHINA'S NEW SOCIALIST COUNTRYSIDE

CHINA'S NEW SOCIALIST COUNTRYSIDE

MODERNITY ARRIVES IN THE NU RIVER VALLEY

RUSSELL HARWOOD

UNIVERSITY OF WASHINGTON PRESS / SEATTLE AND LONDON

This volume includes, with permission, a revised version of material
from Russell Harwood, "Negotiating Modernity at China's Periphery:
Development and Policy Interventions in Nujiang Prefecture," in Elaine
Jeffreys, ed., *China's Governmentalities: Governing Change, Changing
Government* (London and New York: Routledge, 2009), 63–87.

All photographs are by the author unless otherwise noted.

© 2014 by the University of Washington Press
Printed and bound in the United States of America
Composed in Minion Pro, typeface designed by Robert Slimbach
17   16   15   14   13   5   4   3   2   1

University of Washington Press
PO Box 50096, Seattle, WA 98145, USA
www.washington.edu/uwpress

Library of Congress Cataloging-in-Publication Data
Harwood, Russell.
China's new socialist countryside :
modernity arrives in the Nu River Valley / Russell Harwood.
pages   cm. — (Studies on ethnic groups in China)
Includes bibliographical references and index.
ISBN 978-0-295-99325-6 (hb : alk. paper)
ISBN 978-0-295-99338-6 (pb : alk. paper)
1. Rural development—China—Nujiang Lisuzu Zizhizhou.
2. Rural population—China—Nujiang Lisuzu Zizhizhou.
3. Nujiang Lisuzu Zizhizhou (China)—Social conditions.
4. Nujiang Lisuzu Zizhizhou (China)—Economic conditions.
I. Title.
HN740.N85H37   2013
307.14120951—dc23   2013027329

CONTENTS

FOREWORD

STEVAN HARRELL

Nujiang Prefecture is one of the most remote, most sparsely populated, and least-known parts of China. Until very recently, people of the Lisu, Nu, Drung (Dulong), Tibetan, and other small ethnic groups have lived subsistence livelihoods in its deep valleys between precipitous mountain ranges, practicing farming, herding, and forestry. The prefecture stretches for 400 kilometers along the Nu River, for which it is named, and it takes at least six hours to drive along the main highway from the prefectural capital at Liuku to the seat of the northernmost county at Gongshan. From there to the *really* remote northwestern parts of the prefecture, across the Gaoligong mountains to the Dulong valley, there was not even a road until 1999, requiring the Drung people who live in that valley to make a three-day walk just to reach the county seat. Even now, a vehicle journey takes six hours along a dirt road that is narrow, winding, dangerous, and often icy, even in June. Later in the summer, when drivers no longer have to drive gingerly across ice, they still have to drive through waterfalls.

Why should we care about so small and peripheral a place as Nujiang? China calls itself a developing country, and not for the usual reason that "developing" sounds nicer than "poor." China is no longer poor by any standard, but it continues on a decades-long, erratic, but relentless mission of development. Very important goals of this developmental project are to bring modern prosperity to the whole country, to convert even the remotest regions from subsistence to market-based livelihoods, to urbanize the population while maintaining agricultural output and food security, and to improve the "quality" of its population by giving them education, health care, and opportunities to participate in the modern industrial economy. Nujiang, despite its small size and peripheral position, or maybe *because* of its small size and peripheral position, is the perfect case study.

Way off in the corner, Nujiang was late to China's developmental project, late even by Yunnan standards, but it has not escaped. Since the Chinese regime announced the Big Western Development (also known as "Open Up the West") project in 2000, Nujiang too has been developing. The progress, the paradoxes, the leaps and lurches of the multifaceted developmental process in Nujiang, and particularly in Gongshan County, are the topic of Russell Harwood's provocative account in *China's New Socialist Countryside*. Harwood conducted fieldwork in Gongshan between 2005 and 2007, and here he presents us with an account of development there that is at once comprehensive, sensitive, and relevant to the larger issues of China's development.

China's New Socialist Countryside portrays three aspects of the development process—conservation, education, and migration—and shows how they are all connected by a basic logic of development: the idea that poor, peripheral, or even just ethnic minority regions suffer from lack. They lack income and the amenities of modern life, of course, but the reason for this material lack is a more profound lack of scientific knowledge and the spirit of change and innovation. Because the local people are ignorant of science, they do not know how to manage their environment, so the state must step in and be conservationist, imposing reforestation initiatives, payment for ecosystem services programs, and protected natural areas. Both because they are ignorant of science and because they lack the spirit of innovation, the state must step in and provide education to change their backward attitudes. And because another way to gain the spirit of innovation is to come in contact with those who have it, the state must encourage people to leave the backward periphery and travel to China's urban core, where they not only provide cheap labor for factories and construction projects, but, more importantly, learn how to be modern.

By juxtaposing these three wings of the developmental process, Harwood shows us not only how coherent China's overall development project really is, but also how consistent the project is with another project with which Studies on Ethnic Groups in China has been concerned—the project of building a coherent nation out of a multitude of ethnic and cultural groups. Ethnic minorities have to be trained and formed into citizens not only of a united nation, but also of a modern country. It all makes sense, but it raises a larger question: Can China really be multiethnic and modern at the same time? It is certainly possible in theory, since China grants all sorts of cultural and linguistic rights to its ethnic minorities and explicitly rejects "great Han chauvinism" as a basis for development or national unity. At the same time, the economic and educational logic of the programs set out in this book suggests otherwise. The pull of getting off the farm, getting into schools, and going out to factories and construction sites is the pull toward a modernity that seems to have very little room for ethnic variation—the Lisu, Nu, and Drung are told that their ways of managing the biophysical environment are backward and destructive; they are told that the only knowledge worth knowing is the universal knowledge of science and nationalism that they learn in their schools; and even their languages become useless when they are working in Guangdong.

What will happen to the multiethnic population of Nujiang Prefecture and its local livelihoods in the next decade or two is impossible to predict. But by drawing a portrait of the developmental projects of the first decade of the twenty-first century, Russell Harwood has given us much to ponder in the present, as well as a baseline for future research. We are proud to add *China's New Socialist Countryside* to the Studies on Ethnic Groups in China series.

SEATTLE, APRIL 2013

ACKNOWLEDGMENTS

I would first like to thank my family for their enormous support and inspiration. I am particularly grateful to my mother, Susan Harwood, for encouraging me to pursue an advanced academic degree and for her sage words of advice, guidance, and feedback. I would like to thank my father, Errol Harwood, for his generous support and motivation, particularly during my studies. Thanks also to Robyn Daniels for her generosity and guidance. My heartfelt thanks to Kate Harwood, Bruce McGurk, Mia McGurk, Jake McGurk, Jan Harwood, Robert Harwood, and Zhang Xiaomiao. This book is in part dedicated to my late Nana, Betty Mettam.

I also dedicate this book to Geoffrey Davis, my Chinese language teacher at Mount Lawley Senior High School. I am enormously grateful to Geoff, who first sparked my interest in China and China studies. In many respects, the book is a testament to the importance of exposing students at all stages of the education system to the Chinese language, China studies, and Asian studies and languages in general, as well as to the importance of cultivating and supporting educators with skills in these areas. Geoff has the gift of making a subject matter both relevant and interesting to his students. It is because of his enthusiasm and dedication that I ultimately pursued my engagement with China studies. I am also sincerely thankful to Anita Chong at Mount Lawley, who organized our class visit to China in 1993, which firmly cemented my interest in China, for her teaching during my senior high school years. In a period when Australia is looking at ways to strengthen its relationship with China, we should look to the critical, but at times forgotten, role that teachers such as Geoff and Anita have played in building people-to-people linkages with China for more than thirty years. Like most teachers, Geoff and Anita are not driven by fame, vanity, or profit; they are simply dedicated to and passionate about the teaching of the Chinese language and China studies and about engendering that same dedication and passion among their students.

I feel greatly indebted to Gary Sigley, who first took me on as a postgraduate student in 2002 and suggested I focus on the Nu River Valley for my research. While there were certainly times during my fieldwork that I pondered whether a research project in the urban comforts of Shanghai or Beijing might have been a wiser option than working in one of China's most isolated rural communities, I thank Gary for his belief in me and for pushing me to pursue this ultimately highly rewarding research topic. It was an important lesson that the path of greatest resistance, though painful at times, can also lead to the most fulfilling outcomes and life experiences.

Thanks also to Lynette Parker for her practical advice and guidance. I owe a huge thanks to Elaine Jeffreys, who has been a generous mentor and great friend over the years. I am particularly grateful for Elaine's advice on managing the publication process.

I thank my close friends Doug Smith, one of the unsung heroes of Australia's Asian studies community, for his astute advice and observations; Aaron Hales, for helping to keep me sane and in good humor; and Mark Pinoli, for always seeming to know the right thing to say at the right time. I am deeply appreciative of Robert and Myrna Tonkinson's friendship, support, and wise words of advice.

Andreas (Andy) Wilkes's guidance and support greatly enhanced this research project. Andy provided very generous feedback and always responded to my numerous questions and emails with constructive and detailed advice. I have drawn heavily upon Andy's excellent and extensive research on northwestern Yunnan, which you can find listed in the bibliography.

I am greatly indebted to Stevan Harrell for his mentorship and extensive and very helpful feedback on my book manuscript. Steve's own work sets an extremely high standard, and it has been a huge honor to work with and learn from one of the leading scholars in the field. I am very grateful for his belief in me and his support for this book project. To that end, I must also acknowledge the Worldwide Universities Network, which funded my attendance at the 2009 China in the World postgraduate workshop at the University of Oslo. This conference afforded me the opportunity to meet Steve and to discuss my research with him.

A very big thank you to Lorri Hagman, executive editor at University of Washington Press, for her advocacy, for driving this project to publication, and for her generous editorial advice. Thank you also to Tim Zimmermann, Jacqueline Volin, Rachael Levay, David Peattie at BookMatters, and Laura Harger for their meticulous assistance with copy editing, design, and marketing.

Thank you to my academic reviewers, Colin Mackerras, David S. G. Goodman, and Lisa Hoffman, and to two anonymous reviewers of the book manuscript for the University of Washington Press. Their scrutiny and insights have added significant rigor to the book's analysis and arguments.

I would also like to acknowledge the support of the Rotary Club of Matilda Bay, particularly Annie Wearne, Rob Ockerby, Bob Dunn, and Jaap Poll. While not directly linked to this book project, the Rotary Club of Matilda Bay provided financial support for the Safe Path project, discussed in this book's conclusion. Aside from making a tangible contribution to livelihoods in Gongshan, the project also provided me with unintended but extremely useful insights into the machinations of local government and government-community relations in contemporary rural China. My presentations on Gongshan and the path project always elicited stimulating questions and discussion among the club's members that greatly enriched my research experience. Similarly, I acknowledge the generous support of the Jack Family Charitable Trust, Patti Chong, Jen Wheeler, and the Western Australian community for supporting the university scholarship program. These community projects were made possible through the administrative support of the Confucius Institute at the University of Western Australia (UWA).

I would also like to thank the following people: Kath and Ron Mercer, Diao Qigang, He Hongguang, Huang Yingying, Chris Gill, Ivan Roberts, Cecilia Leong-Salobir, Jiang Na, Tamara Jacka, Eva Chye, Judith Berman, Jane Hardy, Craig Mouncey, the staff in the Discipline of Asian Studies at

UWA, Li Jia, Wang Liyong, Zhou Yan, Mao Hongqi, Johanna Hood, and Per Henningsgaard.

Finally, I would like to thank the people of Gongshan for welcoming me into their community and for their generosity, time, and patience. During interviews with local farmers, I was often asked why I was asking questions about their livelihoods and household economies and how my research would affect and/or benefit them. I found these very legitimate questions uncomfortable. It not only made me consider how I would react if a stranger came into my household and began asking questions about my occupation and livelihood; it also made me appreciate that my research was in many ways highly self-indulgent. My research would contribute to academic discourse but was very unlikely to make a tangible contribution to Gongshan society. The path and scholarship projects I discuss in the conclusion were two of the ways that I sought to give something back to a community that has given so much to me. However, I also hope that this book provides a useful and balanced perspective on the challenges and often contradictory demands confronting communities in China's Nu River Valley as they continue to negotiate the rapid and fundamental transformation of their way of life.

My research was made possible by an Australian Postgraduate Award and academic mentorship through the Discipline of Asian Studies at UWA, a UWA Graduate Research School Student Travel Award, a UWA Dean of Faculty of Arts Postgraduate Travel Award, funding provided by UWA's School of Social and Cultural Studies, and a one-month Australia-China Council Residency in Beijing in 2005. Between 2005 and 2006, I undertook a year of further intensive Chinese-language study at Zhejiang University in Hangzhou under a Chinese government scholarship that greatly enhanced my fieldwork and engagement with Chinese language-based texts.

All opinions and views presented in this book are mine alone. I take responsibility for any errors and omissions.

EQUIVALENTS AND ABBREVIATIONS

EQUIVALENTS

1 *jin* = 0.5 kilograms

1 *mu* = 0.0667 hectares, 0.1647 acres, or 666.67 square meters

¥1 Chinese = approximately US$0.125. The equivalent of Chinese yuan to the U.S. dollar reflects a historical average. In recent years, the yuan has appreciated against the dollar. At the time of writing, ¥1 was equivalent to US$0.16.

ABBREVIATIONS

CBIK	Center for Biodiversity and Indigenous Knowledge
CCP	Chinese Communist Party
CCTV	China Central Television
GDP	Gross domestic product
GEB	Gongshan Education Bureau
IUCN	International Union for Conservation of Nature
NFPP	Natural Forest Protection Program
NGO	Nongovernmental organization
NPC	National People's Congress

NTFP   Nontimber forest product(s)
PRC   People's Republic of China
SLCP   Sloping Land Conversion Program
UNEP   United Nations Environment Programme
UNESCO   United Nations Educational, Scientific and Cultural
          Organization
UWA   University of Western Australia
WCMC   World Conservation Monitoring Centre

CHINA'S NEW SOCIALIST COUNTRYSIDE

INTRODUCTION

The road was not just a facility for going and returning; it was also an opportunity to compare conditions and modes of life. It affected the peasants who set out on it, getting them used to strange places, showing them the way, permitting alien notions and a sense of different prospects to germinate in them or in those listening to the tales they told.

—Weber 2007 [1976]: 282

To be modern is to find ourselves in an environment that promises us adventure, power, joy, growth, transformation of ourselves and the world—and, at the same time, that threatens to destroy everything we have, everything we know, everything we are. Modern environments and experiences cut across all boundaries of geography and ethnicity, of class and nationality, of religion and ideology: in this sense, modernity can be said to unite all mankind. But it is a paradoxical unity, a unity of disunity: it pours us all into a maelstrom of perpetual disintegration and renewal, of struggle and contradiction, of ambiguity and anguish.

—Berman 1982: 15

Before 1999, to travel from Gongshan County's poorest and most isolated township of Dulongjiang to the Gongshan county town required an arduous three-day trek along a narrow mountain trail. Today one can travel between these two places by vehicle, following the completion of a ninety-six-kilometer road (see fig. I.1). Situated in a particularly rugged pocket of southwestern China, the new road passes through lush old-growth forests and several climatic zones as it cuts its way through the formidable

FIG. 1.1. Since its completion in September 1999, the Dulongjiang Road has provided vehicle access into and out of one of China's poorest and most isolated
townships (July 2005).

Gaoligong mountain range. While transport into and out of Dulongjiang
has improved dramatically, the journey remains highly treacherous. The
road is frequently cut by wide bodies of rapidly moving water, and landslides are common. Even during summer, some sections remain covered
in snow and ice (see fig. 1.2, in the first chapter). Using a four-wheel-drive
vehicle, it still takes more than six hours to cover the relatively short distance between Dulongjiang and the county town. It is impassable during
the winter months.

Dulongjiang is home to the Dulong (or Drung)—one of China's smallest officially recognized ethnic minority groups—and the road is a stark
symbol of the Chinese Communist Party's (CCP's) ongoing strategy to
socially engineer them and other ethnic minorities into the Chinese
Party-state and industrial economy.[1] The road is not just a conduit for
the transport of goods and services into and out of a remote township.
It also will increasingly channel Dulongjiang's cheap surplus rural labor
toward the coastal-based factories and construction sites that fuel China's
economic development.

The Dulong, along with people from the Lisu, Nu, and Tibetan ethnic minority groups, compose the majority of the population of the Gongshan Dulong and Nu Nationalities Autonomous County (Gongshan Dulongzu Nuzu Zizhixian; hereafter Gongshan). Until very recently, they lived as subsistence farmers, relying on shifting cultivation, hunting, the collection of wild vegetables and medicinal plants, and small-scale logging to sustain their household economies. Gongshan itself is particularly remote, and transport both within and out of the county was once difficult. Across the county's five townships, participation in outward migration for work as well as local off-farm work was extremely limited in the past. However, with new roads such as this one in place, ethnic minority farmers from Gongshan's outlying villages can now participate in labor export programs to China's coastal regions.

One mode of labor export involves local rural governments coordinating with urban-based employers to temporarily transfer teams of surplus rural workers to low-paid urban work assignments, and in September 2008, in what appears to be the first reported case of labor export from Dulongjiang, nineteen local farmers participated in a formal labor export program to Dongguan City, Guangdong (Nujiang Prefecture Labor and Social Guarantee Bureau 2008). Dongguan is one of China's largest centers for manufacturing and has become a prime destination for rural migrants seeking better work and income opportunities during the reform era (1978–present).[2] These migrants generally take up low-skilled production-line work in highly regimented factory environments. Although factory life is in complete contrast to the agricultural livelihood normally experienced by Dulongjiang's subsistence farmers, it offers much higher income than life on the farm.

With that in mind, the new road also can be said to symbolize Gongshan's engagement with modernity. The road has contributed to the collapse of the spatial and temporal boundaries between what was once an isolated rural community and China's modern industrializing economy. With new infrastructure such as this in place, economic and social forces once peripheral to Gongshan are increasingly penetrating and shaping local society (see Giddens 1990: 18–19).

However, the experience of modernity can also be treacherous and dislocating. As on the road journey being made by the farmers in the truck pictured in fig. I.1, there will be many obstacles along the way, and unforeseen challenges lurk around the bend. For example, new outward migration for work opportunities will provide many Gongshan farmers with a more secure financial future. For others, the migration experience may prove traumatic. For all of them, the experience will fundamentally transform their way of life.

This book examines how people living in a rural county at the periphery of China's largely unindustrialized western regions are negotiating the large-scale social and economic transformations associated with recent economic development. It demonstrates that, contrary to expectations that ethnic minority communities in China's western mountainous regions will remain isolated and be left behind, these communities will be increasingly drawn into the industrial economy and dependent on the state.

The examination focuses on Gongshan County. Gongshan is located in northwestern Yunnan, in southwestern China, and is one of four counties that constitute the Nujiang Lisu Nationality Autonomous Prefecture (Nujiang Lisuzu Zizhizhou; hereafter Nujiang) (see maps 1 and 2).[3] Until recently, Gongshan was relatively cut off from the national economy. However, since the late 1990s, economic development has transformed Gongshan's social fabric. This book explores how the implementation and strict enforcement of nine-year compulsory education (*puji jiunian yiwu jiaoyu*), the implementation of environmental conservation programs, the promotion of outward migration for work, and the expansion of social and economic infrastructure have contributed to the marginalization of traditional agricultural livelihoods and the community's closer integration with the national economy and the Chinese Party-state.

Contradictions and tensions underlie modernization in rural China. As a case study, Gongshan demonstrates that whereas rural modernization is associated with the expansion of economic infrastructure, improved access to public services such as education, and the opportunity for members of the rural population to exercise greater autonomy over their livelihoods, it also signals growing entrenchment within the development agendas of China's central government and the expanding market economy. A key objective of the central government's development agendas is the transformation of "low-quality" (*di suzhi*), "unproductive" subsistence farmers into "high-quality" (*gao suzhi*), "productive" industrial workers who can contribute to economic growth and stability. These development agendas reach deeply into contemporary rural society, where

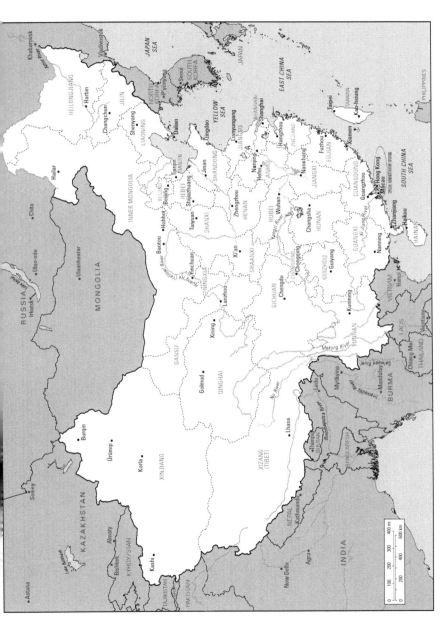

MAP 1. Political geography of the People's Republic of China.

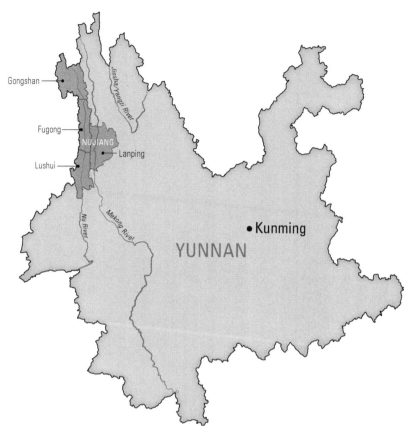

MAP 2. Nujiang Prefecture is located in northwestern Yunnan and is composed
of four counties: Fugong, Gongshan, Lanping, and Lushui.

even the poorest and most geographically isolated rural communities are
entangled in an increasingly dense web of governmental interventions
that are transforming traditional ways of life.

LIFE AT THE PERIPHERY

Gongshan sits at the northern end of the Nu River (Nujiang) gorge—one
of the world's deepest river gorges—and is extremely mountainous.[4] It is
officially recognized as a "poor mountain area county" (*pinkun shanqu
xian*) (Gao 2003: 4), and in 2008 nearly 65 percent of the population, or

23,251 people, were living below the national poverty line of ¥1,067 per year (China Nujiang Gorge Network 2011). Gongshan's 2008 average rural per capita cash income of ¥1,064 (ibid.) was less than one-quarter of the 2008 national average per capita annual net income of rural households (¥4,760.62), and was close to one-fifteenth of the 2008 national average per capita annual disposable income of urban households (¥15,780.76) (National Bureau of Statistics of China Online 2009: sections 9–22, 9–15).

While Gongshan's isolation and extreme mountainous terrain are major barriers to economic development, these conditions have enabled large numbers of plant and animal species to thrive, and today much of Gongshan is included within a biodiversity protection zone known as the Gaoligongshan Nature Reserve.

Gongshan's relatively small population is characterized by a high degree of ethnic diversity. According to official statistics, in 2008, Gongshan's population was 36,075, of whom around 96.5 percent were members of ethnic minority groups (China Nujiang Gorge Network 2011). The Lisu make up more than 50 percent of the county's population, followed by the Nu, 18 percent; the Dulong, 16 percent; the Tibetans, around 5 percent; and the Bai and Naxi, each around 2 percent (Gongshan Government Office/ Gongshan Bureau of Statistics 2005: 3). Illiteracy is pervasive among the ethnic minority adult population, and many are unable to speak standard Chinese (Mandarin, the official language of the People's Republic of China). Officially, around 83 percent of the Gongshan population is engaged in agriculture (China Nujiang Gorge Network 2011).

Gongshan's farmers cultivate some of China's most marginal rural land. Population expansion in the time since China's Liberation by the CCP in 1949 has placed a great deal of pressure on this land. The scarcity of flat arable land means that most households cultivate steeply sloping agricultural land at high altitudes (see fig. 1.4, in chapter 1). There are also few readily exploitable natural resources, and there is limited scope for industry. The majority of households are highly dependent on government subsidies. Agricultural yields are very low, and Gongshan is a deficit grain producer—most households do not produce enough grain to cover their own needs, let alone to distribute to the government as tax. Gongshan has been an ongoing recipient of large-scale government subsidies and technical support since Liberation.

Although access to social services such as education and health care

is gradually improving through campaigns such as "Build a New Socialist Countryside" (Jianshe Shehuizhuyi Xin Nongcun), there are still significant shortfalls in the level of subsidies provided, and most households
remain economically vulnerable. For example, if a serious illness befalls
a household member, it can severely affect the household's productive
capacity and place the members of the household in considerable debt.
In this context, family and fellow villagers play a critical role in lending
money to and supporting households that are facing financial difficulties
and hardship. Informal modes of reciprocal exchange of money, food, and
other resources within families and among hamlet members are a common practice and help to bind communities together.[5]

The high costs associated with health care reflect only one of several
major distortions that exist between local rural income levels and the cost
of basic social services. For instance, while primary and junior high school
tuition is now free for rural households, senior high school tuition and its
associated costs are not. As a consequence, in some of the households surveyed for this book, parents are using most of their disposable income to
keep their children in senior high school (field notes, September 30, 2006,
January 20, 2008). These parents hope that once their children graduate,
they will be able to find well-paid jobs in the county town and help to pull
the family out of poverty. The annual salary paid to mid-level government
work unit employees is equivalent to around eighteen times Gongshan's
average annual individual cash income. However, because poor households located outside the county town are unlikely to have good connec-
tions with local government and there is a general lack of well-paid and
stable off-farm work opportunities in the county town, many high school
graduates return to their rural hamlets. Consequently, parents living in
Gongshan's rural hamlets often view senior high school and its associated
fees as an unnecessary financial burden.

During much of the reform-era geographical isolation, low educational
levels and the inability to converse in standard Chinese kept the mainly
ethnic minority population relatively detached from the large-scale
economic transformation that was affecting other parts of rural China.
Indeed, in other parts of China, temporary rural-to-urban migration has
played an instrumental role in alleviating poverty and creating social
mobility for the rural population. In contrast, until recently it was rare
for people from Gongshan to travel outside the county. The social and

economic environment was defined largely by local conditions, with most children experiencing a life of rural subsistence, as the generations before them had done. The formal education system was underdeveloped and offered limited utility. School completion rates were low.

Gongshan's ethnic minorities are subject to a particularly demeaning official and popular discourse that represents them as "backward" (*luohou*) and of low quality, with their subsistence lifestyles and harsh living conditions representing the antithesis of the development model prescribed by the Chinese Party-state. Governing authorities at all levels call the challenges to development in Nujiang's four counties the "Nujiang issue" (*Nujiang wenti*). According to this narrative, Nujiang's weak environmental carrying capacity, combined with isolation and a "poor," "low-quality" ethnic minority population, is hindering the development of the Nujiang economy. One of the key messages implicit within this narrative is that the traditional, subsistence-based livelihoods and agricultural practices of the local ethnic minority population are environmentally destructive. Critically, this official narrative not only is employed to explain Gongshan's failure to develop; it is also fundamental to legitimizing the government's development agenda for Gongshan's ethnic minority population, which, among other things, includes shifting them away from traditional agricultural livelihoods and toward off-farm work.

Gongshan society has undergone significant social and economic transformation in recent years. Apart from experiencing improvements to social and economic infrastructure, such as the Dulongjiang Road, introduced earlier, Gongshan's population has been subjected to a series of large-scale government development programs. Central among these programs are the implementation of the Sloping Land Conversion Program (SLCP; Tui Geng Huan Lin Huan Cao Gongcheng),[6] the creation and increased policing of the national-level Gaoligongshan Nature Reserve, and the strict enforcement of the nine-year compulsory education policy. The Nujiang and Gongshan governments have been actively encouraging the transfer of household labor away from farming and toward nonagricultural work regimes via the promotion of programs such as "labor export" (*laowu shuchu*).

Here we are seeing not only the transformation of traditional ways of life, but also a shift in the role the local population is expected to play vis-à-vis the state and the encroaching market-oriented industrial economy.

In this new and seemingly neoliberal milieu, local governing authorities expect Gongshan's subsistence farmers to take greater responsibility for improving their livelihoods and "human quality," or *ren de suzhi*, by actively engaging in and contributing to the strengthening of this economy.

There are, however, clearly defined limits to the level of autonomy that local governing authorities are willing to concede to the local population. Although Gongshan's ethnic minority population is being actively encouraged by local governing authorities to improve its human quality, this process is conducted according to a formula strictly defined by the government. Indeed, Gongshan's poor ethnic minority people are considered by the government to have substantially less capacity to improve themselves than other sections of the population. Consequently, they are subjected to significantly more authoritarian forms of government intervention in everyday life.[7]

Nevertheless, even when ethnic minority people from poor communities such as Gongshan engage with the market economy, persistent structural inequalities, particularly in education, severely hinder their capacity to engage in the market on an equal basis. While government discourse promotes education and labor export as avenues for alleviating poverty, improving population quality, and stimulating local economic development, the most that Gongshan youth can realistically aspire to, aside from local government work, is engaging in low-skilled, undervalued production-line work in the coastal-based factories that constitute China's industrial economy.

The analysis that follows is based primarily on ethnographic research I undertook during eleven months of fieldwork in China between May 2005 and January 2008. The fieldwork was composed of two extensive research trips (May–August 2005 and August 2006–January 2007) and one shorter, follow-up trip in January 2008. The ethnographic material is based on household surveys, participant observation, and interviews conducted with officials, teachers, parents, and students. My fieldwork was concentrated in Gongshan's Cikai township (see map 3, in chapter 1, and map 4, in chapter 2), which is also the location of the county town.

Careful negotiation was required to gain official permission to undertake fieldwork in Gongshan, which is part of China's politically sensitive ethnic minority border areas.[8] At the time of my fieldwork, local government sensitivity to outsiders was compounded by ongoing criticism by civil society and the international press of the proposed Nu River damming project. My research access to Gongshan was greatly facilitated by my host university in Yunnan's capital, Kunming, which had links with local government there.[9] Ahead of my departure for Gongshan, the university contacted the local government about my proposed research project. Those conversations led to my meeting with several county government officials soon after my arrival in Gongshan, during which I explained that my research focused on poverty alleviation programs and the "Open Up the West" (Xibu Da Kaifa) campaign in China's western peripheral regions, and that I proposed to use Gongshan as a case study. As a result of this meeting, the county officials provided a letter of introduction, allowing me to conduct research in Gongshan.

I used the Gongshan county town as my base, staying in local hostels at night and traveling to villages and schools by day. I originally had intended to base myself in several villages for extended periods. However, the county officials suggested that I stay in the county town for my own "safety."

Physical isolation presented its own challenges. While transport infrastructure has improved in recent times, the road journey from Kunming to Gongshan takes approximately seventeen hours and requires at least one change of bus. This journey was made more difficult when the road up the Nu River gorge between Liuku and Gongshan was blocked by landslides, which were not uncommon. I generally spent research stints of one month in Gongshan before returning to Kunming for periods of two to three weeks.

The first period of fieldwork (May–August 2005) was particularly difficult, as I had few local contacts and the informants I did meet were reluctant to speak candidly about the impacts of recent development programs. In order to attain a broad overview of social and economic conditions and refine my research threads, I conducted household surveys in several villages of varying proximity to the county town. These included generic questions on income, educational attainment, agricultural output, and the impacts of the nature reserve and the SLCP.

The second period of fieldwork (August 2006–January 2007) was much more targeted and rewarding. Building on my previous household surveys and discussions with local teachers and retired officials, I was able to isolate the key government programs contributing to the transformation of Gongshan society: land reform, mainly via the SLCP; the creation of the nature reserve; education reform, particularly school consolidation and the implementation of nine-year compulsory education; and labor export. I conducted both structured and unstructured interviews as well as further (but more nuanced) household surveys with local farmers, teachers, and officials (both current and retired). I initiated a poverty alleviation project at this time, which provided some particularly useful insights into the machinations of village life and local government; I return to this project in the concluding chapter of this book. This second period of fieldwork also allowed me to consolidate friendships with local families and retired officials, and our informal chats, often over an evening meal, helped me to build a picture of local life as well as to fill in some of the information gaps that inevitably appeared following my daily research trips to villages and schools.

Language presented one of the greatest challenges in conducting ethnographic fieldwork in Gongshan. Although I have a high degree of fluency in standard Chinese, many of the Gongshan-based informants whom I interviewed during the course of the research for this book spoke little or no standard Chinese. I was able to overcome this challenge by employing a local research assistant and translator. "Liu" was born in Gongshan and is fluent in most of the local languages as well as standard Chinese.[10] During most of my interviews, Liu translated from the local language.

THE IMPERATIVE OF MODERNITY AND DEVELOPMENT

In contemporary China, modernity and development not only are implicated in creating and improving material infrastructure such as highways, urban skyscrapers, and mass communication networks, but also are connected with molding human subjects who are useful to the ongoing development and strengthening of the national economy. In contemporary China's "population quality" (*renkou suzhi*) discourse, official and popular narratives privilege modern, urban subjectivity while representing rural China as a backward repository of low-quality human subjects holding back national development. Paralleling neoliberal development regimes elsewhere, there is a growing tendency for government, understood in terms of the "conduct of conduct," or governmentality (Foucault 1991), to use a variety of techniques and forms of knowledge to shape the conduct of people from China's rural ethnic minority communities by evoking and working through their desires and aspirations.

At the same time, government development interventions are relatively blunt instruments for facilitating human improvement and often fail to effectively map the contours of the communities targeted for development.[11] Development interventions from outside China illustrate that although modernity and development are associated with progress, modernization, and the creation of more comfortable material living conditions, they are also connected to social and economic dislocation and the fundamental transformation of community life. Furthermore, in many cases development is associated with a significant power imbalance, with communities having little control or choice concerning the development programs affecting them. Rather, it is something done to them "for their own good."

This book engages with development policy at both national and local levels. Its arguments, however, are based primarily upon ethnographic fieldwork in Gongshan. The fieldwork data illuminate how the Chinese Party-state manifests at the local level of Chinese society. Although central government policy statements clearly inform us of the details and rationale sustaining the development program at a national level, they tell us little about how policy is experienced at a local level. This analysis reveals how "the state has become implicated in the minute texture of everyday life" (Gupta 1995: 375) and illuminates how the state is both constructed and imagined. Primary-school texts used in Gongshan, for example, teach Gongshan children that they are citizens of the Chinese Party-state. During this learning, they also imbibe a "hidden curriculum," learning that they share a common set of values with their counterparts living in prosperous cities in eastern China, even though historically Gongshan's political relationship with China has been highly tenuous.

Deconstructing Modernity and Development

Modernity is a term that can be used to describe the massive ideological, social, and economic shifts that have transpired since the European

Enlightenment. It was during the Enlightenment that scientific rational-
ism emerged to challenge religion as a source of authority for directing
human progress and development. While the term *modernity* is highly
contested in both western and nonwestern contexts, it is usually equated
with a society that privileges scientific progress and human intervention, a
capitalist system underpinned by a modern industrial economy, and freedom from political and religious oppression (Giddens and Pierson 1998:
94). Most important, it tends to reflect a society that "lives in the future
rather than in the past" (ibid.).

Deconstructing "modernity" is important to our understanding of
how modern societies are governed. Under conditions of modernity, the
nation-state represents the hegemonic form of the polity. In this regard, a
distinguishing feature of modern nation-states is their capacity to influence the conduct of disparate populations spread over vast territories via
efficient administrative coordination.

Here, the concept of "governmentality" (Foucault 1991) is a useful theo-
retical tool for excavating the ways in which modern nation-states are
governed. Governmentality is concerned with the modern "art of government," referring to, among other things, the government rationalities, institutions, and techniques geared toward acting upon and through
the conduct and aspirations of the population to achieve the purposes of
the government. It points to the rise of technocracy and reveals how the
"thoughts" of politicians, bureaucrats, and development specialists are
rendered "practical and technical" (Dean 1999: 18).

The identification, categorization, and targeting of specific sections of
the population by government is a fundamental feature of governmentality. Michel Foucault discusses how in Western Europe in the eighteenth
century the "discovery" of the population as an amalgam of individuals
with measurable characteristics facilitated the shift toward this new art
of government. He employs the term *bio-power* to encapsulate the disci-
plining institutions and biological interventions that emerged during this
period and allowed government to survey and act upon the population
in an unprecedented and meticulous manner: "The old power of death
that symbolized sovereign power was now carefully supplanted by the
administration of bodies and the calculated management of life" (1978:
139–40). Foucault describes a process wherein the collection and measurement of information about the population not only improved the state's

capacity to detect societal problems and provide services and supervision conducive to societal well-being, but also provided conditions under which the human capacities of this newly discovered population could be harnessed and optimized by the state. For example, we see the emergence of medical clinics, through which the measuring and recording of different aspects of bodily health and function provided the state with a new, sophisticated mechanism for enacting state power through the population. Similarly, modern education systems are a strategic site for governmental intervention.

This new art of government has greatly facilitated the capacity of modern nation-states to govern and develop national economies. However, while First World economies have thrived as a result of this improved economic capacity, there are also more insidious effects. Foucault's underlying critique of modernity and the modern, liberal nation-state is that rather than engendering conditions for human freedom from state oppression, they actually are a more sophisticated and meticulous form of domination.

Just as modernity is underpinned by the understanding that "progress" is possible and desirable, so modernity is characterized by trauma and dislocation. For example, marginal, rural communities in the developing world find themselves grappling with outside economic and social forces that are generally beyond their control. This scenario is facilitated by a phenomenon that Anthony Giddens describes as "disembedding," wherein "distant events and actions have a constant effect on our lives" (Giddens and Pierson 1998: 98). Major advances in mass communication and transport and the freer flow of capital have bridged spatial and temporal divides among nation-states, as well as between central authorities and marginal communities. Thus even marginal communities are "lifted out" of their immediate economic context and exposed to national and global economic forces, which in turn reshape local contexts (ibid.). On the one hand, this disembedding can provide positive economic and social outcomes for less economically developed rural communities via the provision of better social services and employment opportunities. On the other hand, it can have a deleterious and irreversible effect upon local cultural practices, lead to social dislocation, and marginalize those members of the community who are not equipped to deal with the changes that are taking place.

The ideas of such theorists of modernity as Giddens and Foucault are useful when applied to China, but only with severe modification. Of most significance is their tendency to conflate modernity with liberal democracy and a shift toward indirect forms of government that depend upon acting through the freedom and desires of the population to achieve the ends of the nation-state. This tendency is obviously problematic when examining notions of modernity and government in contemporary China.[12] On the one hand, during China's reform era, we have seen a contraction of authoritarian and direct forms of government intervention in society and a concomitant shift toward more liberal forms of government that depend upon the autonomous choices of the population (see Jeffreys 2009; Hoffman 2006). On the other hand, the CCP continues to maintain a monopoly over the political sphere and still relies upon overt techniques and practices to mold human conduct among some sections of the population (see Sigley 2004). To tackle this apparent contradiction and enable a sophisticated perspective on the ways in which contemporary Chinese society is governed, we need to turn to a nuanced analysis of government, one that blends neoliberal rationalities with authoritarian forms of government intervention (Sigley 2006). For example, Gongshan's poor ethnic minority farmers are subjected to a particularly paternalistic assemblage of government interventions that may be described as "authoritarian governmentality" (Dean 1999: 131–48), as they are regarded by governing authorities as incapable of improving their situation of their own accord. In contrast, we see that urban professionals are endowed with a high degree of autonomy in areas such as educational, work, and lifestyle choices. This also brings to light the hazards of invoking the term *neoliberalism* in our analysis of governance in contemporary China (see Kipnis 2007). Neoliberalism gestures toward small government, greater individual autonomy, and the absence of class differences. Gongshan's ethnic minority farmers are confronted with what appears to be a neoliberal discourse that implores them to, among other things, improve themselves via formal education, move away from their "backward" subsistence-based rural lifestyles and into more "productive" and better-paying off-farm work, and take greater responsibility for their destiny by actively engaging with the increasingly market-oriented economy. In reality, recent reforms in areas including education and agriculture have resulted in government having greater influence over people's lives. These programs have increased dependence upon government and significantly curtailed individual autonomy with regard to the operation of the household economy. Further, even when Gongshan's farmers make the sojourn to coastal areas to take up off-farm work opportunities, deep structural inequalities within the Chinese political economy mean that they do not enjoy the same access to social services as their urban counterparts and are relegated to the lowest-paid, most undesirable work assignments.

If we accept that modernity reflects the social and economic transformation of society as well as the collapse of spatial and temporal boundaries both within and among nation-states, then we can understand development as the vehicle for facilitating these processes. In contemporary times, we see the phenomenon of governmentality replicated in the development regimes of governments and international development agencies.

As with the term *modernity, development* is highly loaded and contested.[13] It is not the purpose of this book to undertake a forensic examination of contemporary international debate about development. However, we can learn from this debate that while it is crucial to acknowledge the power of development policy and interventions to entrench communities within the political and bureaucratic apparatus of the state, it is also critical to note that local actors do not always maintain a passive position and that development policy is subject to local negotiation; indeed, many challenge the dominant and powerful systems of knowledge and practice that are being imposed. Further, optimal development outcomes tend to be achieved when programs are demand-driven and communities are appropriately consulted and engaged.

Through ethnographic examination of the implementation of a series of development programs in southwestern China, this book contributes to our understanding of how development is experienced and negotiated at the local level.

THE CHINESE DEVELOPMENTAL STATE

Marxism remains a central ideology of the CCP.[14] A key premise popularly associated with this ideology is that societies progress through a series of strictly defined stages of material development, beginning with primitive society and culminating in advanced socialist society.[15] Each stage of material development is characterized by a particular mode of production, relations of production, and level of "productive forces" (*shengchanli*) (Stalin 1940: 28–30). Stalin defines productive forces as "the *instruments of production* wherewith material values are produced, the *people* who operate the instruments of production and carry on the production of material values thanks to a certain *production experience* and *labour skill . . .*" (ibid.: 28; original emphasis). Progression to higher stages of material development is dependent upon changes to the productive forces of the population, described by Stalin as "not only the most mobile and revolutionary element in production, but . . . also the determining element in the development of production" (ibid.: 32). During the Maoist period (1949–76), the CCP dismantled all notions of private ownership and actively promoted collectivization as a means of harnessing the productive forces of the population and developing the agricultural and industrial economies.

While there were marginal improvements in the lives of the Chinese populace during the Maoist period (not discounting the deleterious effects of the Great Leap Forward [1958–61] and Cultural Revolution [1966–76]),[16] by the mid- to late 1970s China's leaders were aware that the command economy had generally failed to bring prosperity to the Chinese people. In order to alleviate the rising discontent (particularly in the countryside) and reaffirm the power of the CCP, Deng Xiaoping officially launched a wave of radical economic policies that were intended to modernize China. The Third Plenum of the Eleventh Party Congress, convened in December 1978, marked a major turning point in CCP national development policy. Deng launched a wave of reforms at this conference, signaling a decisive departure from Mao's command economy. China entered a new era, known as "reform and opening up," which promised a better standard of living for the Chinese population.

A crucial outcome of the reform era has been the gradual, though not complete, dismantling of the socialist economy. While a sizeable proportion of the Chinese economy remains in state-owned hands, there has been a substantial expansion of the market economy. A loosening of restrictions on labor mobility has accompanied this shift. Overarching these changes is an increasingly neoliberal approach to economic development wherein Chinese citizens are expected to take individual responsibility for their economic livelihoods. One of the most important outcomes associated with these changes has been the migration of tens of millions of surplus rural laborers to urban areas. These workers have taken advantage of the low-skilled but (in comparison to agricultural work) relatively well-paid work assignments offered by factory managers and construction bosses. Politically, China remains a one-party state. While democratic elections take place at the village level, and there have been experiments with democratic expansion at the township level of government, there is limited space for public participation in forming state policy. The economic system is popularly referred to as socialism with Chinese characteristics or the socialist market economy.

As a result of the reforms initiated in the late 1970s, today many Chinese people experience standards of living that would have been unthinkable thirty years ago. For example, between 1978 and 2005, rural households' per capita annual net income rose from ¥133.6 to ¥3,254.9, more than a twenty-four-fold increase (National Bureau of Statistics of China Online 2006: section 10-2).[17] Reforms there have been credited with removing more than five hundred million people from poverty between 1981 and 2004 (World Bank 2009). The CCP has overseen a dramatic expansion of the Chinese economy, which has in recent years become the world's second largest.

Critically, while many aspects of the economic development agenda pursued by the CCP since 1978 reflect a neoliberal rather than a Marxist ideology, other aspects of this agenda are decidedly nonliberal (see Kipnis 2007), with the Party continuing to represent itself as the only agent capable of providing the social and economic conditions that will enable the Chinese population to improve themselves and achieve higher levels of material and spiritual development.

With this in mind, it is not surprising to find that a development narrative dominates official and popular spheres in China. State-controlled television news programming focuses heavily on stories about economic development and infrastructure projects. Statistics and other economic data demonstrating increases in growth and output accompany these stories. At the grassroots level, this narrative manifests in multiple ways. This includes colorful local government billboards boldly announcing new economic development plans and development goals achieved to date (see fig. I.2). This narrative serves to legitimize the CCP's right to rule.

The Party's state development policy in the contemporary period has

FIG. 1.2. A Nujiang Prefecture government billboard in Liuku, 2006, outlines
the areas that local government will target to stimulate economic development
in coming years. Its text translates as follows: "Scientific and technological
education makes the prefecture prosper / The mining and power-generation
economy strengthens the prefecture / The biological economy enriches the
prefecture / Tourism culture enlivens the prefecture."

two main aspects. The first concerns material improvement and progress:
the creation and fostering of economic conditions to facilitate prosperity
and better living standards for the Chinese people. The second concerns
improving the quality, or *suzhi,* of China's human resources. Population
quality discourse features heavily in the development agenda advanced
by Hu Jintao, who was CCP general secretary from 2002 to 2012. Hu promoted a "scientific concept of development" (*kexue fazhan guan*) in an
attempt to balance the uneven social outcomes associated with China's
rapid economic development.

There is no English term that accurately reflects the connotations of
suzhi (Kipnis 2006a). The western notion of human capital provides a
close approximation.[18] *Suzhi* has come to represent an important index
of human development and is a central feature of the state's exercise of
bio-power over the population. In this regard, the label "low quality" (*di*

suzhi) is invoked to describe those sections of the population considered to embody low levels of cultural and educational sophistication and which undertake activities that contribute minimal economic and cultural value to the Chinese Party-state (see Jacka 2009). Examples of the sections of the population labeled as low quality include poor farmers, rural migrant workers, and ethnic minority people—such as those living in the county that is the focus of this book. These sections of the population are explicitly targeted in campaigns aimed at improving population quality. The dramatic social changes that have taken place in China during the reform era have also contributed to significant public interest in the cultivation of a generation of "high-quality" (*gao suzhi*) child subjects who will be able to deal with the challenges of the modern world (Greenhalgh and Winckler 2005: 44).

China's large rural population has been a major target of population-quality discourse during the reform era; it is often portrayed as a backward, low-quality Other holding back national development and as the antithesis of the modern, productive urbanite residing in major cities such as Beijing, Shanghai, and Shenzhen (Anagnost 1997a). It has been a focus of intellectual and official anxiety, "appear[ing] as a tumorous mass" and "lacking a *consciousness* of development that the post-Mao Chinese state has been striving to foster" (Yan 2003a: 495; original emphasis).

In Gongshan, official and popular discourse suggests that its rural ethnic minority population is an extreme subsection of the low-quality rural population that threatens to destabilize local and national development. Population-quality narratives feature heavily in official and popular discourse, playing a primary role in justifying government intervention in society.

Unequal Development

Population-quality discourse is informed by the substantial social and economic inequality that has accompanied China's economic reform process. During the first two decades of the reform era, the CCP directed both local and foreign investment away from interior and western regions in favor of coastal provinces such as Guangdong, Fujian, Zhejiang, and Jiangsu. The Party called for the "East to get rich," in 1988 instituting the

Coastal Economic Development Strategy (Lai 2002: 433). According to a December 2000 article in the *Economist* entitled "Asia: Go West, Young Han," foreign investment in China's western regions during the first two decades of reform amounted to less than 5 percent of total foreign investment (29–30). Consequently, while communities along or near the eastern and southern coasts prospered, interior and western provinces were largely left behind. According to some estimates, more than 50 percent of China's wealth is concentrated in the hands of a small economic and social elite. Nearly 80 percent of production is concentrated in China's coastal provinces, while only 40 percent of the population resides in these areas (Dirlik 2006: 108–9; Goodman 2008; Naughton 2007).

The central government has become increasingly sensitive to this growing inequality, recognizing that it presents a serious threat to social and economic stability. Consequently, in recent years, rural communities in western China have been subjected to large-scale development campaigns targeted at creating conditions that will bridge the social and economic gap between eastern and western China. "Open Up the West" and the more recent "Build a New Socialist Countryside" are the most prominent of these campaigns.

These campaigns are part of a larger state agenda designed, first, to exploit the natural and cultural resources of the western regions for the purpose of expanding national economic growth and development, and, second, to further entrench the state's control and surveillance of China's peripheral regions, particularly Tibet and Xinjiang. The nominally "autonomous" Tibet and Xinjiang regions maintain a somewhat contentious status within the modern Chinese nation-state. For example, while China's governing authorities consider Xinjiang and its ethnically diverse population to be a part of the modern Chinese nation-state, some sections of its traditional Uighur population refer to Xinjiang as East Turkistan and have been very hostile toward what they regard as Han "colonization" of this region.[19] At times, organized resistance against China's governing authorities has been considerable, and terrorist-type attacks against state institutions have been reported. China's governing authorities are very keen to crack down on these resistance movements (and it has done so quite successfully) and to bring development, prosperity, and "civilization" to the people of Xinjiang.

The "Open Up the West" and
"Build a New Socialist Countryside" Campaigns

"Open Up the West" is the most prominent government program officially targeted at reducing the growing social and economic divide between China's coastal and western peripheral regions. In March 1999, former CCP General Secretary Jiang Zemin declared, during a speech at the Ninth National People's Congress (NPC), that the development of China's western regions was a key strategy in realizing national development and modernization goals (Lai 2002: 436). Launched in 2000, the "Open Up the West" campaign has focused on improving economic and social infrastructure in the less economically developed western and interior provinces and autonomous regions of Shaanxi, Gansu, Qinghai, Ningxia, Xinjiang, Sichuan, Chongqing, Guizhou, Yunnan, Tibet, Inner Mongolia, and Guangxi (ibid.: 432–36). The campaign is a key tenet in the CCP's strategy for entrenching its legitimacy among the ethnic minority groups living in these provinces and autonomous regions.

During its infancy, implementation of the "Open Up the West" campaign was inconsistent and did little to redistribute wealth and investment to China's western regions (see Goodman 2004). However, in more recent times the social and economic impacts associated with "Open Up the West" have become more pronounced, particularly in Tibet and Xinjiang. The central government's recent efforts to link Tibet to the rest of China via railway is an overt manifestation of the "Open Up the West" campaign, not only evidencing the physically transformative power of the campaign, but also underscoring its political and social engineering agenda.[20] Some sections of the Tibetan population have been hostile to growing Han presence in what they consider to be their sovereign territory and continue to call for greater political autonomy from China. While Tibet has been subjected to the political authority of the CCP since the early 1950s, its physical isolation has been a barrier to local economic development during the reform era. However, if all goes according to the CCP's plan, the railway will help to facilitate further economic development in what until now has been a poor and economically marginal area of China. China's governing authorities are clearly expecting that the projected jobs and prosperity associated with this economic transformation will also engender a social and political transformation among the Tibetan population, one that will intensify their integration into the Chinese Party-state and extinguish any desire for greater political autonomy. "Open Up the West" again draws our attention to the hazards associated with applying the concepts of modernity and neoliberalism to contemporary China. On the one hand, the program is designed to enable neoliberal economic conditions in China's western peripheral regions that will provide opportunities for ethnic minority people living in these regions to act with greater economic autonomy, improve themselves, and increase their engagement with China's expanding market economy. On the other hand, it is part of a remarkably unliberal political agenda intended to subdue ethnic opposition and further integrate ethnic minority groups into the Chinese Party-state.

"Build a New Socialist Countryside" is another far-reaching campaign targeted at ameliorating social and economic inequality and engendering political integration. This campaign has directed unprecedented levels of central government funding toward the provision of subsidized social services in rural areas, particularly those located in western peripheral regions. Recent education reforms, including the implementation of free nine-year compulsory education throughout rural China, are a key example of these efforts.

Conservation Programs

In recent times, environmental conservation programs have become a strategic pillar of the central government's development agenda, playing a key role in shifting farmers living in western peripheral regions away from their traditional agricultural livelihoods and facilitating their integration into the market economy. While China's rapidly industrializing economy has been highly efficient in pulling hundreds of millions of people out of poverty and transforming small towns and cities into thriving modern metropolises, its natural environment has suffered extreme degradation (see Watts 2010). Since the late 1990s, the central government has implemented a series of large-scale environmental conservation programs in an attempt to restore China's natural environmental resources. Critically, communities in poor peripheral regions such as northwestern Yunnan are most likely to be adversely affected by conservation programs, prominent among which are a national logging ban and the Sloping Land Conversion Program, which employs subsidies to encourage farmers to convert their marginal agricultural land to forest. Since the 1980s, China has also converted large tracts of old-growth forest into nature reserves. The increased policing of the forest resources within these nature reserves since the late 1990s has impacted communities that traditionally relied upon these resources to augment their household economies. In reducing access to the resources that sustain traditional agricultural livelihoods, these programs have in many cases encouraged farmers to pursue off-farm work in local towns or the industrial cities in China's coastal provinces.

Development and Ethnic Minorities

Ethnic minorities in China are a population subset that is particularly affected by recent development programs. Under Communist rule, ethnic minority groups have been conspicuous targets of government policies centered on integration and population improvement.[21] While in more recent times CCP development policy has contributed to major improvements in social and economic outcomes in ethnic minority areas, including Gongshan, it still tends to be highly paternalistic, and it demeans and subordinates ethnic minority culture to a Han way of life.

Although early CCP policy openly acknowledged and even celebrated ethnic diversity, it also subjected ethnic minorities to a rigid, Marxist-inflected historical materialist narrative that portrayed them as backward, of low productive forces (*di shengchanli*), and a hindrance to national development. Central to this narrative was the notion that societies progress through a rigid, linear index of material development: primitive, slave-owning, feudal, capitalist, and socialist.[22] The Han were placed at the top of this index, with the vast majority of ethnic minority groups placed below them. The Han were represented as the vanguard, responsible for guiding "less advanced" ethnic minorities toward the telos of material development—socialism (Gladney 2004: 13). During the reform era, official concerns about population quality have become enmeshed within this narrative, both informing and providing justification for ongoing government development programs within ethnic minority communities such as Gongshan.

Historically, many ethnic minority communities, including the one that is the subject of this book, maintained a tenuous cultural and political attachment to the Chinese empire. Since 1949, the central government has imposed Chinese national identity upon China's ethnic minorities. Even today, many of China's ethnic minority people share stronger cultural identification with ethnic groups living beyond their national border than they do with their fellow Chinese citizens.

China officially recognizes fifty-five different ethnic minority groups; these groups constitute approximately 8.49 percent of the national population (National Bureau of Statistics of China Online 2011: section 3.5).[23] While there is a high degree of diversity among and within these groups, they are concentrated in the less economically developed western provinces of Sichuan, Qinghai, Guizhou, and Yunnan and autonomous regions of Xinjiang, Guangxi, and Tibet.[24] These groups include the Uighur, Tibetans, Hui, Yi, and Miao. China's ethnic minority population, totaling around 114 million, occupy approximately 60 percent of the country's land area. Many of the areas they occupy are politically sensitive border regions (Mackerras 2003: 1).

Overall, ethnic minorities experience lower standards of living compared to the majority Han population. Inequality between the Han population and ethnic minorities is not just a phenomenon of the Communist era. Over the centuries, growing population pressure and land scarcity in eastern China prompted large waves of Han to migrate west in search of less crowded agricultural land. In so doing, they gradually, though not always peacefully, displaced the less powerful ethnic groups that had traditionally occupied these areas, pushing them away from the fertile plains and toward marginal mountain regions, such as Nujiang.

The definition of *ethnic minority* in China is not straightforward. First, an ethnic label can have significantly different meanings even for people of the same ethnic minority group.[25] Second, the official classification of China's ethnic minority groups has been and continues to be a highly politicized process influenced by official concerns about national unity—in the sense of the unity of the Chinese nation-state.[26] Although I use *ethnic minority* in this book to describe the people who constitute China's officially recognized non-Han ethnic groups, this English term does not accurately reflect the historical and political significance of *shaoshu minzu*. In fact, there is no way to directly translate *shaoshu minzu* into English. *Shaoshu* simply means "small in number." However, *minzu* is more ambiguous. In the Chinese language, there is no semantic demarcation among "people," "nation," "nationality," and "ethnicity": because the single term *minzu* can be used for all of these terms, there is a blurring among the conceptions of nation, nationality, and ethnicity (Heberer 1989: 10–11). For instance, the Uighur and Dulong are both officially classified as *minzu,* even though there are considerable differences in the conception of these groups. Numbering nearly ten million and sharing a strong subjective ethnic identity, the Uighur are the dominant ethnic group in the vast geographical region of China's west known as Xinjiang. As well as sharing a strong ethnic identity, historically the Uighur have also demonstrated a distinctive political identity. Indeed, at various times prior to 1949, Uighur nationalists have attempted to create a Uighur nation-state completely independent of China. Thus it is relatively straightforward for us to conceptualize the Uighur as a "nation" of people, or the "Uighur Nation." Although the Dulong, too, share a subjective ethnic identity, they number approximately six thousand and are concentrated in a minute geographical area in the west of Gongshan. For these reasons it is difficult to conceptualize the Dulong as the "Dulong Nation." Groups such as the Yi further complicate our understanding of the term *minzu.* Large in number and located in the southwestern provinces of Guizhou, Sichuan, and Yunnan, the Yi are officially classified as one of China's *minzu,* yet the "Yi" are actually an assemblage of ethnic groups that when directly compared with one another share neither a common geographical area nor a common subjective ethnic identity in most cases (see Harrell 2001).

When the CCP came to power in 1949, China's ethnic minorities presented a significant policy challenge for the country's governing authorities. Just as the CCP was determined to promote an ideology that ethnic minority groups and the majority Han population were one harmonious entity living within the fabric of socialism, it was also keen to formally acknowledge ethnic minority cultural identity. The CCP settled upon describing China as a "unified country of diverse nationalities" (*tongyi de duo minzu guojia*) (Harrell 2001: 31). In official terms this description accorded ethnic minorities equal status with the Han. However, once the CCP embarked upon its Marxist-Leninist–inspired development agenda for China, any semblance of equality between the Han and ethnic minority groups quickly evaporated.

The Han-dominated CCP saw itself as a modernizing and unifying entity whose role included bridging the development gaps between what it perceived to be backward, less developed ethnic minorities (such as those living in Gongshan) and the more advanced Han population. Universal development and progress were absolutely fundamental to the CCP: while the CCP accepted ethnic diversity, there was an assumption that all ethnic minority groups living within the borders of the Chinese Party-state would conform to its highly prescribed program of universal development. This approach persists today. For example, fig. I.3 shows a government-sponsored billboard on the main road leading into the Gongshan county town. The billboard displays men and women from Gongshan's main ethnic minority groups (Dulong, Nu, Lisu, and Tibetans) wearing traditional costumes. The large red characters at the bottom of the billboard declare: "Unite together to struggle forward, together develop prosperously." Such displays are very typical of political representations of ethnic minorities in China (see Gladney 1998: 2).

The Ethnic Classification Project (Minzu Shibie) was an important initial step in the CCP's strategy to socially engineer China's multiple ethnic groups into the Party-state (see Mullaney 2011). Launched in the early 1950s, the Ethnic Classification Project was a series of expeditions undertaken by social scientists to China's frontier and border areas to investigate and officially categorize ethnic groups on behalf of China's governing authorities. However, rather than being an impartial social scientific investigation of China's complex ethnic tapestry, the Ethnic Classification Project was a reactive, politically expedient exercise designed to accommodate the large, rigid administrative apparatus being developed by the CCP.

For the first-ever National People's Congress (NPC), scheduled for autumn 1954, the CCP had guaranteed at least one of the twelve hundred seats for each officially recognized minority group, with larger groups allocated more than one seat. The inclusion of minority groups in the NPC would provide the newly established CCP with a potent symbol of its commitment to proportional representation of China's minority groups. However, at the time there was still a high degree of uncertainty about China's ethnic composition, making it difficult to apportion seats within the NPC. So when the central government undertook its first official nationwide census of the Chinese population, between July 1953 and May 1954, one of its key goals was to clarify the ethnic composition of China's popula-

FIG. 1.3. Government-sponsored billboard along the main road leading into the Gongshan county town, 2006: "Unite together to struggle forward, together develop prosperously."

tion. Once this was known, the CCP could apportion NPC seats to reflect China's ethnic diversity (ibid.).

Nonetheless, the census results presented the governing authorities with a problem: more than four hundred ethnic groups were identified.[27] If this number had been accepted, minorities would have constituted more than one third of the NPC but only approximately 6 percent of the population.

To ameliorate this situation and more effectively categorize China's ethnic groups, governing authorities organized the Ethnic Classification Project. The underlying goal of the project was to identify a discrete list of groups that could be accommodated within the larger political machinery that was being developed by China's governing authorities. Of the more than four hundred different groups that were identified via the 1953–54 census, fifty-five would eventually be classified as official ethnic minority groups, with the remainder collapsed into one of these fifty-five meta-groups or categorized as Han (which is also a *minzu* but not a minority) (ibid.).

In contemporary China, the notion that "historical" economic bases underpin the material development of different groups of people, and that with an appropriate level of intervention and guidance from Communist governing authorities "less advanced" groups can ascend to higher levels of material development, continues to play a decisive role in shaping policy and attitudes toward ethnic minorities. Government publications emphasize how productive forces and agricultural output in ethnic minority regions have increased under the guidance of the CCP. These reports seek to emphasize the superiority and legitimacy of CCP policy and the backwardness of ethnic minority livelihood practices. In Gongshan, local government officials still commonly describe their work as assisting less developed ethnic minority groups to achieve higher stages of material development, as in this statement made by a Dulongjiang township official in July 2005: "With the help of the CCP and Marxist thought, the people of Dulongjiang are moving from being primitive people to a socialist society. In doing so they are leaping forward and bypassing several levels of development. However, their productive forces are still not very high" (field notes, July 3, 2005).

Autonomy, Affirmative Action, and Economic Development in Ethnic Minority Regions

China's central government officially acknowledged China's ethnic minorities in the 1954 national constitution.[28] Granting autonomy to areas populated by ethnic minority groups was a key feature of central government policy. Autonomy encompassed the right to self-administration and the protection of ethnic minority rights.

However, beginning in the late 1950s there was a dramatic shift regarding the treatment of ethnic minorities, and their special status and privileges were scaled back. Assimilation became the new norm as the highly charged political atmosphere of the Great Leap Forward and Cultural Revolution permeated their communities. Earlier policies directed toward embracing ethnic diversity and difference were supplanted by the dogmatic and often violent application of Communist doctrine, wherein the cultural differences of ethnic minority groups were construed as "class contradictions" that had to be eliminated. National organizations were

shut down and religious practitioners and national intelligentsia perse-
cuted (Barabantseva 2008: 580).[29] The delivery of education in minority
languages was also suppressed. As a consequence of this shift, the social
and economic status of ethnic minorities deteriorated significantly, and
tensions between the Han and ethnic minorities increased (ibid.).

At the beginning of the reform era, the central government became
highly sensitive to social conditions in areas populated by ethnic minorities, realizing that previous policies and the Cultural Revolution not only
had left ethnic minorities largely "underdeveloped," but also had engendered a high degree of antagonism toward the ruling Han elite (Heberer
1989: 6–7).[30] In response, the central government embarked upon a more
strategic policy toward ethnic minorities. The 1984 Autonomy Law was a
cornerstone of the central government's approach, representing "an official upgrading of minorities, their autonomy, and their self-administrative
bodies" (ibid.: 43). This new approach focused on improving social and
economic conditions in ethnic minority regions, as well as on embracing
cultural plurality. For example, article 4 of the Constitution of the People's
Republic of China (PRC) states: "All ethnic groups have the freedom to
use and develop their own spoken and written languages and to preserve
or reform their own folkways and customs" (Central Government of the
People's Republic of China 2004). As of 2007, China had 5 province-level
autonomous regions,[31] 30 autonomous prefectures, and 120 autonomous
counties, covering more than 60 percent of China's total landmass.

Since the mid-1980s, China's ethnic minorities have been a focus of
direct government development programs. Further, according to a Chinese central government white paper entitled "Regional Autonomy for
Ethnic Minorities in China" (Information Office of the State Council of
the People's Republic of China 2005: section IV, part 2), since 1999 the
central government has directed billions of yuan in funding toward the
construction of transport infrastructure in poor rural areas home to ethnic minority people. The Dulongjiang Road, described at the beginning
of this introduction, as well as the Qinghai-Tibet railway connecting the
Tibetan capital, Lhasa, with Beijing, are egregious examples of this process. Ethnic minorities have also benefited from affirmative action policies, which permit most ethnic minorities living in rural areas to have
more than one child and award extra points to ethnic minority students
applying to colleges and universities.

Development policies directed toward ethnic minorities are intended not only to improve their material conditions; they also have a social engineering agenda aimed at engendering, among other things, competitiveness, open-mindedness, and adaptability to the market (Barabantseva 2008: 583). For example, government education and labor programs in Gongshan are explicitly directed at shifting the ethnic minority population away from their traditional livelihood practices and toward practices more compatible with the encroaching market economy.

Whereas conditions in ethnic minority regions have improved considerably during the reform era, autonomous ethnic minority areas are still subjected to political domination by the CCP.[32] For instance, as an officially designated autonomous area, Gongshan is to a large degree administered by locally appointed ethnic minority officials; its titular leader is also a member of a local ethnic minority group.[33] However, the vast majority of these ethnic minority officials are also members of the CCP.[34] More important, these officials have little influence over the higher-level policy decisions emanating from Beijing that directly affect their community. In contemporary China, ethnic minorities, along with the rest of the Chinese population, are still subjected to a top-down system of government that provides extremely limited space for public debate or opposition to government policy decisions. Ethnic minorities remain subordinated to Han culture—ethnic minority diversity is acknowledged and even encouraged, but on terms dictated by the governing authorities. Further, policies enacted since the early 1980s have greatly facilitated the integration of the ethnic minority population into the Chinese Party-state. Indeed, the cooptation of the ethnic minority population into the Party and its development apparatus at the local level has been instrumental in institutionalizing CCP rule in ethnic minority areas such as Gongshan.

However, it is too simplistic to suggest that ethnic minority officials are passively subordinated to CCP policy and Han culture. Indeed, in many circumstances the ethnic minority officials charged with enacting policy on behalf of the Han-dominated governing authorities in Beijing also maintain strong emotional responsibilities and loyalties to the communities that are the targets of these policies. Their predicament can result in a sense of internal tension where they feel "trapped between the state and the local community" (Harrell 2007: 226). On the one hand, they may genuinely endorse the modernization program being pursued by the

Chinese Party-state, believing that external intervention in areas such as education, conservation, and labor allocation will ultimately improve the economic and social position of their community; on the other hand, they feel an emotional obligation to defend the interests, rights, and cultural integrity of their community from the influence of Han culture.

Contemporary Representations of Ethnic Minorities

Reflecting the rigid classification project initiated in the early 1950s, official and popular representations of ethnic minority groups in contemporary China tend to be highly essentialized and simplistic, focusing on specific attributes such as clothing, festivals, dancing, singing, or cuisine that reinforce stereotypes about ethnic minorities (see fig. I.3; Blum 2001). Among the upper leadership of the CCP, it is believed that the "unhealthy mentality" of ethnic minorities is a major stumbling block to their development (Barabantseva 2008: 584). Such perceptions inform the highly paternalistic central government policies directed at ethnic minorities, which in turn perpetuate the construction of ethnic minorities as backward and unable to develop on their own accord.

The growth of ethnic minority cultural tourism during the reform era has exacerbated the exoticization of ethnic minorities. This is particularly so in Yunnan, where ethnic minority culture has become a major target of commodification. The provincial government has promoted Yunnan as a "Great Ethnic Culture Province" since the late 1990s, turning "ethnic minorities' culture from being primarily a signifier of 'backwardness' to a 'resource' to fuel economic development" (Wilkes 2005b: 23). Even in isolated, difficult-to-access areas such as Nujiang, governing authorities perceive ethnic minority culture as a lucrative vehicle for local economic development (see fig. I.2).

Ongoing Resentment among Ethnic Minorities

Although the relationship between the ruling Han elite and the ethnic minority population can generally be characterized as one of cooperation during the reform era, ethnic minorities do not passively accept

Han intervention in their communities. While living standards may have improved considerably in ethnic minority regions since the 1980s, some ethnic minority groups continue to feel a high degree of resentment toward the Han population. This is particularly so in Tibet and Xinjiang, where increased Han migration is viewed by local minority populations as a significant threat to their cultural heritage and is often met with hostile resistance. In recent years this resentment has boiled over into violent riots in which Han migrants have been attacked and murdered and their shops destroyed.

Ethnic minorities also continue to experience much lower standards of living than the majority Han population. Although recent large-scale central government investment in ethnic minority areas has contributed to impressive improvements in economic and social indicators, overall it has been difficult for the central government to promote economic activity and generate off-farm work opportunities in the western peripheral areas occupied by ethnic minorities. Poverty remains a far more serious problem among China's ethnic minority population than among the majority Han population. According to figures published in the *China Daily* in late 2010, although ethnic minorities represent less than 10 percent of the total population, they constitute approximately half of China's rural impoverished population (December 23, 2010b). Further, in 2009, average GDP per capita in ethnic minority areas was two-thirds of the national average (ibid.).

High rates of poverty among the ethnic minority population are reflected in life expectancy and infant mortality figures. In 2000, residents living in a Han-dominated coastal city such as Shanghai could expect to live to an average of 78.14 years. Life expectancy figures were considerably lower in regions where ethnic minorities are concentrated. For example, in 2000, average life expectancy in Guizhou, Tibet, and Yunnan was 65.96 years, 64.37 years, and 65.49 years, respectively. Importantly, these figures were also well below the 2000 life expectancy national average of 71.4 years (National Bureau of Statistics of China 2004: 98). Schuster (2009) highlights the ethnic dimension of this disparity by comparing the health outcomes of Uighur and Han populations in Xinjiang. In 2000, the infant mortality rate among the Han people living in Xinjiang was 13.1 deaths per 1,000 births, while for the Uighur people living in Xinjiang the figure was more than seven times higher, with 101.7 deaths per 1,000 births. Further, the average life expectancy for Uighur people living in Xinjiang was a decade less than that of the Han population (ibid.: 434).

Historically, poverty also has been reflected in the area of education, wherein school completion and literacy rates among the ethnic minority population generally have been much lower than among the Han population. Here, large-scale changes are taking place. The central government recently has set aside unprecedented levels of funding in its efforts to improve access to education in the western peripheral regions, where China's ethnic minority population is concentrated. Key to this reform are the implementation and strict enforcement of free nine-year compulsory education. In Gongshan, these reforms have dramatically increased school enrollment rates, although illiteracy remains a serious problem among the adult population.

WHY GONGSHAN AND WHY ETHNOGRAPHY?

When I began the research for this book in 2004, I was keen to explore the nature and outcomes of development and modernization in peripheral rural communities in China. A literature review revealed that there was a need for such scholarly work. Studying societies from a micro-perspective not only allows us to investigate how development is played out locally; such research also can illuminate the government motivations that underpin development interventions.

Gongshan is ideal for a case study: it is not only at China's geographical periphery, but it is also home to a large non-Han population that, until relatively recently, has been largely cut off from the wide-scale social and economic transformations associated with the reform era. At the time of my fieldwork, Gongshan confronted a series of large-scale government development programs and was increasingly exposed to the forces of the market economy. I was keen to explore how the local community was negotiating these changes.

Upon arriving in Gongshan in May 2005, I was quick to apply popular academic critiques of development to what I was beginning to see in my research site. However, in time, the current arguments failed to account for the nuanced and differential impacts of development in Gongshan. During numerous interviews and surveys, I regularly recorded the grievances of locals regarding the impacts of particular government programs, such as "I'm worried that the diet the students receive at the [new central boarding] school may affect their development" (field notes, December 22, 2006), and "The government should give us ¥150 each a year to protect the nature reserve. We could then stop outsiders from entering. If everybody was compensated, everybody would protect it" (household survey, July 19, 2005). Nevertheless, it was also clear that overall living standards had improved remarkably in Gongshan in the previous two decades, and informants were just as likely to discuss the positive outcomes associated with development programs as they were to note the negative ones.

Development is rarely a neat and precise process, and government policies are a blunt device for dealing with the complexities of human society. There are countless problems associated with the various development interventions taking place in Gongshan, as well as major economic and social benefits. The development programs in Gongshan investigated in this book have caused considerable trauma and change for the local community; they have also benefited most people most of the time. Although Gongshan provides a striking example of the CCP's success in rolling out economic and social infrastructure and alleviating poverty in China's western peripheral regions, it also evidences its top-down, authoritarian approach to development and governance. Gongshan's modernization is taking place on terms dictated by China's governing authorities, with little, if any, opportunity provided to the local community to voice their opinions and shape the policies that are rapidly transforming their way of life. Is freedom the price of rapid economic progress? The absence of full-fledged democratic institutions and transparent government decision-making, as well as a free and open press and civil society, enables the CCP in many cases to bypass public scrutiny and develop and implement policy far more rapidly than governing authorities in other contexts can do. Would Gongshan have achieved its recent economic achievements if more transparent and democratic institutions and processes had been in place? Possibly not. But only time will tell if this approach to development is sustainable in the long term. For instance, how would the local community respond to a major economic downturn and the potential disappearance of opportunities, such as well-paid off-farm work, that were previously promised by the CCP's development model? Would the CCP's narrative that it is the only agent capable of engendering the highest levels of economic and social progress for the Chinese people survive this test? Evidence from other development contexts suggests that the most sustainable development outcomes are achieved when policies respond to local demands via in-depth consultation, when policies are openly reviewed and contested, and when communities take ownership and responsibility for those policies.

1
LIFE AT THE PERIPHERY OF
THE CHINESE PARTY-STATE

An Introduction

The province of Yunnan and its surrounding areas form the present home of numerous tribes, which have been driven towards it in a succession of human waves, and there is probably no district in the world where the tides of humanity have left so varied a deposit as in these mountain tracts forming the frontier lands of two great empires. Whilst the forces of Nature have been driving man from his northern home, the Chinese have been making a steady and irresistible advance from the east, till the high mountainous tracts of Yunnan, Kueichow [Guizhou], and Ssu-chuan [Sichuan] in part, have become the refuge and the home for those whose physical or numerical weakness has compelled them to cede the fertile places of the earth to a more powerful invader.

—Rose and Brown 1910: 250

We now left the river and started up the cliff, climbing high above the torrent; and almost immediately we were introduced to terrifying travel. The ledge along which we trod gingerly passed through a deep slot in the high granite cliffs, and a false step meant a violent death. . . . We followed the glacier torrent for three days, first through semitropical forest, then through Conifer forest, and finally through a chaos of boulders in a wilderness of shrubs. On either side were the high granite cliffs, and from our right streams from the big glacier, the edge of which we could sometimes see high above us, clattered into the valley.

—Ward 1923: 11

Francis Kingdon Ward's account of the extreme conditions that he encountered during a 1922 expedition across the northern reaches of the area that is today known as Gongshan County provides a fitting introduction to one of China's most isolated and inaccessible regions. Ward was an English explorer and botanist who made several research trips through Tibet and southwestern China in the first half of the twentieth century. Botanists were drawn to these areas because of their abundance of unique flora.[1] Gongshan is nestled in the southeastern foothills of the Himalayas, directly below the Tibet-Qinghai Plateau (see map 1, in the introduction). During the most recent Ice Age, its unique topographical conditions provided a safe haven for a plethora of unique plant and animal species. Indeed, today northwestern Yunnan is home to China's densest concentration of plant and animal species, many of which are endemic to the area (Xu and Wilkes 2004).

However, while these topographical conditions formed a rich natural environment, they also shaped a distinct social fabric and now pose a major barrier to economic development. Gongshan is on the geographical periphery of the Chinese state. The county's isolation and rugged, mountainous terrain have, until recently, kept its people relatively insulated from China's rapidly expanding market economy. Compared to other segments of the Chinese population, the mainly ethnic minority people living within Gongshan's borders are very poor.

Historically, the geographical area that we today know as Gongshan represented the absolute edge of Chinese civilization. The indigenous population was subject to overlapping political spheres radiating from both Tibet and the Chinese empire. However, until relatively recently, the local population's connection to the Chinese empire was tenuous. Political administration of the local population was rendered difficult by isolation and rugged terrain, and some sections of the population appear to have been hostile to outside encroachment into the area.

Since "Liberation" in 1949, this situation has changed dramatically. Gongshan society has become deeply enmeshed within China's modernity project, resulting in tremendous social, cultural, and economic change. This modernity project can be summarized as the pursuit of a harmonious, unified, prosperous socialist society through "scientifically based" socialist economic development under CCP guidance. In recent times, central government investment has poured into Gongshan, and major advances in mass communication and transportation infrastructure are collapsing the spatial and temporal boundaries between Gongshan and the world beyond its county border. Importantly, in Gongshan, socioeconomic development is strongly linked with the desire to modernize and raise the "quality" of the local ethnic minority people, whom local governing authorities regard as backward, of low quality, and of low productive forces.

THE GEOGRAPHY AND SOCIETY OF YUNNAN

Far removed from the center of China, it hangs on the ridge of the continent, separated from the basins of the great rivers by chains of mountain ranges. It is not very accessible from the central provinces; and, since distance breeds suspicion, only yesterday the age-old belief was still current that Yunnan was a wild region overrun with beast-like aborigines, in early times. . . . It was also believed that the air of the mountainous country was filled with a lethal vapour which would attack strangers in a mysterious way.

—Fei and Chang 1949 [1948]: 7

Yunnan is one of China's poorest and most marginal provinces. Unique environmental conditions and historical processes have shaped a complex social landscape, and today it is China's most ethnically diverse province. Its geographical position makes it a natural gateway between China and mainland Southeast Asia, and some of the ethnic minority groups living in Yunnan share strong cultural and kinship links with ethnic groups living in Burma, Laos, Thailand, and Vietnam. Substantial numbers of twenty-five ethnic groups (among China's fifty-five officially recognized ethnic minority groups) are found in Yunnan, composing approximately one-third of the province's forty-six million people. Unlike the situation in some of China's other western peripheral regions, Yunnan's main ethnic minority groups have not demonstrated overt opposition toward China's incumbent governing authorities.[2]

Yunnan is home to some of China's highest mountain peaks and some of the world's deepest river gorges. The northwest buttresses the Tibet-Qinghai Plateau and the eastern Himalayas and experiences extremely cold conditions in the winter months. In contrast, the south is home to lush tropical forests and experiences temperate climatic conditions for most of the year. Yunnan is also a conduit for several of the world's major rivers (the Yangzi, Mekong, and Nu/Salween) and is a vital watershed for downstream communities in China and Southeast Asia.

In recent times, the provincial government and large, state-owned power companies have targeted Yunnan's rivers as a major vehicle for economic development (see Brown and Xu 2010; Magee 2006; Xue and Wang 2007; Yardley 2004). The latent hydroelectric potential held by these rivers is a lucrative economic opportunity, particularly for a province such as Yunnan, which has a relatively underdeveloped economy and a large, poor rural population. Major dams already have been built along the Chinese section of the Mekong, and plans are in place to construct a series of cascading dams down the Chinese section of the Nu/Salween. These dam projects underscore the serious dilemmas that Yunnan, and China more broadly, face in balancing rapid economic development with the protection of environmental resources and the interests of local communities. The projects have been the subject of considerable opposition both within and outside of China. According to some nongovernmental organization (NGO) reports, while the Mekong dam projects have provided welcome income for provincial and central government coffers, they have done little to improve the livelihoods of the communities directly affected by them, and in some cases have actually exacerbated their poverty (Xue and Wang 2007: 81–83).

Between the late 1930s and mid-1940s, one of China's preeminent anthropologists, Fei Xiaotong, conducted research in rural Yunnan.[3] He and sociologist Chang Chih-I described Yunnan's diverse ethnic landscape in their study of the province's rural economy.[4] They clearly reveled in the opportunity to research such an ethnically diverse society. For them, Yunnan appeared to be a microcosm of human development: "The whole process of cultural development—from primitive head-hunters to the sophisticated and individualized city-dwellers—can be seen in concrete form. . . . It is here we will see in flesh and blood how the process of modernization is working out" (Fei and Chang 1949 [1948]: 9–10). They describe Yunnan's cultural landscape as a patchwork of atomized ethnic groups in which the Han occupy the fertile plains and the ethnic minorities the more isolated and marginal valleys. Their description also elucidates a high degree of social stratification among ethnic groups. Echoing the observations of other travelers and researchers who spent time in this region during the nineteenth and twentieth centuries (see the epigraphs at the beginning of this chapter), Fei and Chang explain the reasons for this stratification: "Successive migratory waves from different parts of the continent, during the last ten centuries, have pushed the less strong ethnic groups farther into the interior and higher up the mountains" (ibid.: 8). Extreme topographical conditions and dense forest environments exacerbated social isolation. Even in the 1930s, transport infrastructure remained basic and walking was the primary means of human movement within the province. As a consequence, livelihoods were defined largely by local conditions, and people living in remote villages rarely traveled beyond their own valleys (ibid.; Wiens 1967 [1954]: 332). The province's topography filtered the spread of modernization; Fei and Chang (1949 [1948]: 8) describe a distinct technological divide between the increasingly modern provincial capital, Kunming, and the rural hinterlands beyond it.

There are some striking similarities between the accounts from the 1930s and 1940s cited above and life in contemporary Gongshan. During my field interviews in Gongshan, it was common to meet people who had never traveled beyond the Gongshan County border.

Since dynastic times, Yunnan's relationship with China's central governing authorities has been unconventional and its population difficult to govern. In standard Chinese, the name *Yunnan* means "south of the clouds."[5] This name suggests popular and official perceptions of Yunnan during dynastic times. Yunnan was perceived as a dangerous, mysterious, and distant land separate from the "civilized" Chinese empire.

In imperial China, the majority of the population was governed under the prefecture system (*junxian zhidu*), which involved the official appointment of scholar-magistrates to administrative areas across China. Yet in much of Yunnan, including the geographical area we today know as Gongshan, imperial control was often weak or nonexistent: geographical distance from the imperial court, combined with rugged, mountainous terrain and a low tax base, made it impractical to establish a formal administrative apparatus to govern the local population.[6] Instead peripheral areas were governed by "native officials" (*tusi*) on behalf of the imperial court (see Giersch 2006; Herman 1997, 2006; Wiens 1967 [1954]).[7]

Large-scale Han population expansion into southwestern China during the eighteenth and nineteenth centuries fundamentally altered the area's political and cultural terrain.[8] This new wave of migration was stimulated by a combination of growing demand for labor in southwest China and rising population pressure in China's central provinces (Giersch 2001: 74; Lee 1982: 742). In Yunnan, in-migration precipitated a sharp demographic shift—it is estimated that the population grew from four million people in 1775 to ten million people in 1850, with much of the growth coming from Han in-migration (Lee 1982: 729, 742). By 1850, about 60 percent of southwest China's approximately twenty million people were Han (Giersch 2001: 74).

Increased commercial activity and population expansion associated with this large-scale in-migration made it much more viable for the imperial authorities to directly govern the local population, and it is estimated that by the end of the eighteenth century the *tusi* governed only one-quarter of Yunnan (Lee 1982: 728). Many indigenous communities were displaced from their lands during this period. As more migrants moved in, land became an increasingly valuable asset, as well as a potentially lucrative tax base for local officials. In this new milieu, indigenous communities often lacked the financial resources to compete with the more commercially adept Han migrants for access to land.[9]

The last remnants of the *tusi* were dissolved by the CCP in the years immediately after Liberation. Despite pockets of resistance, the CCP was relatively successful at integrating politically and ethnically diffracted frontier regions such as Gongshan into the Chinese Party-state.

Post-Liberation Yunnan

Although significant social and economic advances have taken place under CCP rule, today Yunnan is China's third-poorest province on a GDP per capita basis (*Economist* 2011). The situation for Yunnan's rural population is particularly difficult. In 1996, Yunnan had more rural poor people—7.7 million—than any other province (Mackerras 2003: 67). While this figure has dropped in recent years, the social and economic divide between rural communities in Yunnan and those in coastal provinces is substantial. For example, in 2008, the per capita annual net income (¥6,196.07) of rural households in the coastal province of Fujian was almost double the amount (¥3,102.60) in Yunnan (National Bureau of Statistics of China Online 2009: section 9-22). One of the key reasons for this disparity is Yunnan's low level of rural industrialization. During the reform period, many rural communities in coastal provinces such as Fujian, Guangdong, and Zhejiang have thrived economically as a result of the establishment of export-oriented industries in rural areas. These industries have provided jobs and lucrative nonagricultural income to farmers and local governments. The establishment of these industries has been facilitated by their close proximity to coastal, export-oriented industrial centers such as Shanghai and Shenzhen, as well as a central government development strategy during the first two decades of economic reform that specifically favored the development of coastal regions over that of interior and western regions. In contrast, aside from temporary outward migration for work, Yunnan's farmers and local governments have limited opportunities to generate lucrative nonagricultural income. Yunnan is mountainous and landlocked and is located thousands of kilometers from the nearest seaport, rendering the establishment of export-oriented industries in rural areas less viable than in coastal provinces. The prospects for establishing self-sustaining nonagricultural industry in an isolated, mountainous county such as Gongshan are remote.

Colin Mackerras (2003) contends that Yunnan's extremely mountainous landscape will continue to be a hindrance to development in some areas, stating that many villages will remain cut off and isolated from major transport networks and that "globalisation trends are likely to leave them behind" (67). Evidence presented in this book contradicts Mackerras's assertions. Although there is little doubt that many peripheral areas of Yunnan, including Gongshan, will experience much lower rates of economic development than other provinces, people living in these areas are becoming increasingly entwined with the developmental agendas of China's central governing authorities and the expanding market economy. Indeed, agricultural livelihoods, particularly in marginal areas such as Gongshan, are regarded by governing authorities at all levels as unproductive, environmentally damaging, and providing little, if any, contribution to national economic development. These same governing authorities are keen to move populations residing in isolated mountain areas down from the mountains and toward off-farm work regimes. For example, one of the underlying goals of the nationwide implementation of the Sloping Land Conversion Program (SLCP) has been to push farmers cultivating steep, marginal land in mountainous regions toward off-farm work regimes in towns and cities. Furthermore, outward migration from Gongshan to urban work regimes in China's coastal areas is gradually increasing. This migration is a direct result of China's, and by default Gongshan's, engagement with an expanding global economy.

GONGSHAN

Even by Yunnan standards, Gongshan's physical conditions are extreme; its isolation and rugged terrain have shaped a distinct social, cultural, and economic environment. Even the county's borders are shaped by the region's mountain ranges. Gongshan covers a total land area of 4,506 square kilometers, and its widest east-west axis is 60 kilometers, its longest north-south axis 160 kilometers. Gongshan borders Diqing Tibetan Nationality Autonomous Prefecture's Deqin and Weixi counties to its east, Nujiang's Fugong County to its south, Burma to its west, and the Tibet Autonomous Region's (hereafter Tibet) Chayu County to its north. Approximately 882 kilometers by road from Kunming, Yunnan's capital, Gongshan consists of five townships (*zhen/xiang*): Bingzhongluo, Cikai, Dulongjiang, Pengdang, and Puladi (see map 3). The county town is in Cikai Township and is the site of the county government offices, the county-level work units, and the leading primary and high schools (see fig. 1.1). It is also the county's main commercial and trading entrepôt.

Gongshan's most defining physical features are its extremely steep, mountainous terrain and its deep river gorges. More than 350 mountain peaks are found within the county's relatively small geographical area, with approximately 60 of them over 4,000 meters. More than half the land lies on slopes with a gradient of greater than 35 degrees, and the extreme topography makes agricultural production very difficult. Elevation above sea level within the county varies between 1,200 and 5,128 meters. Three major mountain ranges run north to south through Gongshan. The Biluo range forms the eastern face of the Nu River gorge, delineating the boundary between Gongshan and neighboring Diqing Prefecture's Weixi and Deqin counties and between the Nu and Mekong watersheds. The Gaoligong range runs through the center of the county and forms the western face of the Nu River gorge. As discussed below, the Gaoligong range is a natural barrier between Dulongjiang township and the rest of the county. The Dandanglika range lies in the county's far west, forming the border with Burma.

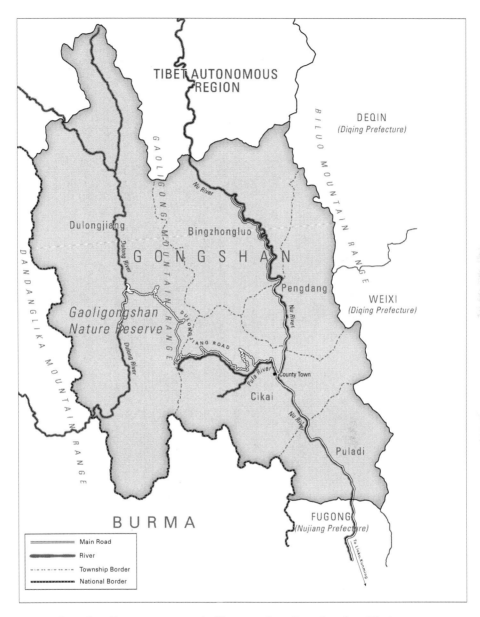

MAP 3. Gongshan County is composed of five townships: Bingzhongluo, Cikai, Dulongjiang, Pengdang, and Puladi.

FIG. 1.1. Gongshan county town lies on the western bank of
the Nu River (January 2007).

The Nu River gorge dominates Nujiang's and Gongshan's landscape.
The gorge cuts sharply though the middle of the prefecture and county:
its fast-flowing, untamed waters begin their journey in Tibet and rush
down Yunnan's western flank via Nujiang before entering Burma (where
the river becomes the Salween) and then emptying into the Andaman Sea.

The Nu River is one of the four major rivers that dissect northwestern
Yunnan.[10] In 1923, Francis Kingdon Ward described the extreme natural landscape carved out by the Irrawaddy, Nu, Mekong (Lancang), and
Yangzi river systems in northwestern Yunnan:[11] "We find then a country
of lofty parallel mountain ranges, separating deep river gorges, and therefore sparsely populated. There are many snow peaks, which stand with
their roots firmly planted in the howling rivers and their heads 12,000

feet aloft. So abrupt is the slope from the river gorge to the summit of the divide that it is the exception to see any of the snow peaks from below. . . . The flanks of the ranges are clothed with forests, and the whole country is a paradise of flowers" (1923: 7). The topography of Gongshan and the surrounding area makes transport into and within the county very difficult. With respect to vehicle transport, Gongshan is a dead end: access into and out of the county is possible only via a single paved road. This road hugs the Nu River gorge for approximately 248 kilometers from south to north, connecting Gongshan with Liuku (the site of Nujiang's prefectural seat) and the rest of the province. Prior to the road's construction in 1973, Gongshan was thirteen days' travel by foot from Liuku (*Gongshan Dulongzu Nuzu zizhixian zhi* 2006: 283). Vehicles now cover the same distance in six to seven hours. The road is periodically blocked by landslides and rock falls, particularly following heavy rain.

The situation in Gongshan's remote Dulongjiang township provides a striking example of the implications of Gongshan's extreme mountain environment. With the Gaoligong mountain range forming a natural boundary between the township and the rest of Gongshan County, each year Dulongjiang is closed off from the rest of the county for up to six months due to deep snow and ice that block road and path access into and out of the township. During my field trip to Dulongjiang in early July 2005, the dirt road had only just been reopened after being closed for six months due to heavy snow and ice. Even in early July, some sections of the road were still covered. Tunnels had been carved out of the ice to allow vehicle access into and out of Dulongjiang (see fig. 1.2).

These same mountain conditions have created a rich repository of plant and animal species. Gongshan's broad elevation range allows several distinct climatic zones to exist within a relatively small geographic area. Combined with geographical isolation, these different climatic zones provide conditions for myriad species to survive. Northwestern Yunnan, which encompasses Nujiang and Gongshan, is home to between one-quarter and one-third of the total animal species in China, and approximately half of the land area is covered with old-growth forest. More than two thousand species of medicinal plants can be found in the area (Xu and Wilkes 2004: 961–62). In recognition of its environmental and cultural significance, an area within northwestern Yunnan was declared a World Heritage Area by the United Nations Educational, Scientific and Cultural

FIG. 1.2. The road connecting Dulongjiang township with the county town. Even in summer, some sections remain covered in snow and ice (July 2005).

Organization (UNESCO) in July 2003. Part of Gongshan County falls within this World Heritage Area.

Prior to Liberation

The name *Gongshan* is a relatively new invention. According to the *Annals of the Gongshan Dulong and Nu Nationalities Autonomous County* (Gongshan Dulongzu Nuzu zizhixian zhi; hereafter the *Gongshan County Annals*), the Yunnan provincial government transformed the Changputong Administrative Committee (Xingzheng Weiyuan) into the Gongshan Government Office (*zhiju*) in 1933 (2006: 9).[12] At the time, a *zhiju* was equivalent to a county. The name *Gongshan* derives from Gaoligongshan, or the Gaoligong mountain range (*shan*), which dominates the local landscape, and it specifically alludes to the county's position at the top of that range.[13] Due to reasons outlined below, Gongshan's current borders are also relatively new.

Pre-Liberation accounts of northwestern Yunnan reveal that the political administration of the population who occupied today's Gongshan was weak, and a high degree of lawlessness prevailed. Administrative borders were often blurred. The population lived a very basic, subsistence lifestyle in a challenging physical environment and was subject to the demands of competing political forces from China and Tibet. What is significant about these accounts is northwestern Yunnan's marginality vis-à-vis the larger Chinese empire. Although China maintained overlapping political control of northwestern Yunnan via the *tusi,* the indigenous population had virtually no cultural identification with or allegiance to the Chinese empire. Adding to these complexities, as early as the middle of the nineteenth century, were French Catholic missionaries entering the area and converting a substantial proportion of the population. Furthermore, although northwestern Yunnan was relatively remote, it became of great strategic interest to colonial powers such as Britain during the nineteenth and early twentieth centuries. During this period, Britain controlled Burma and was interested in extending both its border and its commercial interests into western Yunnan. A paucity of official institutions also gestures to the weak political administration of the local population. Outside of the small number of churches and Buddhist monasteries, there is limited evidence of a formal education system, particularly during the dynastic and early Republican period, in the area at this time. From the perspective of those governing northwestern Yunnan, the local population was simply a source of tax extraction and corvée labor. From the perspective of the Tibetans living in the area immediately north of today's Gongshan, the local population, particularly the Dulong, were an easily accessible source of slave labor.

Another notable feature of these accounts is the high degree of social stratification among the different ethnic minority groups inhabiting northwestern Yunnan. Aside from the small population of Chinese living in the area, the Tibetans were at the top of the political hierarchy, and they enjoyed much higher standards of living and maintained a dominant political hold over the local population. The Nu and Dulong people were not politically organized and offered limited resistance to the demands of competing forces from Tibet and China. For example, the Dulong appear to have been unable to prevent the Tibetans from enslaving members of their community. Conversely, the Lisu demonstrated a high degree of resistance to Tibetan and Chinese domination. Even though today the

Lisu are Gongshan's dominant ethnic group, evidence suggests that during the late Qing and early Republican periods their presence in this area was minimal, and they were concentrated farther south, in the areas we today know as Fugong County and Lushui County. The Lisu occupying the area immediately south of today's Gongshan were particularly hostile to outside incursion into their territory (Rose and Brown 1910: 255–58).

The Lisu have demonstrated a fierce desire for independence from the Han and from other ethnic minority groups for at least several centuries (see Daniels 1994). Today the Lisu are concentrated in Nujiang Prefecture. However, according to historical records, as early as the Tang dynasty (618–906), the Lisu were concentrated farther east, in an area between southern Sichuan and northwestern Yunnan. Over the centuries, they were pushed by more powerful ethnic groups and ever-growing numbers of Han migrants toward increasingly peripheral areas of the Chinese empire and beyond. Nevertheless, the Lisu's reaction to Han incursion into their native areas was not passive. For example, in 1821, Lisu living in an area of Yunnan immediately south of Sichuan led a series of uprisings in response to Han appropriation of Lisu land that resulted in the killing of more than five hundred Han settlers (ibid.).

Few historical accounts describe conditions in northwestern Yunnan prior to 1949. Among the most useful are those provided by French missionaries who established themselves in this region in the mid-nineteenth century (Gros 1996, 2001). These accounts note that the local population was subject to the demands of several systems of political administration. Although the area was officially administered on behalf of China by Naxi *tusi* based in Weixi to whom the local population provided taxes and corvée labor, Tibetan *tusi* from the north also extracted taxes and corvée labor from the local population (Gros 2001: 6–8). Chinese cultural influence among the indigenous population clearly was limited, and "while Tibetan influence was not homogenous, it was part of [the] common, cohesive structure of northwest Yunnan" (Gillogly 2006: 58).

According to missionary accounts, when the French Catholic Father Renou first entered the region in 1854, Chinese control was tenuous (Gros 2001: 9). The local population was entrenched in a debt system that bonded them to Naxi and Tibetan *tusi*. Slavery was closely entwined with the debt system, and some accounts suggest that slaves were sometimes provided as tribute to Naxi *tusi* (ibid.: 18).

Conditions immediately south of today's Gongshan, in the area now known as Fugong County, were particularly hostile and lawless. In 1905, George Forrest, a keen botanist, escorted a Mr. G. Litton, a fellow of the Royal Geographical Society, on an expedition through the area. Forrest describes the conditions they encountered: "Since leaving Hsia-ku-dé [Jiakedi] we found that the country increased in wildness every march, and the inhabitants in squalor, poverty, and barbarism. . . . There is no sort of government or control of any sort or kind, by any Chinese or other chief. . . . The villages are nearly all at war with one another; few of the people have ever in their lives been more than a day's journey from their own huts; suspicion, rumour, and terror sit enthroned among those limestone ridges" (1908: 250, 261).

When Ward visited northwestern Yunnan in 1913, conditions appeared much the same as those described by the French missionaries and Forrest. *Mystery Rivers of Tibet* (1986 [1923]) is an account of an expedition in which Ward attempted to cross from China into Burma via northwestern Yunnan. His expedition was thwarted by a combination of hazardous weather and unstable political conditions. According to Ward's account, Chinese troops were embroiled in battles with Tibetans in the area immediately north of today's Gongshan as the Chinese government sought to take political control of Tibet. The Chinese officially controlled the area that encompasses today's Gongshan, but governance of the local population was very tenuous, with only a rudimentary provision of troops stationed in the area. Indeed, the area appeared to suffer from a high level of lawlessness. For example, in his account of a later expedition through the same area in 1922, Ward makes specific mention of the practice among Tibetans living in the north of today's Gongshan and across the border in Tibet of capturing and enslaving people from Dulongjiang. In fact, he suggests that the Dulong tattooed the faces of young women aged fourteen to seventeen years specifically to discourage Tibetans from capturing and enslaving them (Ward 1923: 14). The practice of tattooing appears to have ceased after 1949 as today tattoos adorn the faces only of elderly Dulong women.

Although the study and collection of plant species were Ward's main preoccupation during his earlier expedition through today's Gongshan, he also made detailed observations of social, economic, and political conditions. While some of these observations indicate that there have been minimal social and cultural changes since 1913, others reveal major changes. For example, Ward notes that "the mountains are not cultivated to any height above the river and the population is scanty, though small villages are built wherever a torrent debouches into the main valley" (1986 [1923]: 195–96). Any visitor to Gongshan today will note that farmers cultivate very steep, sloping plots of land at elevations well above river level. The disparity between current practices and Ward's observations suggests a significant increase in population pressure over the past hundred years.

Ward describes local living conditions as basic: "The people appear to live entirely on buckwheat cakes and maize meal porridge, though there are plenty of cattle, pigs and fowls. These, however, are kept for religious festivals" (ibid.: 196). He notes the local inhabitants' conspicuous lack of warm clothing during the winter months and describes an encounter with a party of Dulong people who had just trekked across the high, snow-covered Gaoligong mountain pass separating what we today know as Dulongjiang township from the Nu River valley: "They were an uncouth crowd. Their hair hung matted over their dirty faces, giving the men a girlish appearance. They possessed only two garments apiece, a sort of hempen blanket worn round the waist like a skirt, and another thrown over the shoulders and tied across the chest. . . . They carried light loads in bamboo baskets, long spears, big Shan *dâhs* [knives] in open wooden sheaths, and war-bows, with a span of four or five feet" (ibid.: 211–12).

Ward notes that approximately one hundred families inhabited what is today's county town. He observes that although most of the families were Lisu, there were also several Chinese shops and houses (ibid.: 219). Nevertheless, modern modes of commerce and trade in what is today's Gongshan were limited. As Ward traveled farther south into the Nu River valley, social and political conditions deteriorated. He traveled as far as Latsa Fort, a small military outpost that was most likely just north of the current border separating Gongshan and Fugong counties. This fort, which was manned by approximately forty soldiers and appeared to be one of the few sources of overt Chinese political control, played a strategic role in quelling Lisu tribes to the south, who at the time were highly hostile to Chinese encroachment (ibid.: 238–39). A Chinese soldier described the difficulties involved in controlling these tribes: "When we come along . . . they all run away, and we cannot get porters. We fight with them every year round Latsa, but they hide in the jungle and shoot at us with poisoned arrows, and we never see them. When we do reach the village we find it empty. Everyone hates the Lisu" (cited in ibid.: 228). Disease was also a serious problem in this part of the valley. Of arriving at Latsa, Ward writes: "What a dreary sight was this valley with its sodden ruined crops bowed in the fields, its empty huts and dying people" (ibid.: 238). His account of the misery and primitiveness of the people is meant to signal the clear "need" for modern British colonial administration.

Modes of formal tax extraction were in place at the time, even if enforcement proved difficult. During a visit to the Chinese administrative office, or *yamen*, in Changputong (today known as Bingzhongluo), Ward saw a Chinese tax collector arrive with a party of porters.[14] He had just returned from Dulongjiang, where he was collecting taxes from the local population. No mention is made of the success of the tax-collecting episode (ibid.: 253).

Ward's account also reveals that the Tibetan district of Tsawarong, immediately north of today's Gongshan, was regarded by the Tibetan and Chinese governments alike as militarily strategic to control of Tibet (ibid.: 276). At the time of Ward's 1913 expedition, hostility between the Tibetans and Chinese was particularly fierce. From the Tibetan perspective, the Nu and Mekong rivers represented strategic lines of defense against Chinese incursion into Tibet.

In 1932, a Yunnan provincial investigation team traveled to northwestern Yunnan to record the political, economic, and social conditions there.[15] Their report provides detailed insights into conditions in pre-Liberation Nujiang. Importantly, the account is free of the CCP's official interpretation of political and economic conditions prior to 1949. The report suggests that Chinese attempts to pacify the local population became more effective in the decades following Ward's 1913 visit:

The upper Salween from Lu-shui Hsien [Lushui County] up to Ch'ang-p'u-t'ung [Bingzhongluo] is principally inhabited by Li-su [Lisu] and Nu-tzu [Nu]. Prior to the murder of a German missionary here in the Manchu period, the whole area was a wilderness virtually unknown to the Han-Chinese. Li-su and Nu-tzu frequently killed Chinese or Min-chia [Bai] people who came into the area. A small force of Chinese soldiers, sent to the Fu-kung [Fugong] area after the Republic, was attacked with poison arrows. Garrisons have been stationed at Fu-kung (then Shang-p'a) and Chih-tzu-lo,[16] a day's trip south, ever since. Pacification of the area after an attack by the tribesmen in 1917 brought peaceful relations thereafter. . . . Neither the Li-su nor the Nu-tzu care much for rice, their staple food being maize, which was cooked for eating. The tribesmen had become quite addicted to alcoholic drinks, and much of the imports of the Han-Chinese merchants pertain to this commodity. The Li-su are largely farmers living in the higher elevations, planting the mountain slopes. Those that live on the valley plains plant paddy also and use Chinese methods of farming in contrast to the firefield [slash and burn/swidden] methods of the moun-taineers. They hunt a great deal and engage themselves out as coolies, espe-cially farther south in the T'eng-yueh sector of the Salween. . . . The Li-su are self-reliant and have a democratic social structure although in some areas they were oppressed by the t'u-ssu [*tusi*] who ages ago were imposed upon them by the Han-Chinese. The Nu-tzu are shifting cultivators like the Li-su mountaineers, planting such crops as buckwheat, maize, white potatoes, and sorghum millet. . . . Since the Hsien [*xian* = county] system was introduced here, the t'u-ssu had been restricted in his powers and there no longer were positions of headmen under him. The social system had continued much the same after the abolition of the headmen system, and remnants of the slavery system remained. . . . The children of slaves remained slaves, and the class difference between masters and slaves was sharp. (Segments translated in Wiens 1967 [1954]: 326–27)

Although Nujiang's political environment has undergone significant changes since 1949, the social and economic conditions described in this account are not significantly dissimilar to current conditions. One of the striking features in this account is the reference to alcohol abuse among the ethnic minority population. In contemporary Gongshan, alcoholism is widespread and contributes to social dysfunction.

Religion

Christianity has had a long and deep influence upon northwestern Yun-nan society. In 1854, Father Renou established the first missionary pres-ence in Yunnan's northwestern border region (Gros 2001). The French missionaries were part of the Tibet Mission, created in 1846 with the goal of converting Tibet to Christianity, following Pope Grégoire XVI's decision to make Tibet an autonomous Catholic mission (ibid.: 2). Due to an ongoing dispute between Tibet and China at the time, access to Tibet's interior was impossible. Instead, the missionaries planned to use the border region as a site for future expansion into Tibet (ibid.).

The missionaries appear to have been quite successful, converting a significant proportion of the population living in this region to Christianity. The missionaries began sourcing converts by buying members of the local population out of enslavement, and thus their initial success appears to have had more to do with providing the possibility of escape from economic obligations to abusive *tusi* than with a genuine desire to convert to Christianity (ibid.: 9–14).

At the start of the twentieth century, Protestant missionaries also entered northwestern Yunnan. The legacy of this early missionary presence persists today (see Zhao 2008). While it is difficult to obtain official statistics regarding the size of Gongshan's Christian population, anecdotal evidence suggests that Catholicism and Protestantism are widely practiced. A large church sits on the hill above the Gongshan county town, and large congregations attend its weekend services. Smaller churches are a common feature in Gongshan's hamlets and villages. Nevertheless, religious practice is closely policed by the local governing authorities. For example, all churches must be officially approved by the state, and children are not allowed to attend church services until they complete high school. Members of the CCP are forbidden to practice religion.

The "Official" History

Alternative historical accounts of Gongshan are scarce, and today Chinese government publications and government-endorsed pseudo-academic literature monopolize the telling of local history. According to the *Gongshan County Annals* (2006), from the time of the Western Han (206 BCE–25 CE) until the Republican period, Nujiang's territory was controlled and administered by *tusi* from neighboring regions. The county was "liberated" by the CCP on October 8, 1949. As the following excerpt from the *Gongshan County Annals* reveals, Gongshan's official history is overlaid with a Communist Liberation narrative, which articulates that prior to 1949 the people living in the area we today know as Gongshan maintained a low level of social development and were oppressed by feudal forces. The CCP represents itself as a benevolent liberating organization that freed the local people from this oppression and helped them to achieve a higher level of material development:

> The ethnic minority people of Gongshan once launched unyielding and unrelenting uprisings and struggles in order to oppose the *tusi* from past dynasties, slave owners, imperialism, and Republican rule. However, due to a lack of advanced classes and correct guidance from their political party [*xianjin de jieji jiqi zhengdang de zhengque zhiyin*], they were defeated each time. In August 1949, Yunnan's Northwest Defensive Army officials, under the leadership of the CCP, led an armed force across the Biluo mountains from Weixi and entered Gongshan. Using stealth and speed, the Communist forces surrounded the armed force stationed in Cikai, forcing them to lay down their arms and surrender. . . .
>
> Gongshan's Liberation on October 8, 1949, demonstrated the end of its people's enslavement under imperial and Republican rule, and a transition to a new period of united nationality equality. However, social economic development was very slow. There were a number of reasons for this: Gongshan is in a border area; historically, nationality relations had been complicated; and primitive, backward productive forces and production levels were still holding back the development of the local people. Although a private market system had developed in Gongshan, land ownership had not been centralized, the majority of land still belonged to primitive household communal systems, and the division of classes was not clear. Class divisions were particularly unclear among the Dulong people, who had yet to undergo the disintegration of their primitive commune stage of development. Low productive forces and production levels were the main factors restricting the development of Gongshan society.
>
> The Party's goal was to fundamentally change Gongshan's poor and backward conditions. However, because of the unique social [and] historical characteristics of its nationality people, the Party and government decided not to implement land reform. Rather, there would be a direct [but] gradual transition to socialism [that would take place under the following conditions]: via party leadership and the strong support of the nation; by relying on poor farmers, the unity of other working people, education and reform, cultural work, organization, and cooperation; by gradually raising the people's production level and political consciousness; by strengthening socialist

factors; and by gradually abolishing the primitive and backward exploitative elements not advancing production and nationality development. . . .

In the fifty years since the creation of the autonomous county, under the leadership of the Party and people's government and the strong support of the country, Gongshan has gradually changed its primitive and backward agricultural production methods. For instance, swidden agricultural production methods have gradually been developed into the use of fixed agricultural methods, water channeling, and terracing. (*Gongshan County Annals* 2006: 2–4)

This description is typical of official accounts of Gongshan society, which are used to justify ongoing government intervention among the local population. Since 1949, the CCP has presented itself as the only agent capable of guiding the social and economic development of the local population. Harnessing the productive forces of the local population is central to these efforts. More recently, economic development policy has had more of a neoliberal orientation, as it is increasingly geared toward providing conditions under which the local population will take responsibility for improving their situation. This involves, among other things, improving access to educational services and encouraging farmers to shift toward "more productive" off-farm work.

Contemporary Society

Following the foundation of the People's Republic of China in 1949, Gongshan's population grew quite rapidly. The county's 1953 population of 17,134 nearly doubled to 33,395 by 1990 (*Gongshan County Annals* 2006: 58). Although official population growth since 1990 has been very low (rising to just over 36,000 by 2008 [China Nujiang Gorge Network 2011]), official accounts indicate that the post-Liberation population growth has placed a severe strain on the natural environment. According to the *Gongshan County Annals,* prior to the Republican period, there are no concrete, historical population data for Gongshan (2006: 58). However, by 1918, Gongshan had a reported population of 6,516 people. The population grew to a reported 10,404 by 1947. These pre-Liberation population figures need to be treated with caution because establishing accurate population figures was often dif-

FIG. 1.3. A typical Gongshan hamlet (July 2005).

ficult at this time. It was in people's economic interests not be counted in population surveys and censuses in order to try to avoid paying taxes.

In contemporary official and popular discourses, Gongshan's populace is generally referred to in pejorative terms, often being described as poor, backward, of low quality, and having low productive forces. Local governing bodies play a particularly paternalistic role with regard to the development of the population. Indeed, official documents are deeply permeated by the historical materialist discourse introduced earlier. These official documents emphasize Gongshan's primitive, backward, and feudal past. A key issue that these documents repeat again and again is the low productive forces that existed among Gongshan's ethnic minority communities prior to 1949. Productive forces are used as a measure of an ethnic minority group's level of development, as well as their "potential" to develop further. Descriptions of the Dulong people are particularly pejorative. The *Gongshan County Citizens' Civilized Handbook,* which was prepared by the Gongshan County Communist Party Propaganda Department, explicitly outlines appropriate forms of conduct for the people of Gongshan. This document was distributed among the local population by the county government in the lead-up to National Day celebrations in 2006. The opening page states:

Whether our country's national strength is strong or weak, our economic development large or small, depends more and more on whether the quality of our workers is high or low. This is because people are the most active and positive elements of the productive forces.

Within the creation of a socialist spiritual civilization, raising people's quality is one of spiritual civilization's most fundamental problems. The basic goal of creating a socialist spiritual civilization is [to] cultivate socialist citizens with ideals, morals, culture, and discipline, as well as [to] raise the moral quality and scientific cultural quality of all of the nationalities.

This year is the fiftieth anniversary of the establishment of the Gong-shan Dulong and Nu Nationalities Autonomous County. Our county will hold grand celebrations to show its bright achievements over the past fifty years. To contribute to the county's celebrations and provide a good image of Gongshan to the outside world, from today [onward] every Gongshan citizen has an obligation and responsibility to increase your quality, eliminate bad habits, and advocate civilization (*Gongshan Xian gongmin wenming shouce* 2006: 1)

Narratives such as this are central to legitimizing the relatively high degree of direct governmental intervention among the Gongshan community. They imply that, unlike other, "higher-quality" sections of the population, the people of Gongshan are uncivilized, maintain bad habits, and require ongoing direction from government on how to conduct themselves appropriately and make a valued contribution to national development.

The Local Economy

> The problem is that the people here are too poor. They have
> to depend upon government support.
> —Senior official of the Gongshan Education Bureau,
> field notes, January 28, 2008

Prior to 1949, Gongshan's population relied on swidden agriculture, the collection of wild plants, and subsistence hunting. Despite recent improvements in living standards, Gongshan's formal economy remains small and relies heavily on outside financial assistance. Today governing authorities at all levels employ the term "Nujiang issue" to articulate the interconnected challenges to economic development in Nujiang Prefecture, including population growth, isolation, ethnicity, religion, poverty, and ecology. Central to this narrative is the notion that Nujiang's severely limited environmental carrying capacity and "poor," "low-quality" ethnic minority population have held back the development of the Nujiang economy (Chen Xiang, May 16, 2006).

Since 1949, Gongshan has been a target of ongoing development programs, which have intensified in recent years. After 1949, Nujiang received special attention from governing authorities because it was perceived to have particularly backward social and economic conditions. Agricultural specialists were sent to the area to train local farmers in what the government considered to be more advanced agricultural methods. For example, farmers were encouraged to shift away from swidden agriculture and toward fixed agricultural production methods.

In the first forty years after 1949, agriculture, forestry, and raising livestock formed the base of the Nujiang economy (Gao 2003: 15). However, it has been difficult to develop industry and income in Gongshan in particular and in Nujiang in general. The *Nujiang Lisu Nationality Autonomous Prefecture Survey* (Nujiang Lisuzu zizhizhou gaikuang) states that, following Nujiang's Liberation in 1949, agricultural production levels remained low (1986: 178). Industry was developed, but because it developed from a zero base, production levels were low. After 1949, the party and government adopted an economic principle of "taking little and giving more" (*shao yao duo gei*) toward the local ethnic minority population and implemented a policy of light or no taxes.

However, by the mid-1990s, nonagricultural industry remained largely underdeveloped in Nujiang (Zhang, Chen, and He 1997: 116). As noted earlier, in many other parts of China the establishment of industry in rural areas has been instrumental in raising rural household income and local government revenue. Geographical isolation is obviously the main reason that industry has been unable to gain a foothold in Nujiang, although official accounts stress that the low quality of the local population is also a key reason. According to Zhang, Chen, and He: "The labor quality of the agricultural population in Nujiang's four counties has restricted labor from being diverted to different regions and nonagricultural industries.

Nujiang's population quality [*renkou suzhi*] is the lowest in the province. It will be very difficult to change this scenario in the current era" (ibid.: 116). Today the Gongshan economy is characterized by a high degree of social and economic inequality. For example, there is evidence of a wide income and opportunity gap between people living in the Gongshan county town, who are generally employed in government jobs, and those living in rural hamlets. There is also an economic divide between farmers living in close proximity to the county town and those living farther away. For instance, in 2008, farmers living in Cikai township (the site of the county town) earned an average of ¥1,136 per person per year, while farmers living in remote Dulongjiang township earned an average of only ¥805 per person, around two-thirds of Cikai's average per person income (China Nujiang Gorge Network 2011).

Recently local livelihoods have been further complicated by a series of state development programs. These programs, which include the SLCP, a logging ban, and the creation and policing of a nature reserve, have severely affected traditional agricultural and cultural practices as well as the capacity of local community members to generate income.

Agriculture

Several officially endorsed Chinese accounts describe challenges confronting Nujiang's largely agricultural economy, all of which highlight the dilemma of trying to balance economic development with a fragile ecology. These accounts tend to lay most of the blame for Nujiang's problems upon the agricultural practices of the local population rather than on governing authorities' past development policies. They are generally written with local and higher-level governing authorities in mind, not only reflecting the goals of those governing authorities, but also serving to bolster their ongoing developmental agendas for areas such as Nujiang. In the case of Nujiang, this agenda involves further integrating the ethnic minority population into the national economy and Chinese Party-state, which includes transferring farmers away from what governing authorities describe as "unproductive" agricultural work and toward "productive" off-farm work.

Gao Yingxin (2003) is an agricultural technician who was sent to Nujiang Prefecture in 1957 to assist with the development of the local economy. He spent several decades in China's border areas and has written extensively on economic and social conditions in Gongshan. In 1992, Gao coauthored an article with Wang Daming and Tang Qingping in which they state that balancing a fragile ecology while also trying to develop agricultural, forestry, and livestock industries was one of the greatest challenges to economic development and poverty alleviation strategies in Nujiang (cited in Gao 2003: 15–16). Today this challenge is encapsulated in the phrase "Nujiang issue."

Gao notes that conditions in Nujiang are particularly challenging to the development of the local economy: "The mountains are high and the water rapid, agriculture takes place on steep slopes, the agricultural environment is unusually fragile, it is a remote area, it is inaccessible, social conditions are comparatively backward" (ibid.: 3).

Nujiang's land area covers 22,050,000 *mu,* or 1,470,735 hectares. Over three-quarters (76.3 percent) of this total land area is on slopes with a gradient of at least 25 degrees. Furthermore, 40 percent of this total land area is 3,000 meters above sea level and is unsuitable for cultivation. Technological limitations in Nujiang also render unsuitable another 29.51 percent of total land area, lying between 2,400 and 3,000 meters above sea level. In 1995, only 3.3 percent of Nujiang's total land area was under cultivation (Zhang, Chen, and He 1997: 121), and because most of this area is on steep slopes, agricultural output is very low. Cultivating land on steep slopes also contributes to soil erosion and landslides, compromising the long-term viability of agricultural land. Furthermore, by the late 1980s, conflict between the increasing population and the limited and finite amount of arable land was becoming pronounced. Summarizing the problem, Gao states: "With almost no reserve land available to open up and with population increase, the conflict between people and the ecology is becoming increasingly pronounced" (2003: 32). Following the introduction of the SLCP in Gongshan in 2003, most land on slopes with a gradient of greater than 25 degrees has been converted to forest and cash crops. (The SLCP will be discussed in greater detail in the following chapter.)

Since 1949, the human footprint in Nujiang has grown substantially and has affected forest coverage, significantly increased the amount of steeply sloping land under cultivation, and contributed to an increase in wide-scale landslides. Prior to 1949, Nujiang had a population of 140,000 (Zhang, Chen, and He 1997: 122), who cultivated approximately 1.13 per-

FIG. 1.4. An example of steep, sloping agricultural land in Gongshan (May 2005).

cent (250,000 *mu*) of Nujiang's total land area, about one-third of the 1995 figure. However, between 1954 and 1986, Nujiang's agricultural popula-tion grew from 203,000 to 365,000 people, a 79.8 percent increase. At the same time, the area of land under cultivation expanded from 517,950 to 717,000 *mu*, a 38.4 percent increase (Gao 2003: 10). Gao notes that agricul-ture has had a significant impact on Nujiang's forest coverage, particularly in areas below 2,500 meters close to the river gorges (ibid.). According to official figures, between 1949 and the mid-1980s, Nujiang's forest coverage decreased from 50 to 34 percent (ibid.).

Population increase has resulted in a rise in the amount of steep agri-cultural land under cultivation. In fact, in 1995, 42.4 percent of Nujiang's agricultural land was on slopes with a gradient of greater than 25 degrees (Zhang, Chen, and He 1997: 121). The practice of cultivating steep, slop-ing land was particularly acute in Lushui, Fugong, and Gongshan coun-ties. According to Gao, in the mid-1980s, 68.2 percent of agricultural land in these three counties was on slopes with a gradient of greater than 25 degrees (2003: 20). In the most extreme case, land was cultivated on a slope with a gradient of 52 degrees. These practices created serious soil erosion and rockslides (ibid.). Large landslides did not occur prior to 1949 (Zhang, Chen, and He 1997: 122). Today evidence of landslides is highly

conspicuous.[17] The cultivation of land on steep slopes was strictly out-
lawed by the central government in 1999 following major flooding on the
Yangzi River the previous year.

Based on research conducted in the 1980s, Gao argues that rapid population increase reduced the amount of land available for agricultural
production (2003: 32). Up until the mid-1990s, Nujiang had the highest population growth rate in Yunnan (Zhang, Chen, and He 1997: 129).
Between 1979 and 1988, Nujiang's total population grew by 21.2 percent,
to 418,000 people. However, during the same period, the area of agricultural land grew from 678,000 to 715,000 *mu*, an increase of only 5.5 percent (Gao 2003: 32). Gao attributes this relatively minor increase to the
Household Responsibility System (Jiating Lianchan Chengbao Zeren Zhi),
officially implemented by the central government in the early 1980s (ibid.).
He notes that this new system encouraged the local population to increase
productivity and revenue. As a consequence, more land was opened for
agricultural production. However, this appears to have had a deleterious
effect on the local environment, so that newly opened land quickly became
untenable. In the early 1980s, the amount of land under cultivation spiked
to more than 760,000 *mu*, falling back to just over 700,000 *mu* by the
end of the decade (ibid.). In 1988, the average amount of agricultural land
per person in Nujiang, 1.71 *mu*, was higher than provincial and national
averages. However, within this average, only 0.99 *mu* was on land with a
gradient of below 25 degrees. By the mid-1990s, this figure had dropped
slightly, to 1.65 *mu* per person (Zhang, Chen, and He 1997: 130). Less than
20 percent of this land was paddy field.

Nevertheless, agricultural production has increased significantly since
1949. For example, in 1954, total agricultural production was 44,000 tons.
By 1986, agricultural production had more than doubled, to 99,570 tons.
Official figures also indicate that agricultural productivity has increased:
annual grain production per *mu* rose from 84.8 to 138.9 kilograms over the
same period. Agricultural output per person increased from 216 to 247 kilograms (Gao 2003: 310). However, although agricultural yields have increased
substantially since 1949, they are low when compared to provincial averages
(ibid.: 316). Population increase and a fragile ecological environment mean
that Nujiang has been unable to produce enough grain to sustain its population. For example, in 1985, Nujiang's average agricultural output per *mu*
for a single harvest was only 99.6 kilograms, slightly more than half the

provincial average of 188 kilograms. Furthermore, average annual agricultural output per rural person was only 247.5 kilograms, well below the provincial average of 310.5 kilograms (ibid.). According to figures cited by Gao, between 1957 and 1985, national grain allocations to Nujiang increased from 1,920 to 27,835 tons, a 14.5-fold increase (ibid.: 308). Further highlighting the inability of the local rural population to grow enough grain to sustain themselves, in 1985, the government distributed 8,365 tons of grain to Nujiang's rural population, approximately 22 kilograms per person (ibid.).[18]

Importantly, nonofficially endorsed accounts of livelihood practices in Nujiang also highlight the prefecture's low agricultural yields and the conflict between nature and the local population. Research by Xu Jianchu and Andreas Wilkes published in *Biodiversity and Conservation* suggests that Nujiang's per capita agricultural output increased significantly in the 1990s (2004: 969). Nonetheless, these authors also note that livelihood conditions in upland areas in northwestern Yunnan in general remained difficult, with nearly one-third of households reporting inadequate food levels for at least one-third of the year (ibid.: 966). Households purchased their remaining food requirements with cash generated through the collection of nontimber forest products, small-scale timber felling, and grazing livestock, all of which negatively impacted local biodiversity (ibid.).

Overall, Nujiang Prefecture has been heavily reliant on external subsidies and financial support. Poor soil quality, hazardous terrain, and population pressure severely restrict agricultural yields. Indeed, under China's Household Responsibility System, households are required to provide a quota of their agricultural output to the state. They can then sell any surplus on the free market. Thus the majority of farming households are surplus producers. The figures cited from Nujiang, on the other hand, indicate that local farmers are deficit producers and cannot even grow enough grain to sustain their own households—the policy of providing a quota of agricultural output to the state is generally waived in poverty-stricken areas such as Nujiang.

CONCLUSION

Prior to Liberation in 1949, the ethnic minority population who occupied the area we today know as Gongshan maintained limited cultural and political connection with the Chinese empire, whereas contemporary accounts represent the local ethnic minority population as full-fledged citizens of the Chinese Party-state. Since 1949, the Gongshan population has been a major target of development programs geared toward their integration into China's political and economic fabric. These programs have been underpinned by a pervasive narrative that represents the local population as poor, backward, maintaining low productive forces, and incapable of developing themselves—a narrative that has also served to legitimize CCP intervention in Gongshan. Over the past decade, there has been a dramatic upscaling of government intervention here, in which conservation, education, and labor programs, combined with significant improvements to social and economic infrastructure, are disembedding the people of Gongshan from their local context and further integrating them into the expanding market economy and Chinese Party-state.

2

NATURE RESERVES AND REFORESTATION

The Impacts of Conservation Programs upon Livelihoods

China is now experiencing many pollution hazards that only emerged during the middle or late stages of industrialization in developed countries, and no more sustainable environmental capacity is left to sustain the current pattern of economic growth. In the next 15 years, China's population will reach 1.46 billion and the GDP will quadruple. The expansive growth of the economy and population will bring huge pressures on resources and the environment.

—Yang Dongping 2007: xxxvii

When officials view situations such as that in the Dulongjiang, they mostly see extreme poverty, "backward" ethnic culture and the environmental destruction caused by creating swidden fields. Meeting "rights to subsistence" and "rights to development" are prioritized, and the focus of officials' efforts is on ensuring that basic food needs are met while introducing "advanced" and "scientific" agricultural production technologies. In this view, Dulong culture has nothing to offer the future.

—Wilkes and Shen 2007: 80

The CCP's legitimacy hinges upon its capacity to deliver sustained economic growth, social stability, and better livelihoods for the people of China. The continuing deterioration of China's natural environment is a serious challenge to these aspirations. Indeed, it is estimated that the economic costs associated with air pollution alone account for between 3 and 8 percent of China's GDP (Yang Dongping 2007: xxxviii). In an attempt to balance conservation with development, the CCP has implemented a series of large-scale conservation programs. Poor, marginal rural communities such as Gongshan are the most likely to be adversely affected by these programs.

The concept of governmentality, which provides us with a particularly useful tool for excavating the ways in which modern societies are governed, may be applied to conservation programs recently implemented in Gongshan, which not only are intended to conserve physical natural resources, but also are implicated within the broader social engineering agenda of China's governing authorities. In Gongshan, this agenda involves transferring so-called backward, low-quality, and unproductive farmers away from agricultural work and toward off-farm work in cities and towns, and, in doing so, facilitating the integration of a formerly peripheral ethnic minority community into the national economy and Party-state. These conservation programs are legitimized by a government narrative that represents the local rural population as the most serious threat to the natural environment and as being incapable of maintaining sustainable livelihoods without government intervention. Although this phenomenon is not unique to China, the techniques and practices associated with conservation programs in Gongshan are relatively blunt, and in some cases ineffective, instruments for influencing the conduct and aspirations of the local population.[1] Furthermore, it appears that these programs have had limited success in terms of conservation.

Three major conservation programs affect agricultural practices and access to resources in Gongshan: the Natural Forest Protection Program (NFPP), the Sloping Land Conversion Program (SLCP, also known as "Grain for Green"), and the creation of the Gaoligongshan Nature Reserve. These programs have significantly redefined local livelihoods. Despite Gongshan's geographical isolation and economic underdevelopment, its people find themselves increasingly detached from their local context and grappling with fundamental changes to their livelihoods and agricultural practices that are beyond their control. Policy goals also appear to be incongruent with the economic and social realities of the communities targeted by these programs. While conservation programs promise long-term benefits for China's environment, they can also contribute to increased economic marginalization and welfare dependence among those community members ill-equipped to deal with these changes. For example, whereas conservation programs such as the SLCP are designed to move farmers toward off-farm work in cities and towns, in poor ethnic minority rural communities such as Gongshan, members of the local adult population often do not have the skills and knowledge necessary to engage in off-farm work. These programs do not always result in improved conservation outcomes, either: in many cases, the tree species selected for conservation programs are not suited to local conditions. As a consequence, many areas nominally reported to authorities as forested are in fact barren wasteland, significantly undermining the promised environmental benefits of these conservation efforts.

This scenario also reflects the contradictory demands placed upon the local community. On the one hand, government constantly dictates to local parents that they must keep their children in school. They are told that a full education will ensure that future generations will not experience a life of poverty. However, in imposing strict conservation policies, the government has severely affected the capacity of households to generate the income required to support their children's education-related costs. The household economic burden associated with the first nine years of education has decreased substantially in recent years; nevertheless, education still is the largest economic outlay for many household economies.

The programs demonstrate the Party-state's present dilemma of trying to balance rapid economic development with environmental conservation. During the first two decades of the reform period, China's natural environment was often neglected as governing authorities pursued swift industrial development. The central government appeared to be pursuing a policy of "get rich first, clean up later." However, by the end of the 1990s, the central government realized that the ongoing damage to China's environment was not sustainable and that it threatened the long-term prosperity of the nation. As a consequence, over the past decade and a half we have witnessed a big shift in the Party-state's attitude toward environmental conservation.

Nevertheless, conservation programs have exacerbated ecological destruction in some cases (see Harkness 1998). The first case study presented in this chapter, "Zala" hamlet, demonstrates that the creation of the Gaoligongshan Nature Reserve has actually escalated the exploitation of ecological resources.[2] The boundaries and codes of conduct outlined in official conservation policy are not rigorously enforced and are easily circumvented at the hamlet level. Our second case study, focusing on the isolated hamlet of "Talaka," demonstrates the ways in which geographical isolation and inadequately resourced monitoring agencies can render conservation programs ineffective. The Talaka example highlights the coercive limits of the Chinese Party-state as well as the contradictory policies associated with development in poor rural communities.

The recent promotion of hydroelectricity production provides further evidence of the contradictory development policies being pursued by the governing authorities in Nujiang. The prefectural government has strongly endorsed plans to construct a series of large-scale cascading dams down the Nu River as a vehicle for generating income and stimulating Nujiang's underdeveloped economy. However, the construction of these dams is likely to have a severe impact upon Nujiang's unique and fragile ecology as well as the livelihoods of the local population.

CHINA'S DEVELOPMENT DILEMMA: BALANCING CONSERVATION AND ECONOMIC GROWTH

China has a critical shortage of naturally forested areas, and its biodiversity is seriously threatened. One of the major challenges to the conservation of naturally forested areas and biodiversity is the large, generally poor populations living in and around China's forested areas. While China's population as a whole has increased approximately two and a half times since 1953 (the year of the first official census), the population living in forested areas has increased five times. Increased population pressure combined with wide-scale industrial logging in forested areas has resulted in significant reductions in natural forest cover and serious soil erosion problems (Zhang et al. 2000: 2135). The areas with the densest concentration of biodiversity are also home to some of China's poorest rural communities. On the one hand, these communities find themselves subject to popular and government discourse telling them that they are poor and backward and must develop. On the other, they are confronting conservation programs that have removed their access to the resources necessary for household economic development.

China's current development dilemma stems from a history of unbridled environmental destruction. China is home to one of the world's oldest continuous civilizations, and its natural environment has been under pressure from human habitation for several thousand years. In recent times, an extremely large populace, coupled with rapid industrial development, has placed severe strains on the fragile natural environment. Although China has a large land area, more than half of it is highly mountainous. China also has one of the world's lowest ratios of arable land per person. One-third of China's land is at altitudes over 2,000 meters above sea level (Smil 1984: 5). As Smil notes, "No other large populous nation has so much of its territory in high mountains" (ibid.: 4–5). China's forest volume per person is approximately one-eighth of the world average (Elvin 2004: 20).

Since dynastic times, China's forests have provided the fuel for economic development and have been subject to wide-scale human intervention. Forests were not only cleared for new farmland and settlements; they also provided fuelwood for households and industry and timber for the construction of houses, ships, boats, and bridges (ibid.). As early as the eleventh century, there was an awareness of fuel shortages associated with deforestation in central eastern China (ibid.: 20–21).

Deforestation escalated during the Maoist period as the Party-state engaged in a "war against nature" to fuel rapid industrial expansion and increase agricultural production (see Shapiro 2001). Although China's first nature reserve was officially created in 1956 and efforts were made to reforest vast areas of the country, environmental conservation was not a government priority during the Maoist period, and reforestation efforts were largely ineffective (Harkness 1998: 913–14; Murray and Cook 2002: 48–53).

China's rapid economic growth over the past three decades has translated into increased pressure on the country's forestry resources and biodiversity. For example, average annual timber consumption nearly doubled between the mid-1970s and early 1980s (Harkness 1998: 914). The increased pressure on China's forest resources is attributable to the "recommodification of the natural world since 1978," whereby resources that had been strictly controlled under state monopolies became subject to market forces (ibid.: 915). Nontimber forest products (NTFPs), including wild medicinal plants, flowers, and mushrooms, have become highly commodified during the reform era and now are an important source of cash income for rural communities living in or near natural forests. In some cases, the commodification of these resources has exposed peripheral rural communities to powerful economic forces beyond their local realm. For example, exposure to lucrative foreign markets resulted in the sudden commodification of matsutake mushrooms in northwestern Yunnan in the mid-1980s (see Yeh 2000). Previously, matsutake mushrooms had held little economic value for local rural communities, but from the mid-1980s onward, improved local transport infrastructure and rising demand among wealthy Japanese consumers have induced wide-scale, and sometimes unsustainable, exploitation of these mushrooms.[3]

From the early 1980s onward, increasing concerns about forest destruction and the loss of biodiversity within China has led to efforts to preserve existing forests and promote reforestation. For example, by 1993 the number of nature reserves had increased to more than 760, and they covered 6 percent of national territory (Harkness 1998: 917). Furthermore, official restrictions were placed on timber use. For example, starting in 1983, timber was officially prohibited from being used as industrial fuel or floorboards or to build coffins, stairs, or bridges (ibid.: 916).

Today nature reserves form the backbone of China's efforts to prevent biodiversity loss (McBeath and Leng 2006: 106). These are areas of land with artificial boundaries that limit human activity and prevent the exploitation of resources. Areas are generally nominated as nature reserves because of their unique biological characteristics. By 2005, China had close to 2,200 nature reserves, covering 14.8 percent of its land area. There are plans to increase the number to 2,500 by 2050, which will cover 18 percent of the land area (Xu and Melick 2007: 320).

In western China in particular, poor rural communities have experienced major changes to their livelihoods because of nature reserves. While western areas such as Yunnan, Guizhou, and western Sichuan are home to China's densest concentration of plant and animal species, they are also home to China's poorest people.

China's efforts to reforest and promote environmental conservation appear impressive on paper. However, these efforts have not been accompanied by effective management, financial support, or enforcement (Harkness 1998; Xu and Melick 2007). Most of China's nature reserves are in poor, isolated areas of the country. The local governments in charge of managing and policing reserves generally do not have the financial and human resources to effectively undertake these activities (Harkness 1998: 918). These poorly funded provincial and county governments are expected to shoulder the burden of managing and policing reserves without a concomitant increase in financial support or training from higher-level governments (Xu and Melick 2007: 321). Consequently, local governments often regard reserves as an administrative burden (Harkness 1998: 918). The inability of underfunded nature reserve offices to effectively police and manage reserve resources often results in reserves becoming "paper parks," so that their resources continue to be plundered. This can actually cause further harm to protected areas because the newly prescribed management and policing associated with nature reserve protection are not as effective as traditional, more inclusive community forestry conservation and management practices (Harkness 1998; Xu and Melick 2007).[4]

CHINA'S REFORESTATION PROGRAMS

China's nature conservation efforts have been augmented by the Natural Forest Protection Program (NFPP; Tianran Lin Ziyuan Baohu Gongcheng) and the Sloping Land Conversion Program (SLCP; Tui Geng Huan Lin Huan Cao Gongcheng). These programs are designed to protect old-growth forests, to forest barren wasteland, and to convert agricultural land to forest, and China's western areas are a major focus of their work. Central to both of these programs is their reliance on nominal reporting of increased forest coverage as a proxy for progress (Trac et al. 2007: 277). A number of case studies suggest that these programs' effectiveness as conservation measures has been highly uneven and that, in some cases, they have been a complete failure, challenging official accounts that the programs have led to widespread increases in forest coverage (Trac et al. 2007; Weyerhaeuser, Wilkes, and Kahrl 2005).

The Natural Forest Protection Program

Two major conservation activities underpin the NFPP: a national logging ban and reforestation. The program can be traced back to central government reforestation efforts of the late 1970s. However, it was not until late 1998 that the central government began investing heavily in the NFPP in an attempt to systematically restore China's forested areas and to protect water and soil resources in the watershed areas of its major rivers (Mallee 2001: 6–7).

In 1998, the middle reaches of the Yangzi River experienced severe flooding, resulting in the loss of more than three thousand lives and serious environmental and economic damage. The flooding was officially attributed to high levels of silt in the river system, linked to soil erosion resulting from deforestation in the Yangzi's upriver catchment areas. The major culprits for the high levels of erosion and river silting were said to be farmers in the upland watershed areas of western China, who over the past decades had opened up agricultural land on slopes with a gradient of greater than 25 degrees (ibid.: 7). Recent research challenges this attribution, suggesting that while deforestation in upriver catchment areas did lead to localized erosion and buildup of silt, this silt did not flow downstream and cannot be directly correlated with the flooding of the middle reaches of the Yangzi (see Henck 2010).

In late 1998, in response to this crisis, a number of provinces, including Yunnan and Sichuan, placed a blanket ban on logging in natural forests in accordance with the NFPP; over the ensuing two years, the central government invested heavily in the program. In December 2000, the central government announced that it would invest nearly ¥100 billion (approximately US$12.5 billion) over the following ten years in an effort to both protect existing forests and expand China's forestry coverage. Eighty percent of this funding would come directly from the central government (Mallee 2001: 6).

This policy has had a substantial impact on livelihoods in areas where households and governments had relied heavily on logging for income. Indeed, in southwestern China, some county governments had relied on logging for 80 percent of their tax revenue (ibid.: 7).

The NFPP has been incorporated within the Open Up the West policy. There are five central tasks in this policy; the second of these emphasizes the need to "earnestly strengthen the protection and construction of the ecological environment" (*Qieshi jiaqiang shengtai huanjing baohu he jianshe*) (China.com, August 19, 2007).[5]

The Sloping Land Conversion Program

Closely affiliated with the NFPP is the Sloping Land Conversion Program. The SLCP is one of the biggest changes to agricultural life since the founding of the PRC. Essentially, the SLCP provides subsidies to farmers in return for converting their steep, sloping agricultural land into ecological forests, economic forests, or grasslands. According to the State Forestry Administration definition, *ecological forest* comprises timber-producing forests, while *economic forest* comprises orchards or plantations of trees with medicinal value (Xu et al. 2004). Farmers receive grain subsidies, cash payments, and free seedlings for converting their land. If farmers convert to economic forests, they receive subsidies for five years. If they convert to ecological forests, they receive subsidies for eight years. In the Yangzi River Basin, farmers receive 150 kilograms of grain per *mu* (0.0667 hectares) per year as compensation. In the Yellow River Basin, farmers receive 100 kilograms of grain per *mu* per year. Farmers also receive ¥20 (approximately US$2.50) cash per *mu* per year. In recent years, farmers in some areas have received cash instead of grain as compensation. The SLCP is taking place on a massive scale and is one of the world's largest ecological conservation projects. The program was originally targeted to affect nearly fifteen million hectares of land and forty to sixty million households (Uchida, Xu, and Rozelle 2005: 247).

Although the SLCP is targeted at restoring soil and water systems in fragile ecological areas, it also has a social engineering agenda. According to a State Forestry Administration report, the program aims to shift farmers away from environmentally damaging agricultural practices and toward what governing authorities regard as more sustainable and productive activities, such as raising livestock and engaging in off-farm work (Xu Zhigang et al. 2004: 318).[6] Thus, for millions of farmers the program is a fundamental transformation of their way of life and potentially means closer integration into China's industrial economy.

The SLCP has had the greatest impact in western provinces such as Sichuan and Yunnan, which have a high concentration of farmers cultivating land on slopes with a gradient of greater than 25 degrees.[7] Farmers participating in the program are particularly concerned about how they will generate income and sustain their households when they stop receiving government subsidies in five to eight years. This scenario will begin to change in the years ahead, as implementation and strict enforcement of nine-year compulsory education in China's western peripheral regions expand the pool of farmers eligible for off-farm work in the long term. For now, though, the future for adult farmers remains open.

THE IMPACTS OF CONSERVATION PROGRAMS IN NUJIANG AND GONGSHAN

Until the early 1980s, Nujiang's forest resources, including those in Gongshan, were targeted as lucrative fuel for local economic growth. During the 1960s, government policy declared, "Take forest as the key, and fully develop forestry and grain" (*Yi lin wei zhu, lin liang bing ju, quanmian fazhan*). In the 1970s, new government policy declared, "Take forest as the key, and fully develop forestry, grain, livestock, and medicinal plants" (*Yi lin wei zhu, lin, liang, mu, yao quanmian fazhan*) (*Gongshan County Annals* 2006: 262).

Since the early 1980s, a series of programs has been put in place to preserve Gongshan's ecological resources. However, it was not until the late 1990s that the county government, in alignment with national conservation policies, made serious efforts to preserve Gongshan's local ecology. According to contemporary official sources, the county government still views Gongshan's ecological assets as one of its greatest potential resources; however, the county government is now promoting conservation rather than exploitation. The importance that the county government now attributes to ecological preservation is summarized by Gongshan County Secretary Zhu Yuhua: "Gongshan's advantage lies in its ecology. Gongshan's development relies on its ecology. Increasing farmers' revenue relies on ecology. Therefore the protection of Gongshan's ecology is the key to opening up its development" (*Yunnan Daily Online*, January 23, 2007).

According to official figures, Gongshan's forest coverage has increased significantly over the past two decades due to reforestation efforts. These figures declare that forest coverage has increased from 48.2 percent in 1984 to 77.2 percent today and claim that over the past fifty years, more than 410,000 *mu* (27,347 hectares) of land has been reforested, over 1,700,000 trees have been planted, 3,935,000 *mu* (262,464.5 hectares) of forestry resources have been protected under the NFPP, 180,000 *mu* (12,006 hectares) of collective forest have been created, and 47,000 *mu* (3,134.9 hectares) of agricultural land have been converted to forest in accordance with the SLCP (Xinhuanet, September 26, 2006). Associated with these policies are government efforts to move villagers down to lower altitudes from upland villages. These official figures need to be treated with a high degree of caution, however. Although notionally, large areas of former agricultural land have been converted back to "forest," in many cases the tree species that have been planted have not thrived. In fact, many of the areas that have been "reforested" actually resemble barren wasteland (see figs. 2.1, 2.3, and 2.4).

Moreover, conservation development policies in Gongshan are often highly contradictory, and they unfairly attribute environmental problems to the agricultural practices of the local population. For example, government officials have identified the development of hydroelectricity via both small- and large-scale dams as a key vehicle to ensure ecological preservation in Nujiang. The Nujiang Prefecture party secretary, Jie Yi—the most powerful person in the prefecture—made the following statement to reporters: "Nujiang's fragile ecological environment unsustainably supports a large population. Nujiang is not facing an ecological protection problem, [but] rather an ecological rehabilitation problem. Ecological restoration forces people to relocate. Converting land to forest and restoring ecology requires people to invest money. It is urgent to develop hydroelectricity to protect Nujiang's ecology. Why are we so determined? Because there is no other way out" (*Yunnan Daily Online,* quoted in Wang et al., January 13, 2006). The party secretary essentially is arguing that the production of hydroelectricity via large-scale dam projects is the only mechanism that will provide Nujiang with the high level of income necessary to effectively restore the local ecology. These sentiments were echoed by Shi Lishan, deputy director of the new energy department under the National Energy Administration, at a meeting in Beijing in early 2011 following an official announcement that the central government was resuming plans to build a series of large cascading dams down the Nu River (*China Daily,* February 1, 2011). In response to suggestions that the dams would damage Nujiang's ecology, he said that the ecology along the Nu River had already been damaged by local farmers who cultivated the steep slopes above the river, and he implied that these farmers were responsible for depleting all of Nujiang's forests below 1,500 meters and increasing its susceptibility to natural disasters. He stated: "Some people say that Nujiang people are not growing grain, but brewing disasters. . . . So proper development of the river is crucial to improving local people's lives and protecting the environment" (ibid.).

These official statements, one by a central government official and one by a lower-level prefectural official, are further articulations of the "Nujiang issue" narrative that ascribes Nujiang's low level of economic development and its environmental problems mainly to the livelihoods and agricultural practices of the local ethnic minority population. This narrative not only serves to legitimize government intervention; it also deflects attention from the highly deleterious environmental impacts associated with the government's development policies. Governing authorities point to Nujiang's ethnic minority farmers as the single biggest threat to local ecology, even though it was these same governing authorities who began efforts to exploit the prefecture's natural resources in a damaging way and who continue to do so today.

Based on experiences in other parts of China, it is highly unlikely that these so-called conservation development policies, particularly the development of hydroelectricity via the construction of dams, will translate into positive outcomes for the people of Gongshan and the local environment. As noted earlier, according to nongovernmental assessments, the nearby Mekong River hydroelectric dam projects have done little to improve local livelihoods and in some cases have exacerbated poverty (Xue and Wang 2007: 81–83). Furthermore, according to some estimates, of the sixteen million people who have been displaced by hydropower projects in China since 1949, more than 60 percent now live below the poverty line (ibid.: 82).

Although the Chinese government has not publicly released the results of the Environmental Impact Assessment performed for the proposed dams project, there can be little doubt that the construction of these dams would have a devastating impact upon local ecology. Even if these dams are built at altitudes below those at which Nujiang's unique ecological resources are found, they will submerge prime agricultural land and, in so doing, push farmers farther up the mountain slopes and toward these resources. An independent investigation conducted by the International Union for Conservation of Nature (IUCN) in conjunction with UNESCO also suggests that the proposed dams will negatively impact local ecology (Lopoukhine and Jayakumar 2006).

The Gaoligongshan Nature Reserve

In the decades following Gongshan's Liberation, forestry resources were regarded as fuel for economic growth (Wilkes 2000). Forestry products, including medicinal plants, were specifically targeted for economic exploitation. However, due to poor transport infrastructure and logistical constraints, it was not until 1979 that forestry industry began to take off. By the 1990s, forestry resources were the bedrock of the Gongshan economy, providing a large revenue stream for local government, income for local households, and profits for local and outside businesses (ibid.).

Nevertheless, although forests were targeted for economic exploitation, there was also evidence of increasing conservation concerns starting in the mid-1980s. In 1986, the Gaoligongshan National-Level Nature Reserve (Gaoligongshan Guojia Ji Ziran Baohu Qu) was created. The reserve covers more than 50 percent of Gongshan's territory and is one of China's richest repositories of plant and animal species. A number of stations were established by the County Nature Reserve Bureau to police the nature reserve and prevent villagers from accessing its resources. The creation of the reserve imposed an artificial barrier; the threat of legal punishment was used to deter villagers from accessing forestry resources, hunting, and grazing livestock (ibid.). However, it was not until the late 1990s that the policing of the reserve's resources began in earnest. More effective surveillance contributed to a considerable decline in household income in communities within or near the reserve. At the same time, evidence suggests that increased surveillance has done little to deter outsiders from exploiting the reserve's resources. The reasons for this are explained below.

The Three Parallel Rivers UNESCO World Heritage Area has been inscribed on top of the Gaoligongshan Nature Reserve area. In accordance with a request from the Yunnan provincial government, the World Heritage Area is above 2,000 meters in elevation and, as a consequence, does not encompass the Nu River's fast-flowing waters, which are coveted by provincial authorities as a key resource for economic development via dam construction and hydroelectric power generation (Brown and Xu 2010: 779). The UNESCO World Heritage Area system convention "seeks to encourage the identification, protection and preservation of cultural and natural heritage around the world considered to be of outstanding value to humanity" (UNESCO 2007). The Three Parallel Rivers Area was officially inscribed in July 2003; it covers nearly 1.7 million hectares of northwestern Yunnan and includes the watersheds of three of China's major rivers, the Nu (Salween), Lancang (Mekong), and Jinsha (Yangzi). The World Heritage Nomination report notes the unique biological criteria that formed the basis upon which the Three Parallel Rivers Area was nominated and accepted:

> Northwest Yunnan is the area of richest biodiversity in China and may be the most biologically diverse temperate region on earth. The site encompasses most of the natural habitats in the Hengduan Mountains, one of the world's most important remaining areas for the conservation of the earth's biodiversity. The outstanding topographic and climatic diversity of the site, coupled with its location at the juncture of the East Asia, Southeast Asia, and Tibetan Plateau biogeographical realms and its function as a N-S corridor for the movement of plants and animals (especially during the ice ages), marks it as a truly unique landscape, which still retains a high degree of natural character despite thousands of years of human habitation. As the last remaining stronghold for an extensive suite of rare and endangered plants and animals, the site is of outstanding universal value. (IUCN n.d.: 10)

The World Heritage Area is believed to contain more than 25 percent of China's animal species (IUCN n.d.: 2–3). Many of these species are classified as endangered. The World Heritage Area is also home to more than six thousand species of plants, six hundred of them endemic to northwest Yunnan (ibid.). The Gaoligongshan Nature Reserve is one of many protected areas included in the World Heritage Area. The conservation strategy associated with the World Heritage listing emphasizes the need to balance conservation with economic development. We see clear evidence that this program not only is aimed at protecting natural resources, but also is influencing the conduct and aspirations of the communities affected: "The guiding principles are ecological equilibrium, between man and nature, ecological conservation and conformity to existing laws. The plan is to preserve the ethnic cultures, focusing on certain villages, retaining their biological, cultural and landscape diversity while developing their economic potential in environmentally friendly ways. Staff training and public awareness programs are planned, and programs for monitoring by satellite and aerial photography, and on site [monitoring] of the hydrology, ecology, fires, pollution, forest disease and tourist movements" (UNEP/WCMC 2003).

The World Heritage listing does not provide direct financial funding to the protected area, and it relies on existing governing institutions to ensure ongoing protection. Nevertheless, at present it remains unclear whether the listing translates into better protection for plant and animal species and sustainable outcomes for people living in or near the World Heritage Area. Indeed, the listing appears to provide further justification for local government efforts to relocate poor rural communities out of the area.

UNESCO and the IUCN have been concerned about the lack of transparency and openness regarding hydroelectric dam construction in the Three Parallel Rivers Area (see Lopoukhine and Jayakumar 2006). As noted earlier, the provincial government has identified hydroelectricity production as a key driver of economic development. Local governments are pursuing hydroelectric dam construction projects in the Three Parallel Rivers Area even though these projects would severely compromise the biological and cultural assets of this region.

In Gongshan, the creation of the Gaoligongshan Nature Reserve and its subsequent inclusion in the World Heritage Area have resulted in poorer outcomes for local communities and ongoing unsustainable exploitation of nature reserve resources. Similar to the situation in other reserves, the Gaoligongshan Nature Reserve has suffered from insufficient financial support, and its resources are still being exploited by local villagers as well as outsiders (Wilkes and Yang 2000a, 2000b).

The creation of the Gaoligongshan Nature Reserve has also marginalized communities living in or near the reserve by prohibiting access to income-generating resources such as timber and medicinal plants. In Gongshan, anecdotal evidence suggests that nature reserve resources continue to be harvested despite intermittent policing by the Nature Reserve

Bureau staff and village-based forest guards. One reason for ineffective surveillance and policing is a lack of incentive for locals to report people who are illegally extracting resources from the reserve.[8]

While it was difficult to find informants who would openly admit to the ongoing exploitation of nature reserve resources, some informants did disclose that people from their hamlet continued to access the nature reserve to collect medicinal plants and other NTFPs. Furthermore, along the main thoroughfares of the county town it is common to see locals and outsiders openly selling orchids, medicinal plants, and protected animal species extracted from the reserve.

Exposure to market economic conditions appears to be one of the main factors that have contributed to the overexploitation of local natural resources in Gongshan. Under the command economy, NTFPs and timber offered households limited financial utility. However, under market economic conditions, these resources are transformed into lucrative generators of household cash income (also see Hoang 2009). During the reform era, households have become increasingly reliant upon cash income, not only to meet government obligations such as education costs for children, but also to purchase the growing array of goods and services available under the market economy. According to a village-based informant in Gongshan, in 2001 the price paid for wild orchids reached ¥100 (approximately US$12.50) per plant. This is a very large sum of money in a community where the average rural per capita cash income in 2008 was ¥1,064 (China Nujiang Gorge Network 2011). The sudden increase in orchid price resulted in the wide-scale stripping of orchids from the nature reserve by local farmers. Consequently, today it is very difficult to find orchids there. The stripping was driven by increased demand for orchids from outside collectors. According to the informant, locals sold orchids to middlemen, who took them back to cities such as Kunming, Shanghai, and Beijing to sell at much higher prices (field notes, July 6, 2005).

In some cases, the ongoing exploitation of medicinal plants and other NTFPs by local households also reflects their practical response to the high-priced goods and services delivered through government institutions and the market economy. For example, apart from providing villagers with a valuable source of cash income, medicinal plants are an important substitute for expensive medical treatment at local hospitals and medical clinics (ibid.).

CASE STUDY ONE: "ZALA"

The Gongshan hamlet of Zala is an example of the impacts of the Gaoligongshan Nature Reserve on the area. The creation and increased policing of the reserve have affected some communities more than others, and
poor rural communities such as Zala that relied heavily on the reserve's
resources have suffered. The importance of the reserve to poor households
cannot be overstated. In earlier times of hardship, the resources there provided insurance against starvation.

Zala is a poor, isolated hamlet in the west of Cikai township, approximately three hours' walk up the Pula River from the county town (see map
4). No roads directly link it with the rest of Gongshan. The hamlet sits at
1,900 meters, approximately 475 meters above the Pula River. Zala sits
directly on the border of the Gaoligongshan Nature Reserve. Production
and income levels are low (Wilkes and Yang 2000a: 2). In 1999, Zala had
41 households, which is approximately a sixfold increase in the number of
households since 1949. In 1999, average income was ¥629, approximately
75 percent of the Cikai township average and ¥170 below the national
poverty line (Wilkes and Yang 2000b: 36). The NFPP has strengthened
restrictions on logging. Prior to 1999, 80 percent of Zala households were
engaged in logging. One family could make ¥2,000 to ¥3,000 from logging each year. However, following the construction of the Dulongjiang
Road, the Nature Reserve Bureau built an inspection station next to the
county town. Timber being brought out of Zala and surrounding areas
had to be taken through this inspection station. From that time onward,
villagers have been unable to sell timber (Wilkes and Yang 2000a: 8).

One newspaper report suggests that the logging ban has actually exacerbated environmental destruction in Nujiang, as the ban induced farmers
to open up more agricultural land in order to compensate for the income
loss associated with the logging ban (Wang et al., January 13, 2006). There
is veracity to such reports. However, they also reflect local government
prejudice against the rural ethnic minority population, which is perceived
not only as poor, backward, and engaging in a method of agricultural
production that does not contribute to economic development, but also as
dependent upon the "advanced," "scientific" intervention of government
if it is to interact with the local environment in a sustainable manner (also
see Hoang 2009).

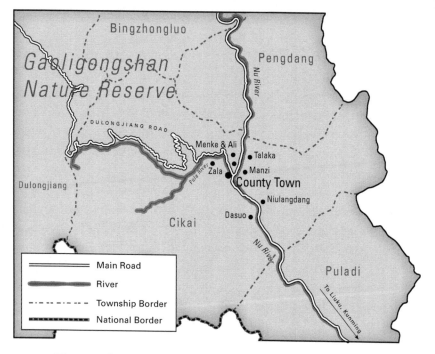

MAP 4. Cikai township. Menke, Ali, Zala, and Talaka are pseudonyms for towns.

According to an investigation conducted by Andreas Wilkes and Yang Xuefei in 2000 (2000b), most households were reliant on the nature reserve's natural resources. NTFPs collected within the reserve contributed between 10 and 60 percent of household income (ibid.: 43). Resources that could be sold for cash included matsutake mushrooms, fragrant mushrooms (*xiangjun*), and *sanqi,* as well as more than twenty types of wild vegetables and wild honey (ibid.: 37). These resources provided both cash income that villages could use to compensate for their insufficient grain levels and wild vegetables to eat during times of grain shortage. Importantly, household cash income generated through the sale of NTFPs such as these was used to pay for government-imposed services, including education (ibid.: 43).

Despite the creation of the nature reserve in 1986, resources continue to be exploited by local villagers and outsiders. The villagers' relationship with the reserve resources is summarized as follows:

The villagers are very clear that they are not able to take the resources within the nature reserve. But at the same time they are very clear the resources within the nature reserve are also very important for maintaining their livelihoods and increasing income. Because villagers normally do not have enough grain (grain harvests are low, because apart from natural disasters, nature reserve animals also destroy their crops), the villagers rely on the natural resources within the nature reserve to supplement their food supply and increase income, and ensure that they have enough foodstuffs. (Ibid.: 43)

The current approach to reserve management serves neither community development nor national conservation interests. The situation has been compounded by the poor relationship between the community and the organizations responsible for managing the reserve (Wilkes and Yang 2000a: 2). Several NTFP species within the reserve face serious threat, and many other NTFP species have declined in recent years. For example, *tushan* (*Taiwania flousiana*) is a national protected species, but in the nature reserve area close to Zala there were only about thirty *tushan* trees left in 2000 (ibid.). Increases in prices paid for medicinal plants and wild mushrooms have led to the disappearance of four species. Apart from local villagers, people from Fugong, the county directly south of Gongshan, also collect large quantities of medicinal plants and mushrooms (ibid.).

A villager described the problems associated with the imposition of the nature reserve: "The government should give us ¥150 each a year to protect the nature reserve. We could then stop outsiders from entering. If everybody was compensated, everybody would protect it. We do not bother stopping outsiders entering at the moment" (household survey, July 19, 2005). Such compensation is very limited. According to an article published in the *Yunnan Daily Online* (cited in Wang et al., January 13, 2006), the Forestry Bureau compensates farmers for crop losses associated with wild animals, but only for 10 percent of such losses. Furthermore, protection services have to cover vast areas with extremely limited human and financial resources, so it can take several days for Nature Reserve Bureau staff to undertake a return trip by foot to the core areas of the reserve. Limited funding makes such trips very difficult. Speaking with *Yunnan Daily* reporters about these issue, He Runcai, the director of the

Prefectural Forestry Bureau, stated: "We have to beg for finances. Apart from salaries, we have very limited funds to cover other expenses" (quoted in ibid.).

I had originally intended to revisit Zala during my final follow-up fieldwork visit to Gongshan in January 2008 in order to conduct several more in-depth interviews with villagers. However, Zala was snowed in and inaccessible for the duration of my visit. As a consequence, my research assistant made two return visits to Zala on my behalf in February and March 2008. During these visits, he conducted in-depth interviews with two households. Data from these interviews reinforce the findings of Andreas Wilkes and Yang Xuefei (2000a; 2000b) indicating that the creation and increased policing of the reserve have significantly affected local household economies. Furthermore, the data highlight how nature reserve resources provided vital insurance against occasional falls in agricultural output as well as natural disasters.

Reflecting the day-to-day challenges of life in contemporary Gongshan, the large snowfall of late January 2008 had badly damaged Zala's infrastructure, and the hamlet's electricity supply had not been restored when my research assistant made his first return visit on February 11.

Zala Household One

The first household defines itself as Dulong and is composed of three persons: a mother and her two sons. The father of the household died from illness four years prior to my research assistant's field interview. The eldest son attends university in Kunming. His university fees are paid for through a scholarship awarded by a provincial tobacco company. Prior to the increased policing of the nature reserve, the household generated most of its income via the cultivation of a large amount of agricultural land (they did not specify its area) within the reserve boundary, as well as the sale of medicinal plants and wild vegetables collected from the reserve.

However, following the increased policing of the reserve, the family can no longer access the large amount of agricultural land that they used to cultivate there. They also are no longer able to collect medicinal plants and wild vegetables. Furthermore, because the land they used to cultivate within the reserve boundary was defined as illegal, they were not able to receive compensation for that land when the SLCP was introduced in Zala.

Today the household subsists upon 3.5 *mu* of land, 20 goats, and 4 pigs, as well as a government subsidy for the small amount of agricultural land (1.5 *mu*) outside the reserve boundary that they converted following the implementation of the SLCP. The family complained that apart from the relatively small amount of SLCP compensation, they have received no other compensation from government for the loss of household income associated with the creation and increased policing of the reserve. They also complained that wild animals from the reserve damage their crops. However, because of the intensification of conservation laws, they do not have the right to hunt these animals (field notes, February 11, 2008).

The Zala Hamlet Leader's Household

On March 20, 2008, my research assistant visited the hamlet leader's house. The leader was appointed to his position in May 2007, and his household is composed of three persons: the leader himself, who is Nu; his wife, who is Lisu; and their son. Like the previous household, this household complained that their income had decreased significantly and said that life was much harder than before policing intensified. They reported that their household income and general situation are more difficult now than they were prior to the increased policing of the nature reserve. The income they generate from cultivating land is unstable. Raising goats and cows is also more difficult than before. After 1998, their access to timber, NTFPs, and hunting was increasingly curtailed. In 2000, access was completely cut off. Since then, household income has decreased by 40 percent. Previously, an average household could make ¥1,000 to ¥3,000 per year from the reserve resources. This income source has now evaporated.

They also reported that following the increased policing of the reserve and implementation of the SLCP, some wild animal populations have recovered. Consequently, crop damage by wild animals has increased. Moreover, the SLCP has reduced access to pastoral land for raising goats and cows, further affecting the ability of local households to generate income (field notes, March 20, 2008).

The creation and subsequent policing of the Gaoligongshan Nature

Reserve have thus had a destabilizing impact upon local livelihoods. Historically, the resources that now fall inside the reserve boundaries provided households with insurance in times of need. As the resources within
the reserve became increasingly commodified during the reform era, they
provided households with an important source of cash income that was
used to pay for government-imposed services such as education. While
the government imposed much heavier restrictions upon the extraction
of reserve resources from the late 1990s onward, this appears to have done
little to serve either national conservation or local community interests,
with both locals and outsiders continuing to exploit reserve resources. One
of the underlying reasons for ongoing exploitation is the contradictory
demands placed upon the local population by government. On the one
hand, local households are subject to governmental demands to "develop."
This encompasses, among other things, incurring large financial costs in
order to pay for education-related expenses. On the other hand, households have not been provided with adequate alternative income streams
to compensate for the loss of income caused by the creation of the reserve.

The Sloping Land Conversion Program in Gongshan

The SLCP has fundamentally altered Gongshan's agricultural economy,
and although the SLCP has generally been positively received by the local
community, some households have benefited from the program more
than others. The SLCP also appears to be linked to an escalation of social
problems such as dependence, boredom, and alcoholism. The implementation of this program in Gongshan highlights how national development
policies created in Beijing often fail to map the economic and social realities of the communities that will be affected by the changes.

As most agricultural land in Gongshan is located on slopes with a gradient of greater than 25 degrees, the SLCP has had a big impact on local
livelihoods. In Gongshan, households have converted their land to either
ecological forest or to cash crop/economic forest. Golden bamboo (*Phyllo-
stachys aurea*; see fig. 2.1) was the species selected for economic forest,
and *donggua shu* (*Alnus nepalensis*) and Yunnan pine (*Pinus yunnanensis*)
were the main species selected for ecological forest. There was another

ecological forest program attached to the SLCP in Gongshan that affor-
ested or reforested land using "ecological" tree species.[9]

According to official reports, between 2002 and 2005 approximately
60 percent of Gongshan's rural households converted part of their land in
line with the SLCP (Digital Countryside—Building the New Countryside
Information Network 2008). Golden bamboo was selected as the main
species for conversion. The Prefecture Forestry Bureau made this decision
arbitrarily, without taking local environmental conditions into account
(see Wilkes 2005a). Indeed, it appears that golden bamboo is not suited to
local soil and weather conditions, and it is failing to grow in many areas
(see figs. 2.1 and 2.3). There also appears to be a high level of uncertainty
among farmers and government officials about whether they will be able
to harvest the golden bamboo in five to eight years' time, when they will
stop receiving government subsidies. Although local government officials
were unable to provide a definitive explanation regarding eventual user
rights for the golden bamboo, a local hamlet leader explained to me that
"half is the government's and half is ours" (household survey, July 9, 2005).
Some farmers believe that they will be permitted to sell the bamboo on
the open market.

Even if farmers are eventually permitted to harvest the bamboo, there
are concerns that they will be unable to generate any income from it, as
the species of bamboo selected is not thriving in Gongshan and is unlikely
to produce substantial harvests. Furthermore, Gongshan is a long way
from major markets, rendering the transportation costs of bamboo and
bamboo products out of Gongshan very expensive and impractical. A case
study of the attempts made by a county government in southwestern Sichuan to integrate the isolated township of Baiwu into the market economy
via apple production is a sobering reminder of the hazards associated with
exposing poor rural communities to market forces. Engaging in apple
production failed to account for local economic, social, and logistical constraints and actually left some farmers worse off (see Ho 2004).

In Gongshan, most farmers appear to be satisfied with the short-term
outcomes associated with the SLCP. Households are receiving adequate
compensation and no longer have to engage in substantial agricultural
work. Their main concern is what will happen after they stop receiving
state subsidies.

FIG. 2.1. Golden bamboo planted on converted agricultural
land near the county town (December 2006).

Dulongjiang township provides a useful case study for assessing the
impacts of the SLCP on traditional livelihood practices. Since the 1960s,
the government had been actively encouraging Dulongjiang households
to give up their rotational/swidden land in favor of stable agricultural
land, which the government perceived to be a more advanced and productive basis for agricultural production. However, it was not until the
early 2000s that large-scale financing provided through the SLCP enabled
local governing authorities to realize this and other social engineering
goals, such as moving farmers into off-farm work. The implementation
of the SLCP has been more comprehensive there than in other townships,
and although it has been successful in improving food security, it has significantly increased community dependence upon government and has

altered livelihood practices that had traditionally defined Dulong identity (Wilkes and Shen 2007; Shen et al. 2010).

Traditional agricultural practices in Dulongjiang are summarized by the Center for Biodiversity and Indigenous Knowledge as follows: "For centuries, the Dulong have been dependent on agricultural production, with hunting, fishing and gathering as important supplementary activities. . . . Dulong agriculture is mainly rotational agriculture, in which a patch of forested land is selected, cleared and then cultivated. After cultivation for 1–3 years, forest is left to regenerate" (CBIK 2006: 3). When the SLCP was first implemented in Gongshan in 2002, the county government diverted most of the grain quota for the first year toward Dulongjiang. Following the implementation of the program, approximately 66 percent of Dulongjiang's agricultural land was converted to forest in return for subsidies. The converted land was traditionally used for rotational farming and located mainly on slopes with a gradient of greater than 25 degrees. Importantly, although rotational land represented approximately two-thirds of the land used by the Dulongjiang population for agricultural production, it composed only a very small proportion (approximately 0.33 percent) of Dulongjiang's total land area (ibid.: 3–4). This challenges the notion that the people of Dulongjiang were engaging in deleterious agricultural practices and were placing unsustainable pressure on local natural resources.

The formula used to allocate subsidies in Dulongjiang was unique. Whereas households in other townships (as well as the rest of the country) are allocated subsidies that are calculated according to the amount of land converted, in Dulongjiang, households were awarded subsidies on a per capita basis. Thus all rural inhabitants (adults and children) were allocated 180 kilograms of paddy rice per year until 2011, although these grain subsidies were later replaced by cash payments (Shen et al. 2010: 206; Wilkes and Shen 2007: 78). In addition to the SLCP subsidy, local government made direct cash payments to villagers to assist household economies (Shen et al. 2010: 206).[10]

The SLCP has essentially forced farmers to convert their rotational fields, along with a portion of their permanent land, to ecological forest in return for grain subsidies. Following implementation of the SLCP, each household has only a small amount of permanent land allocated for agricultural production (Wilkes and Shen 2007: 78).

Prior to the implementation of the SLCP, Dulongjiang households sub-sisted upon swidden agricultural production, hunting, NTFP collection, and animal husbandry (Shen et al. 2010). Following the implementation of the SLCP, traditional forms of agricultural production, NTFP collection, and animal husbandry have decreased substantially, with households now heavily dependent upon state cash subsidies. One notable impact of the SLCP upon Dulong culture is a change in dietary practices (see ibid.). Prior to the SLCP, the Dulong diet consisted of a range of tradi-tional grains such as millet, buckwheat, and finger millet. Paddy rice was not part of the traditional Dulong diet. The cultivation and consumption of these traditional grain species were considered not only part of a bal-anced, healthy diet, but also a defining characteristic of Dulong culture. However, since the SLCP, traditional grains have disappeared from the diet of many Dulong people. There are two main reasons for this. First, households have discontinued planting some traditional crop species, as these species either do not grow on stable land or have lower yields on stable land as compared to swidden land. Second, paddy rice is the grain provided by the state via the SLCP and by default has become the main staple in the Dulong diet. Many Dulong elders feel that these changes in dietary and agricultural practices have removed an important part of what it means to be Dulong.

The SLCP has also impacted religious rituals. In non-Christian areas in the north of Dulongjiang, the clearing of forests for swidden agricul-ture was preceded by religious rituals performed by shamans. These ritu-als were employed to gain the support of spirits for a good harvest. With the implementation of the SLCP, such rituals have disappeared, and local elders are concerned that knowledge about such rituals will not be passed on to the younger generation (ibid.: 208–09).

Nonetheless, as in other parts of Gongshan, overall the Dulong people are satisfied with the short-term benefits of the SLCP (Xiao 2005). They have a stable, guaranteed source of grain and are not required to under-take as much agricultural work as they were in the past. That said, they are also much more dependent upon the government to sustain their household economies. Here it behooves us to examine the social engi-neering agenda behind the implementation of the SLCP in Dulongjiang, an agenda that in many respects is not in the long-term interests of the Dulong people and their culture. The SLCP appears to have provided the

Gongshan County government with a convenient mechanism to address its own developmental agenda for the ethnic minority people of Dulongjiang. Indeed, a major outcome of the SLCP in Dulongjiang is the abolition of swidden agriculture. Local governing authorities have always regarded swidden agriculture as backward, unproductive, unscientific, and a key indicator of the primitive stage of historical material development.[11] They hold this opinion despite evidence suggesting that swidden agriculture has been used sustainably for several centuries by the population living in the area that we today know as Dulongjiang township (see CBIK 2006). Another critical outcome of the SLCP is that it is has significantly increased Dulongjiang's surplus rural labor population, as the local population now needs to devote much less time to agricultural production to maintain their household economies. Local government is turning to education reform and labor export programs as a means to transform this surplus rural labor into "productive" off-farm workers who will contribute to national and local economic development.

CASE STUDY TWO: "TALAKA"

In December 2006, I spent two days in Talaka hamlet, conducting interviews with local households about economic conditions and the impacts of the SLCP. I first became aware of Talaka after discussions with a local teacher, Ye, and other Gongshan residents. Ye had been Talaka's primary school teacher for ten years until the school's recent closure. He now teaches at a primary school in the county town. Ye has several relatives living in the hamlet and is an uncle of the Talaka hamlet leader. He recommended that I visit Talaka because the conditions in the hamlet were particularly difficult. He explained that the land there was very marginal and produced low agricultural yields. Gongshan residents also reported that conditions in Talaka were so severe that households had resorted to charcoal production to supplement their low agricultural incomes. I was escorted to Talaka by Ye and my research assistant.

While conditions in Talaka are generally difficult and there are very limited income-generating opportunities, the SLCP has considerably altered the local socioeconomic environment. I conducted in-depth interviews with three households, including the household of the village leader. Some households have benefited substantially from the SLCP, with SLCP subsidies essentially replacing income losses associated with the earlier logging ban. Other households appear to be worse off than they were before the ban. In some instances, households recently have begun household-level charcoal production to recoup household income that was lost as a consequence of the ban.

Talaka's physical isolation appears to be a barrier to local governing bodies' effective supervision of local resource extraction. Talaka hamlet lies on the eastern side of the Nu River at approximately 3,000 meters above sea level (see map 4). It is not connected to the rest of the county by road or electricity, although some households have electricity supplied by small hydropower units. An increasing number of households use mobile phones. The hamlet is reached by first walking upstream from the county town for one hour and then ascending a steep mountain path for another hour. Talaka is dotted by a number of large walnut trees, with maize and vegetable fields filling pockets of land between houses (see fig. 2.2). Households are scattered over a large area. The mountains above Talaka rise to over 4,000 meters and are covered in dense old-growth forest that begins at approximately 3,500 meters.

According to my research assistant, Talaka's electricity supply problem is discussed every year when the county government holds its annual meeting. But every year they conclude that it is too difficult and expensive to supply Talaka with electricity. Installing the lines would cost too much for the county government to cover on its own. The hamlet is connected to a water supply from a concrete tank two kilometers away, but the flow is not strong enough to reach every household. This water supply system was first installed in 1997 as part of a poverty alleviation program supported by the Gongshan Poverty Alleviation Office, the Education Bureau, and the Hydropower Bureau. But the system fell into disrepair and was subsequently repaired in December 2005 by the Hydropower Bureau as part of another poverty alleviation program. When I inspected the tank, it was contaminated with tapeworm.

Talaka is home to 116 villagers occupying 41 households. Although most villagers are Lisu, there are also Nu, Tibetan, and Dulong people living there. The village is also home to one Han woman who married into the village from Lushui County. According to Ye, the adult popula-

FIG. 2.2. Talaka hamlet, approximately 3,000 meters above sea level (December 2006).

tion is generally unable speak standard Chinese, but the children learn it through the formal education system. This phenomenon reflects recent improvements in access to Chinese language–based education.

The hamlet's population has increased approximately fourfold since 1960. According to Ye, this population increase is attributable to natural population growth rather than the migration of new households into the hamlet. The highest rates of population growth took place during the pre-reform period. According to the hamlet leader, population pressure is a problem in Talaka: "Three months ago, six more households were added due to marriage and the creation of new households. . . . Now there are not enough resources to go around. Now there is not enough water to supply the village of over one hundred people. As households divide [due to marriage], the amount of land [per household] also decreases" (field notes, December 9, 2006). It appears that this population increase has yet to impact Talaka's primary school–aged population, as the hamlet's single-teacher primary school was recently closed due to low enrollment. Local school-aged children board and study at either Cikai Primary School or

Gongshan High School, both of which are two hours' walk from Talaka. Ye indicated that Talaka's primary school could be reopened if there are enough students in the future.

According to the hamlet leader, the average yearly household income is approximately ¥2,000. On a per capita basis, income is just below the Gongshan average. Maize is the main agricultural crop, and households also raise pigs and chickens for personal consumption. None of Talaka's villagers is engaged in off-farm work; physical isolation and lack of effective communication infrastructure mean that it is difficult for villagers to receive information about off-farm work opportunities. Talaka is on the far side of the Nu River from the nature reserve, and households have not relied on resources now located within the reserve to supplement household income. Thus income and livelihoods in Talaka were not affected by the recent increased policing of reserve resources.

Prior to the logging ban, Talaka's households relied heavily on logging for household income. I was told that three or four years prior to my visit, households began engaging in household-level charcoal production to compensate for income losses associated with the ban. Just as Talaka's isolation is a barrier to off-farm work opportunities and its barren high-altitude landscape makes crop production difficult, these factors also are barriers to the local government's supervision of local practices, particularly the illegal felling of trees for charcoal.

Today the main source of income for Talaka's households is annual subsidies received through the SLCP. Land was converted in 2004; altogether the hamlet has converted over 320 *mu* (21.34 hectares) of agricultural land, mainly to golden bamboo. In 2005, the government began allocating cash instead of grain for SLCP subsidies. Households now receive ¥240 (approximately US$30) per *mu* of converted land per year. More than 100 *mu* (6.67 hectares) of land is still used for agricultural production. The financial benefits associated with the SLCP vary significantly from one household to another. Some households had much more land opened up for agricultural production compared to other households prior to the implementation of the SLCP. As a consequence, there is a considerable imbalance in the distribution of subsidies among local households. For example, one household's total annual SLCP financial subsidy is five times higher than some other households' subsidies.

According to the hamlet leader, the largest amount of land converted by an individual household was 21 *mu*. The smallest amount of land converted by an individual household was 4 *mu*. The household that converted 21 *mu* still has 10 *mu* of land under cultivation, meaning that prior to the implementation of SLCP, the household had 31 *mu* of land under cultivation. The household receives ¥5,040 in cash as SLCP subsidies from government each year, more than five times the amount received by the family that converted 4 *mu* of land. According to both Ye and the hamlet leader, this household grew maize on the 21 *mu* of land prior to conversion. From my discussions with Ye and the hamlet leader, it appears that until 2001 there were no restrictions on cutting and clearing forest to open new agricultural land. Consequently, this particular household cut and cleared a large area. The ¥240 per *mu* per year calculation is based on areas with much higher agricultural yields than Talaka. Thus, because the land in Talaka is particularly marginal and produces low yields, this family receives substantially more financial benefit from SLCP subsidies than they did from growing maize.

According to Ye, even prior to the introduction of the SLCP, families did not earn any cash income from agriculture. The maize and other vegetables they grew on their land were used for raising pigs and chickens, as well as for personal consumption. Talaka is a long distance from the county town, and this distance and the terrain make impractical the regular transportation of fresh meat and vegetables to and from the market for sale.

Since the logging ban and agricultural cultivation restrictions, the production of charcoal is one of the very few income-generating opportunities for Talaka's residents. Charcoal is the main fuel used for household heating and cooking by county town residents. Nevertheless, this does not mean that charcoal production is a lucrative industry. Indeed, it is not the main income source for households, but merely supplements SLCP subsidies. Data gathered from households in Talaka indicate that charcoal production is highly labor intensive; furthermore, households earn only about ¥10 per day from this activity. For a household of four people, this equates to only ¥2.5 per person per day.

Households produce charcoal in manmade kilns dotted on the mountainside above the hamlet. To reach the first charcoal production area, we had to walk approximately two kilometers upriver from Talaka. From that point, we made a gradual ascent up the mountain, encountering more charcoal kilns the farther we ascended. Most kilns are at the bottom of

FIG. 2.3. Agricultural land recently converted to golden bamboo in Talaka (December 2006).

FIG. 2.4. Agricultural land recently converted to *donggua shu* (*Alnus nepalensis*) in Talaka (December 2006).

FIG. 2.5. Charcoal kiln located approximately 3,500 meters above sea level (December 2006).

timber slides: trees are felled at the top of the slides and then are either carried or rolled down the slides to the kiln area below. Some kilns were in operation during our visit.

Households engage in charcoal production for several months each year, starting in early winter. This hard labor requires carrying the charcoal for two hours from the kilns back to Talaka, and from Talaka to the county town for two more hours. Men normally carry baskets weighing 120 *jin* (60 kilograms), women 100 *jin* (50 kilograms). According to the hamlet leader, the whole process takes about fifteen days, with seven to eight days for burning and another seven to eight days for transportation to the county town. Only the chestnut tree (*lishu*) is cut down and used to make charcoal. Trees are cut from old-growth forests and are not replanted by the villagers; the forest regrows naturally. Other trees are not cut down, minimizing the impact on forest resources. The County Forestry Bureau does issue tree-felling permits for private charcoal production and housing construction. Villagers are charged ¥20 for every cubic meter of wood felled.[12]

However, interviews with local household members and the hamlet leader suggest that most of the households do not have official permits for the trees they fell to produce charcoal. In fact, the Forestry Bureau does not issue permits for the level of charcoal-related tree felling taking place in Talaka; and even if they did, the small financial returns associated with charcoal burning mean that it would not be economically viable for these people to purchase permits. Revealing the loose monitoring and supervision associated with tree felling in Gongshan, Ye stated: "Even though it is illegal, they still do this a little bit. Some households have official permission [through the Forestry Bureau]. If households only cut a small amount, then they do not need to apply" (field notes, December 9, 2006).

My research assistant also indicated that government supervision of local logging practices is largely absent: "The management office is not going to come all the way up here to check on them, are they?" (ibid.). On most days, a large group of local farmers can be seen in the middle of the county town openly selling large quantities of charcoal to town residents. The local government appears to turn a blind eye to this practice.

The Talaka Hamlet Leader's Household

The hamlet leader's household is composed of four people: the leader, his wife, and their two sons. One son attends grade four and boards at Cikai Primary School. The other son is not yet of school age. Reflecting the tendency among the Gongshan population to avoid venturing outside their local environment, the hamlet leader had not traveled farther south than the county town. He had not heard of the labor export programs available to local farmers.

I asked the leader how life today compared to life prior to the implementation of the SLCP: "Life is a bit better following the introduction of the SLCP. We can use our spare time to make a bit of extra money" (field notes, December 9, 2006). The hamlet leader indicated that his household makes ¥700 to ¥800 per year from charcoal production. This work consumes seventy to eighty days of household labor each year, equating to ¥10 in revenue per day. The household converted 8 *mu* of land through the SLCP and still has 4 *mu* of land under cultivation. Based on this information, the household's yearly income is ¥2,620 to ¥2,720 per year (¥655 to ¥680 per capita), which is below the county average at the time.

The household started burning charcoal three years previously. I asked the hamlet leader how the household's pre–logging ban income compared to their current income: "Our previous income was much higher. In 1998 our household income was as high as ¥6,000." Much of this income came from logging. The hamlet leader was asked if he had an opinion regarding the ban. "No opinion. We follow what the government says." When asked if life was harder now compared to the time before the ban was introduced, he responded, "Yes. Our income is not enough. We do not have enough money to buy what we need" (ibid.).

Talaka Household Two

The second household we visited is also composed of four people: a husband, a wife, and their two sons. The household converted 17 *mu* of land through the SLCP and has another 10 *mu* of land under cultivation, on which they grow maize for personal consumption. The family also has four small pigs under the house, as well as a number of chickens. The household does not engage in charcoal production, and their entire income derives from SLCP subsidies. Their total household income is ¥4,080 (17 *mu* x ¥240).

One son is in his second year of junior high at Gongshan High School. The elder son is in the army and is stationed in Chongqing. The younger son's schooling costs ¥50 to ¥60 per month, and sometimes as much as ¥100 per month; the money is used to purchase his clothes and daily necessities. The father described the financial impact of school-related expenses upon the household: "It is quite a large economic burden on the family" (ibid.). The father was in the army from 1980 to 1985, based in Liuku, but he receives no pension. He was born in Talaka, while his wife is from Lushui County. When the husband was asked whether he had ever engaged in off-farm work, he responded: "No, I was tricked by outside bosses several times in the past, so I do not take part in laboring. I work at home." Even though the family previously had relied heavily upon income from logging, the father stated: "Our current income is higher than before."

The family clearly values education for their children. The younger son indicated that he wanted to attend senior high school. The parents indicated that they wanted him to attend university upon finishing senior high school. When asked whether they would have difficulties paying for his senior high school fees, his father responded: "Our economic situation isn't very good. We'll have to try to save some money to send him to senior high school." Discussing the potential hurdles to his educational aspirations, the younger son stated: "I'd like to attend university. But the fees are very high. I'm not sure if I'll be able to. I'd like to study a foreign language." When asked how life today compared to life twenty years ago, the father responded: "Life's much better now. There weren't enough clothes back then" (ibid.).

Talaka Household Three

Household Three is also composed of four people: a husband, a wife, and their two sons. The husband is Talaka's deputy leader and accountant. The sons attend grades one and two of junior high at Gongshan High School. We met the members of this household during our inspection of the charcoal kilns: as we walked along a steep, slippery path at approximately 3,500 meters, we were passed by the mother and her sons descending the mountain with baskets of charcoal on their backs. We met the husband at the household's charcoal production site, 50 meters farther uphill. When we arrived at their two large kilns, the husband had just started another burning cycle and smoke was streaming out of the kilns. Next to the kilns was a covered hut containing bedding for one person, two baskets of charcoal, a chainsaw, and a fire.

The husband confirmed that they had converted 21 *mu* of land through the SLCP and were receiving over ¥5,000 per year in cash subsidies from the government. He said that they also earn approximately ¥1,000 per year from charcoal production and that they make charcoal for one to three months per year. According to the husband, it takes the household approximately ninety days to make ¥1,000 from charcoal production. While only one household member is required for the burning process, the whole family is involved in carrying the charcoal to the county town for sale.

The husband said they had been making charcoal for more than one year. When asked why the family had started producing charcoal, the husband responded: "Life was difficult. We started so that we would have enough spare cash [*lingyongqian*] to support our children" (field notes, December 10, 2006).

I asked whether he had a permit to cut trees for charcoal production. He said that he did not have a permit but applies for one when he needs to cut down trees for personal household construction. Again my research assistant reminded me that even though this household was engaging in illegal activity, the government was unable to effectively monitor what took place in Talaka.

I asked the husband how the household's current income compared with their pre-logging ban income: "We used to be involved in logging. Our income is about the same as it was prior to the start of the logging ban." Considering the very substantial subsidies the household receives through the SLCP, this statement is not surprising. When I asked the husband whether the household's current income was enough to support them, he responded: "No. We need a lot of money for our children's education." He said that he hoped his sons could attend senior high school. I asked what he hoped his sons would do when they finished high school. He responded: "Attend university" (ibid.).

Even though this household has an annual income of more than ¥6,000, they still claimed that this was insufficient to cover costs for a family of four in contemporary Gongshan. The waiving of junior high school tuition and boarding fees under the compulsory education policy meant that the costs associated with keeping their two sons in junior high school equated to approximately ¥100 for each son per month. Over a school year, this would translate to approximately ¥2,000. This would leave them with a relatively high surplus income. Nevertheless, once their sons enter senior high school and later proceed to university, the financial burden will increase dramatically. Thus, in the near future, the majority of this household's income will be devoted to education costs unless they can find new income sources.

Again, the case studies of Zala and Talaka reveal the contradictory demands placed upon Gongshan's rural population. On the one hand, households respond to governmental demands to develop, which, among other things, requires them to ensure that their children receive a full education. On the other, the local resources that households rely upon to generate cash income to pay for services such as education have been severely restricted. Even with the new, free nine-year compulsory education policy (discussed in the next chapter) in place, education is still a considerable financial burden for households. As a consequence, households engage in illegal activities to supplement household income.

At first glance, the ongoing exploitation of nature reserve resources and illegal felling of trees for charcoal production seem to gesture toward overt local resistance to the imposition of national development policies. However, in examining the motives that underlie this resistance, we detect a compelling scenario. Many parents who engage in these illegal activities do so to ensure that their children achieve a full education and can access lucrative off-farm employment. This outcome reflects full compliance with (rather than resistance to) the overarching social engineering agenda of China's central governing authorities.

CONCLUSION

Conservation programs are a component of the CCP's social engineering agenda for China's rural population, and ethnic minority people living in poor peripheral areas such as Gongshan are the most likely to be affected by these programs. In Nujiang, governing authorities have identified local ethnic minority communities as the key culprits behind local environmental problems such as deforestation, erosion, and landslides, even though it was these same governing authorities who guided the past rural development programs that created these problems. In employing narratives such as the "Nujiang issue" and connecting Nujiang's environmental problems with the local ethnic minority population, governing authorities not only deflect attention from their role in contributing to these problems; they also provide legitimacy for government programs targeted at shifting farmers away from traditional agricultural livelihoods.

Here the recent decision to proceed with the construction of a series of large, cascading, environmentally destructive dams down the Nu River is a demonstration of the true nature of development priorities in Nujiang and China more broadly. China's governing authorities are primarily concerned not with the protection of Nujiang's rare biological resources, but with economic development and human progress. The traditional livelihoods of Nujiang's ethnic minority farmers are anathema to China's governing authorities. From their perspective, these livelihoods evidence a primitive stage of human development and directly challenge the CCP's development agenda for China. Programs such as the SLCP, and now the construction of the dams, promise to generate large quantities of local income and create economic conditions wherein Nujiang's farmers will no longer be dependent upon traditional, subsistence-based agricultural livelihoods for survival. In the government's vision for Nujiang, ethnic minority people will live not in isolated rural hamlets such as Zala and Talaka, but in modern apartment buildings in county seats such as Gongshan. Their children will attend centralized boarding schools, where they will receive a standardized education. Through this education, they will learn that the agricultural livelihood pursued by their parents' generation was "backward" and a "remnant of a primitive society." They will also learn that high-quality and valued Chinese citizens are not those who engage in agriculture, but those who are willing and able to contribute their labor power to the construction sites and factories of China's modern industrial economy and help to strengthen the Chinese Party-state.

3

ALL IS NOT AS IT APPEARS

Education Reform

Chinese state education attempts to achieve a high degree of cultural and political homogenization for several reasons: to make communication possible among different parts of the country, to ensure the integration of peripheral areas into the Chinese state, to promote patriotism and loyalty to the CCP, and, in a broader sense, to "improve the quality" of or to "civilize" the presumably more "backward" parts of the population.

—Hansen 1999: xii

In comparison to provincial and prefectural averages, in Gongshan basic education is still lagging behind [*zhihou*]. . . . Backwardness in education has created low-quality workers, produced scientific and cultural backwardness, and seriously held back the development of the economy and society.

—*Nujiang News,* November 16, 2005

Until recently, school completion rates among Gongshan's ethnic minority population were very low. The high costs of participating in formal education, combined with a perception that it offers limited utility, caused many ethnic minority students to drop out of school and return to the family farm before completing the standard nine years of compulsory education. However, beginning in 2004, Gongshan implemented a series of wide-scale national reforms aimed at enforcing participation in the mainstream education system: the consolidation of schools (*jizhong banxue*) and free

nine-year compulsory education (*puji jiunian yiwu jiaoyu*). Local governing authorities regard the low educational levels of the Gongshan population as a major stumbling block to the county's development. These same
authorities have outwardly embraced these education reforms as the key
to unlocking the "potential" of this population, preparing them for insertion into China's industrializing economy and stimulating local economic
development. The reforms have reduced the financial burden of education
for Gongshan's households and will most likely contribute to improved
economic livelihoods in the long term. However, in socializing Gongshan's ethnic minority population to the institutions and rationalities of
state education, the reforms also will tighten their integration into the
political fabric of the Chinese Party-state.

In contemporary China, the formal education system is a crucial tool
for governing the population and reinforcing national unity, with the
education of ethnic minorities a major priority of the CCP (see Hansen
1999; Lin 2007; Mackerras 1995). The Chinese education system not only
manifests as a physical site where students are provided with technical
instruction in areas such as mathematics, standard Chinese, and science;
it also is a strategic government technology for influencing the conduct
and aspirations of the population (see Kipnis 2011). Some analysts suggest that China's transition from a socialist command economy to a more
open and market-based economy weakened the Party-state's influence
over some aspects of the public domain. While the Chinese Party-state
has fully embraced modernization and rapid economic development, it
is also sensitive to the potential social and political instability associated
with modernity. In response, central government authorities in China
have become "obsessed with a kind of 'moral planning,' trying to regulate
and control the changing behaviours, norms, and values that follow in the
wake of modernization" (Bakken 2000: 19). The formal education system
represents a strategic and enduring site for this type of moral planning.
No other formal state institution captures such a large slice of society
within a relatively regimented and uniform social and political sphere for
such a long period of time.

Moral planning is entwined within a larger "human quality" (*ren
de suzhi*) discourse. During the reform era, China's central governing
authorities have become fixated on improving population quality, regarding human quality as not only central to China's material and spiritual

development, but also as "a core element in attempts to control the Jugger-
naut" of modernity (ibid.: 5). Reference to population quality is a conspicuous feature of official and popular discourses; moreover, it has provided
the Party-state with a useful mechanism to deflect liability for the serious
social and economic inequalities that have emerged during China's reform
era (Murphy 2004). The poverty and inferior educational outcomes that
persist in peripheral rural areas such as Gongshan tend to be attributed
to the "low quality" and "cultural backwardness" of the local population
rather than to geographical isolation and structural inequalities associated
with CCP policy. In Gongshan, a generally demeaning population-quality
discourse targeted at the local ethnic minority population features prom-
inently in official speeches, newspaper articles (such as the one quoted
in this chapter's epigraphs), school textbooks, and the slogans painted
in bright red characters on the whitewashed walls of official buildings.
It serves as a constant reminder to Gongshan's ethnic minority people
that, from the government's perspective, they are poor, backward, of low
quality, and a hurdle to China's economic development. Within this context, government development programs, such as the strict enforcement
of compulsory education, are presented as opportunities for Gongshan's
ethnic minority people to raise their quality and strengthen the nation.

CHINA AND EDUCATION IN HISTORICAL CONTEXT

Born in 551 BCE, Confucius had a profound influence on the Chinese
education system. He developed a philosophy that extolled the virtues of
harmonious kinship and emphasized self-cultivation and unquestioned
acquiescence to a strictly defined social hierarchy (see Cleverley 1991 [1985]:
4–12). Today Confucianism is still popularly cited as the glue holding Chinese society together.[1] Chinese philosophy and culture assume that "all
persons are potentially perfectible through education," that "the educational environment determines whether or not an individual will be good
or evil, and [that] educational reform is a key to solving urgent social and
political problems" (Bakken 2000: 85). Nevertheless, although Chinese
society has placed strong emphasis on education and self-cultivation for
several millennia, universal access to cost-effective, formal, comprehensive education in both rural and urban China was not achieved until 2007.[2]

In imperial China, the civil service examination system (*keju*) dominated the educational terrain. Although attempts were made during the late Qing and Republican eras to provide a more comprehensive and politicized school system, formal comprehensive education remained out of reach of the majority of the population. Wealthy clans and villages were able to provide schooling for their boys and young men; however, the bulk of China's rural population and urban poor were cut off from formal education.[3] Economic mismanagement, corruption, and civil and national wars during the Republican era severely impeded the development of a comprehensive and effective education system. According to some estimates, in 1949, only 25 percent of the elementary school–aged population was attending school, and the illiteracy rate for the entire population was more than 85 percent and was particularly high among women and the rural population (Cleverley 1991 [1985]: 69).

Educational provision improved dramatically after the CCP gained political control of China in 1949. China's predominantly illiterate rural population presented an enticing prospect for the CCP, which was determined to inscribe a new ideology of national political unity and social cohesion upon China's fragmented population. Indeed, the CCP saw beyond the functional role of education, and sought to utilize it as a key political tool to promote its socialist ideology. Nonetheless, the CCP has also struggled to effectively implement formal comprehensive education, particularly in rural areas.

THE EDUCATION SYSTEM UNDER CCP RULE

Apart from their other characteristics, the outstanding thing about China's six hundred million people is that they are "poor and blank." This may seem a bad thing, but in reality it is a good thing. Poverty gives rise to the desire for change, the desire for action and the desire for revolution. On a blank sheet of paper free from any mark, the freshest and most beautiful characters can be written, the freshest and most beautiful pictures can be painted.

—Mao 1966 [1958]: 36

When the CCP took control in 1949, the country was still economically, socially, and ideologically fractured. The goal of the CCP was to construct a "Communist state populated by a new Communist man [*sic*]" (Ridley, Godwin, and Doolin 1971: 24). The construction of modern socialist society was the first step toward achieving this goal. However, it was not only a material process; it also involved attempts to cultivate a "spiritual" sense of socialism in the hearts and minds of the people living within the borders of the Chinese state (ibid.). Formal education was seen as a particularly useful vehicle for socializing the Chinese people to CCP ideology and policy. The young in particular were considered ideal candidates for ideological conversion, and the primary school became a strategic site to cultivate the "successors to the revolution" (ibid.: 25–26). This social engineering agenda continues to echo loudly across China's education landscape (see fig. 3.2).

A feature of CCP educational policy in the first couple of years after Liberation was the extension of "eliminating illiteracy classes," or *sao-mangban* (Thøgersen 2002: 152–56). These classes were delivered on a part-time basis via nighttime and winter sessions, offering the rural adult population an opportunity to attain a functional level of literacy in standard Chinese. The classes still exist and are an important feature of Gong-shan's education system.

Nevertheless, it was not until 1956 that serious efforts were made to eliminate illiteracy in rural areas.[4] These efforts were precipitated by Mao's transformative economic agenda for rural China. In July 1955, Mao initiated a dramatic shift in policy direction by calling for the mass, rapid collectivization of agriculture. A literate rural populace was identified as an important precondition for the effective collectivization of agriculture.

Thus, in March 1956, "China's most ambitious national literacy campaign" was introduced (Peterson 1994: 113). The Central Committee and State Council adopted a new anti-illiteracy decree that "called for complete elimination of illiteracy among rural fourteen- to fifty-year-olds in China within seven years" (ibid.). Education for the rural population was delivered via collectively organized "people-run" (*minban*) schools, while education for the urban population was delivered via government-sponsored state-run (*gongban*) schools (ibid.: 116). There was a clear demarcation in the content and quality of education delivered via these different forms of schooling. Whereas a state-run education provided a comprehensive educational base, people-run schooling focused on expanding literacy and providing the educational knowledge necessary to work as a member of the newly formed production teams. The "Two Basics" anti-illiteracy policy, introduced by the CCP in the 1990s at the height of the economic reform period, closely resembles this early campaign. The Two Basics refer to the universalization of nine years of basic compulsory education and the elimination of illiteracy among youth and adults between fifteen and forty-five years of age (Zhang and Zhao 2006: 262–63). Thus, although the first concrete attempt made by the CCP to eliminate illiteracy in rural areas was made in 1956, fifty years later illiteracy continued to be a serious policy problem in some areas for China's central governing authorities.

Like other sectors of the formal economy, the education system deteriorated significantly during the Cultural Revolution period (1966–76). Across the country, class struggle took precedence over all other aspects of public life. Teachers were accused of being "bourgeoisie" and often were subjected to violent persecution. Many schools were closed during this period, and those that remained open were converted to people-run schools (Peterson 1994: 116). It was also during this chaotic period that urban youth were sent down to the countryside to learn from what Mao perceived to be the more ideologically "clean" rural population.

THE REFORM ERA

In the reform era, we see a return to a more instrumentalist role for education. Political education still forms a key pillar of the Chinese education system. However, in the wake of the Cultural Revolution, education policy shifted toward the training of experts, with education increasingly utilized as a critical government technology to instill discipline and morality among the population and to mold high-quality human subjects who could contribute to the "material and spiritual development" of the Chinese Party-state (see Ministry of Education of the People's Republic of China 1995: Article 1; Bakken 2000; Murphy 2004). Although children are exposed to less political propaganda than they were in the past, "the Party is always there," reminding them that it "is the organizing principle and supreme power that makes it possible for China to make scientific and economic progress and win international glory" (Thøgersen 2002: 225).

In 1986, China unveiled the Compulsory Education Law, which stipulated standard nine-year compulsory education for all Chinese children.

Nine-year compulsory education consists of six years of primary school and three years of junior high school. However, the new law was calibrated to local conditions, with less economically developed areas of the country given more time to achieve compliance. Gongshan did not achieve compliance with the compulsory education law until October 2007, and even then its compliance was questionable.

The education of the rural population has received particular attention during the reform era, with governing authorities perceiving the task of transforming rural children into Chinese citizens as particularly challenging (Murphy 2004: 15). This reflects a broader sense of ambivalence: on the one hand, the rural population is represented as a reason for China's failure to achieve modernity, a hurdle to economic development, and a threat to stability; on the other hand, its abundant, cheap, flexible labor has been a critical ingredient in China's rapid economic and industrial expansion. In this context, the CCP sees itself as playing a decisive role in harnessing the productive forces of the rural population and engendering social and economic stability, with formal education at the center of these efforts (Anagnost 1997b: 86–87).

ETHNIC MINORITY EDUCATION

Accessing full and effective education is particularly difficult for ethnic minority people living in China's less economically developed western peripheral regions, and school completion and literacy rates among the ethnic minority population have been much lower than among the Han population (Xue and Shi 2001). This has made access to off-farm work opportunities and upward economic mobility difficult (Postiglione 2006: 3–5). Many ethnic minority populations are in isolated, less economically developed parts of the country, rendering the provision of quality comprehensive education difficult.[5]

Ethnic minorities continue to present a particular policy problem for the CCP. Historically, education has been regarded as a critical mechanism for modernizing and integrating ethnic minorities living in China's peripheral regions (see Mackerras 1995), and "it is an acknowledged aim of minority education to confirm the unity of the PRC and patriotism towards it" (Dilger 1984: 156). Policy documents indicate that the CCP still considers ethnic minorities to be a threat to national strength and cohesion. These same policy documents promote increased investment in education in ethnic minority areas and the transmission of scientific knowledge and moral education to ethnic minority people as essential to building national cohesion and economic strength (Ministry of Education of the People's Republic of China 2002).

Since 1949, ethnic minorities have been subject to state-sponsored preferential treatment policies (*youhui zhengce*) in education (Sautman 1999). The formal education of ethnic minority cadres was one of the strategies used to integrate the ethnic minority population into the CCP. Formal education was regarded as a particularly useful vehicle for transmitting scientific knowledge to "less-developed" ethnic minority communities. At the same time, the CCP emphasized the need to take local conditions and cultural characteristics into account when carrying out education work in ethnic minority areas. On June 8, 1950, Premier Zhou Enlai declared to a national education conference: "Our education is national education, and must take the form of the nationalities. . . . Our country is a multinationality country, and we must pay attention to our brother nationality characteristics and form. The brother nationalities should study each other's good qualities. Only then will scientific knowledge be transmitted down to the nationality people" (quoted in Teng and Wang 2001: 294).

Following the Second National Nationality Education Conference, held in Beijing in June 1956, there were also calls to bring education in ethnic minority areas to the same level as that enjoyed by the Han by eliminating illiteracy and implementing compulsory primary school education in ethnic minority areas (Teng and Wang 2001: 297). During the economic reform period, ethnic minorities have paid lower school fees, have had access to subsidized boarding fees and remedial classes, and have had bonus points allocated to their raw entrance score (*gaokao*) when applying for university (Sautman 1999: 173–77).

At the beginning of the twenty-first century, ethnic minority education remained a key policy problem for the central government, with illiteracy and dropout rates among the ethnic minority population much higher than among the Han population (Lin 2007: 935). Lin explores the ways in which inferior educational outcomes among the ethnic minority population are articulated by Chinese officials and researchers (2007). For example, during a speech at the conclusion of the Fifth National

Minority Education Working Conference, in March 2003, Chairman of the State Ethnic Affairs Commission Li Dezhu stated: "The 'three backwards' [*san ge luohou*] divide ethnic minority areas from the rest of the country, particularly eastern coastal areas. The 'three backwards' refer to a backward level of production development, a backward level of cultural development, and a backward level of livelihood. . . . The three backwards are intimately related to backward development of education in ethnic minority areas" (2003). While central governing authorities are justifiably concerned that low levels of educational attainment in ethnic minority areas will extend poverty and that efforts must be made to address this deficit, Li Dezhu's speech conflates poverty with minority culture and devalues ethnic minority people and their role in Chinese society (Lin 2007: 947–48).

Until recently, school attendance rates in Gongshan were low, particularly at the high school level. Although high financial costs associated with education were a major factor that contributed to low attendance, they were not the only one. Gongshan is geographically and economically isolated, and local economic conditions are depressed, so there are few off-farm work opportunities. As a consequence, parents often regard education as offering limited utility to the household economy and keep their children out of school. Aside from the local government's own accounts, information on Gongshan's educational environment prior to 1949 is very limited. Official accounts need to be treated with a degree of caution. Like the comments by the chairman of the State Ethnic Affairs Commission quoted above, they are deeply influenced by the historical materialist narrative. Reflecting official representations of other aspects of Gongshan society, the accounts contrast the primitive and unsophisticated cultural attributes of the local ethnic minority groups to the superiority of CCP policy.

THE HISTORY OF EDUCATION IN GONGSHAN

According to the Gongshan Education Bureau's (GEB) report (2006), prior to Liberation there were very limited formal education opportunities in Gongshan, and the local population was illiterate in standard Chinese.[6] The GEB's account states that the Dulong, Nu, Tibetan, and Lisu minorities in Gongshan did not have their own written languages.[7] In the absence of a formal writing and numerical system, their system for recording and counting things consisted of "notching sticks and tying knots" (*kemu jishi, jiesheng jishu*).[8] We see the first signs of official education in the summer of 1910, when two Chinese-language schools were established in Cikai and Geputong. However, it seems that these schools were accessed by only a very small section of the population. During the Republican period, the government established four primary schools in Gongshan. According to the GEB account, these schools were "unsuccessful in cultivating any talent" (ibid.: 2) despite attracting more than 290 students. By the time the Republic fell from power in 1949, all of these schools had already closed down and school materials had been looted. Prior to 1949, Gongshan did not have a standard school education system, and there were no high school or university students among the ethnic minority population (ibid.). The GEB report summarizes the situation as follows:

> Due to historical, natural, and regional reasons, prior to Liberation there was no formal conception of education [in Gongshan], and the nationality countrymen living within the county never received a real education. Following Liberation, our education progressed directly from a primitive stage to a socialist [system of] education. The starting point for education was very primitive. However, under the strong leadership and radiant nationality policy of the CCP, as well as the hard work of several generations of workers over fifty years, educational facilities have been established and widened, resulting in an outstanding achievement. (Ibid.: 3)

Accounts such as this one fail to acknowledge the sophisticated indigenous knowledge developed and transmitted by the local population prior to Liberation. This knowledge was essential for engaging in agricultural production and sustaining a livelihood in extremely difficult environmental conditions; in many cases, it has proved superior to the "modern" and "scientific" agricultural techniques introduced to the area by the CCP after 1949.

Despite "not having any funds or teachers" (ibid.: 2), the People's government established one primary school in Cikai in 1950. In 1958, Gongshan also established a junior high school and nursery school. By 1970, Gongshan had a senior high school, and a complete high school system was established. The official account states that prior to the Third Plenum of the Eleventh Party Congress (1978), Gongshan's education was divorced from the realities of local rapid economic development. Following the Congress, there appears to have been a move toward major educational reform with the introduction of a policy calling for "adjustment, reform, consolidation, improvement" (*tiaozheng, gaige, zhengdun, tigao*) (ibid.: 3).

The official GEB account does not provide attendance rates prior to 1990. However, by 1990, the official primary school attendance rate was 82.6 percent. In the same year, the county had a combined secondary school population of 737 students, with 624 in junior high school and 113 in senior high school. Since 2000, a number of campaigns have been implemented at the local level to try to reduce illiteracy and to improve primary and high school attendance rates. For example, a 2003 program to "sweep away illiteracy" (*saomang*) shows continuity with education interventions launched by the CCP in the 1950s. These campaigns appear to have had some degree of success. According to official accounts, between 1995 and 2005, the number of students attending junior and senior high school nearly doubled, even though the county's overall population increased only marginally. By 2006, attendance rates for primary school, junior high school, and senior high school were 96.8 percent, 65 percent, and 35 percent, respectively (ibid.). Nevertheless, based upon the household surveys I conducted in "Menke" and "Ali" hamlets (see below), these figures, too, need to be treated with caution.[9] Even if we accept that in 1990 the attendance rate for primary school was 82.6 percent, it is unlikely that these students completed primary school and/or were taught by qualified teachers in standard Chinese.

In 1950, Gongshan did not have any formal teachers. By 2006, the county had 115 secondary teachers and 315 primary school teachers. All junior and senior high school teachers and more than 50 percent of primary school teachers held at least a technical college qualification (*zhuanke biye*), and most senior high school teachers held an undergraduate qualification (ibid.).

Even though formal educational levels in Gongshan have improved significantly over the past sixty years, illiteracy remains widespread among the rural adult population, with illiterate members of the community having few opportunities for upward economic mobility. In December 2006, I surveyed educational levels among adults (whose ages ranged from twenty-one to eighty years) in a sample group of nine households in Ali hamlet (total number of hamlet households = twenty-five) and another sample group of thirteen households in Menke hamlet (total number of hamlet households = thirty-two). These surveys were carried out between December 18 and 24, 2006, using random household selection. Both hamlets are close to the county town and schools (see map 4).

Among the sample groups from the Ali and Menke adult populations, the average number of years of school attendance was 4.5 years and 2.8 years, respectively. In Ali, nearly one-quarter of adults surveyed had never attended school, while approximately one-third had completed more than six years of schooling. In Menke, nearly half of the sample adult population had never attended school, and slightly less than 10 percent had completed more than six years of schooling. Furthermore, in both hamlets, just over half of the sample from the adult populations said that they were unable to communicate using standard Chinese. Among those who said that they could communicate using standard Chinese, half indicated that their ability was limited.

RECENT CHANGES: FREE NINE-YEAR
COMPULSORY EDUCATION FOR RURAL CHINA

In 2004, Gongshan's education environment began to undergo a major adjustment following the implementation of the consolidation of schools and free nine-year compulsory education policies. These policies have reduced the financial burden of education while also increasing the capacity of China's governing authorities to act upon and through the conduct and aspirations of Gongshan's ethnic minority population.

Since 2001, central government authorities have invested heavily in a major educational reform known as the Two Basics—the universalization of nine years of basic compulsory education and the elimination of illiteracy among youth and adults between fifteen and forty-five years of age (Zhang and Zhao 2006: 262–63). Nonetheless, until recently, in many poor rural areas this policy existed in name only due to inadequate levels of the funding required for effective implementation. Fiscal decentralization and inadequate funding in rural areas prevented millions of rural children from attaining full education, even though nine years of compulsory basic education has been explicit in Chinese law since 1986 (ibid.: 263).

Thus, when China's central governing authorities announced in December 2005 that there would be free nine-year compulsory education for all of rural China by 2007, this was one of the most revolutionary changes to education policy of the reform era (National Compulsory Education Fee Reform Leading Office n.d.). China's less economically developed western areas have been the initial target of this policy, which will facilitate the successful implementation of the Two Basics in rural areas, since school fees and medical fees often are the most substantial financial burdens for poor rural households. The importance that the central government attaches to education reform in rural areas such as Gongshan is captured in a statement made by State Councilor Chen Zhili to an education conference on November 30, 2006: "Only when rural schools are reformed and the quality of education is increased will: (1) the 'Build a New [Socialist] Countryside [policy]' provide high-quality workers [*gao suzhi de laodongzhe*]; (2) the educational problems of hundreds of millions of rural children be solved; and (3) rural society become stable" (quoted in *China Education News* [Zhongguo jiaoyu bao], November 30, 2006).

The implementation of free nine-year compulsory education in rural areas is underpinned by the New Rural Compulsory Education Assured Funding Mechanism (Nongcun Yiwu Jiaoyu Jingfei Baozhang Xin Jizhi) (National Compulsory Education Fee Reform Leading Office n.d.; Wang 2008). This reform has seen the central government direct unprecedented levels of funding toward educational services in rural areas, particularly those in less economically developed western regions. Associated with this reform is the "two exemptions, one subsidy" (*liang mian yi bu*) policy measure. It aims to ensure that students from poor households receive exemption from textbook fees (exemption one) and tuition and miscellaneous fees (exemption two), and are allocated a monthly subsidy to cover their living expenses while boarding at school (subsidy).[10]

Another feature of increased funding for education in China's less economically developed western regions is the consolidation of the local school system. Between 2004 and 2007, the central government contributed ¥10 billion to the building and rebuilding of boarding schools for rural students (Zhang and Zhao 2006: 267). This increase in funding has enabled the closure or downsizing of small village-based schools and the relocation of students to central boarding schools. The shift to centralized schools is a principal strategy for governing and acting upon the conduct of the school-aged population. The "enclosed method of school-ing" (*guanbi shi*) characteristic of these centralized schools intensifies the capacity of the state to act upon the conduct of the rural school-aged pop-ulation. This method of schooling is particularly regimented, "with time, space and relations among individuals structured so that children learn to regulate their conduct in ways that 'turn them into material' (*chengcai*) for modernization" (Murphy 2004: 11).

Compulsory education reform in rural areas is enforced through grassroots campaigns targeted at measuring results and ensuring com-pliance. Compliance is achieved through a combination of coercion and surveillance that extends from the National People's Congress down to the village level (Zhang and Zhao 2006: 264–65). The central government's administration and funding of the Two Basics program are strength-ened through an accreditation and inspection system, first established in 1993, which is summarized as follows: "Inspection and accreditation is conducted once a year to assess educational expenditures, school enroll-ment and facilities, teachers' qualifications, and educational quality. The inspection procedure normally begins with a county's self-evaluation. The county then applies to the provincial inspection authority for a field inspection. Once the province reaffirms the county's accomplishment of the goals of universal basic education and literacy (measured by specific criteria), a certificate is granted to the county. In addition, the National Education Inspection Office also conducts field trips to re-evaluate the counties randomly" (ibid.).

THE SCHOOL STRUCTURE AND ITS CONSOLIDATION

Historically, the equitable provision of school-based education across Gongshan has been challenged by a number of factors, including the extreme topography, a widely dispersed population, and limited govern-ment fiscal capacity. Beginning in 2004, Gongshan's schools were con-solidated in order to try to redress this imbalance. Increased funding for school infrastructure and student care is associated with this consolida-tion. The school consolidation policy is being implemented nationwide, as it is intended to reduce educational costs and standardize the delivery of education across the country (see Chan and Harrell 2009; Kipnis 2006b).

Consolidation has had a big impact on Gongshan's social fabric and has intensified the government of everyday life. Again, this brings to light the paradoxes associated with China's reform process and the hazards of applying concepts such as neoliberalism to the changes that are taking place. While the market economic reforms pursued by the CCP gesture toward greater freedom and the withdrawal of the state from society, we actually see evidence of more government intervention in the everyday life of the population, particularly among those sections of it who are regarded as underdeveloped and a threat to national stability.

The consolidation of primary schools is one of the biggest and most controversial changes affecting Gongshan's educational environment in recent years. It has gone some way toward solving Gongshan's considerable educational shortfalls, but it has also created a new set of social challenges, as we will see in the case study of consolidation in Cikai township, the location of the Gongshan county town.

Until September 2005, there was a wide distribution of primary schools in Gongshan. In 2000, there were more than one hundred of them scattered across the county. Many of these primary schools were single-teacher schools (*yishi yixiao*), which sometimes served a single hamlet and sometimes served a cluster of hamlets. By July 2006, close to thirty single-teacher schools had been closed across the county, in line with the school consolidation policy. Many other schools were downsized as part of the policy (GEB 2006: 7).

In Cikai township, students from either closed or downsized schools were sent to board and study at Niulangdang, a newly expanded central boarding primary school. Niulangdang Primary is on the eastern bank of the Nu River, about two or three kilometers south of the county town. Most rural students living in Cikai township now study and board at Niulangdang Primary for grades two to four. Some village-based schools have been maintained for grade one students.

When they reach the end of grade four, the Niulangdang students transfer to Cikai Primary, where they study and board for grades five to six. Cikai Primary is the county's best primary school and is in the county town. At the time of my research, Niulangdang Primary and Cikai Primary were receiving an additional ¥45 per rural student per month from the central government to cover boarding expenses. The schools are a long distance from the village homes of most of their students. For instance,

FIG. 3.1. Heiwadi Primary School is one of Gongshan's few remaining single-teacher schools (December 2006).

even when traveling by vehicle, students from Shuanglawa village have to travel for up to one hour from home to school.

In general, children living in the county town with an urban/town household registration (*chengzhen hukou*) study at Cikai Primary for grades one to six. Cikai Primary also has a special nationality class (*minzu ban*) for grades five to six, consisting of talented rural ethnic minority children who have been hand-picked by the school from across the county.

One exception to the consolidation policy is Manzi Primary School, a nonboarding rural school that teaches grades one to four for children living in Manzi village. This school is on the other side of the Nu River from the county town (see map 4). Prior to the consolidation, Manzi Primary taught grades one to six. However, Manzi's students now transfer to Cikai Primary at the end of grade four to complete their primary schooling. Despite its close proximity to the county town, Manzi is classified as a rural school and does not receive as much financial support from the county government as schools based in the county town do. For example, although teachers at Cikai Primary receive financial bonuses from the County Finance Bureau, Manzi teachers receive none. Teachers at Manzi

FIG. 3.2. Main entrance to Niulangdang Primary School, with a sign reading: "Display a school style of rigorous dedication, realism, unity, and creativity. Work hard to cultivate the builders and successors of the socialist cause" (December 2006).

are also less likely to have full-fledged teaching qualifications, and they receive little ongoing training. According to my research assistant, local teachers do not consider Manzi a desirable place to work; teachers based at Cikai Primary tend to look down upon the Manzi teachers; and Manzi teachers aspire to transfer to Cikai Primary. Nevertheless, student results at Manzi are only slightly lower than those at Cikai.

Gongshan's educational terrain is in a state of constant flux. When I conducted follow-up fieldwork in Gongshan in January 2008, the situation at Manzi Primary had again changed. During the 2007–08 school year, its student population contracted further as students beginning the grade-four school year were shifted to Cikai Primary. As a consequence, Manzi was providing education only for grades one to three, and the number of teachers had contracted from eight to six. The reason Manzi had not been closed down and consolidated along with other schools was that it provided educational services for a particularly large student population drawn from thirteen hamlets, and the county school authorities did not have the financial capacity or physical space to accommodate these students at the new centralized boarding school.

Reasons for the Consolidation

According to the GEB, the scattering of schools in Gongshan created a number of problems, including low-quality teaching, an uneven distribution of resources, and poor educational outcomes (2006: 7). Indeed, many of Gongshan's single-teacher schools catered to more than one grade level in the same classroom. As teachers had to divide their teaching and preparation time among students from different grade levels who studied in the same classroom, they were often under considerable stress, and the overall efficacy of their teaching was reduced.

Problems associated with single-teacher schools appear widespread. Some of these problems were outlined by Xu Jialu, vice-chairman of the National People's Congress, in an interview with CCTV's *Policymakers Speak* (Juece zhe shuo) program in 2006. He related an experience from several years previously when he had visited schools in Yunnan. At that time it was reported to him that there were more than ten thousand single-teacher schools in the province. He indicated that the teachers working in these schools had considerable burdens. For instance, they often had to teach a group of students spread across four separate grades: there might be two students from each of the four grades in a single classroom. Furthermore, the teachers' role extended beyond teaching in the classroom; they also had to cook, boil water, and grow vegetables for the students.

In Gongshan, evidence suggests that prior to the consolidation, teachers often had to devote considerable amounts of their own time and energy to developing creative strategies to overcome the lack of effective government support. The experience of a teacher based at a single-teacher school in Ali hamlet prior to the consolidation provides a good example. Before the consolidation, this interviewee taught grades one to two in one classroom to students from Ali and Menke hamlets. The school is a special case because it was built with funds provided by a Hong Kong magazine group. His salary of ¥800 per month was also paid for by the group. The teacher did not have formal qualifications.

During an informal discussion, the teacher told me that the school had

FIG. 3.3. Ali's single-teacher school has been closed as a consequence of the consolidation (July 2005).

little or no money: "We do not receive one cent from the local government and do not even have money to buy a broom" (field notes, June 3,
2005). He then explained that he and the local community had to employ
creative methods to deal with the school's poor financial situation. One
involved climbing to the top of the mountain above the school to gather
medicinal plants, which they would then sell in the county town, earning
¥20 to ¥30 per day, which was used to buy shoes for the students, at ¥5 per
pair. Toward the end of our discussion, the teacher lamented: "[The offi-
cials] spend several hundred yuan on meals every night and drive around
in very expensive cars. Why can't they buy less expensive cars? We don't
even have enough money here to pay for electricity. We used to pay ¥6 per
year; now we are expected to pay ¥100. We only have two light bulbs! So we
told them [the electricity company] that we don't want to be supplied with
electricity anymore. We don't receive any money from the government.
They won't even buy us a basketball" (ibid.).

Official privilege is a conspicuous feature of Gongshan's political economy. The county government office parking lot is filled with expensive
four-wheel-drive vehicles that are used mainly to ferry government officials around the county for government work. While such vehicles are
essential for traversing Gongshan's rugged terrain, they serve more than

this practical function. On one occasion, a senior local government official had his private driver provide me with a lift back to the county town in his government vehicle. The vehicle's interior was particularly luxurious, and a DVD player and television screen recently had been installed to keep its occupants entertained during long journeys.

As well as being poorly funded and resourced, village-based primary schools posed travel problems for those children living a long distance from the village. A case in point is Dasuo Primary (see map 4), a village-based school that previously had taught grades one to six for local rural students. Following the consolidation, this school provides classes only for grade one. Dasuo's teacher stated that prior to the consolidation, some students were spending a total of six hours walking to and from school each day. This was because the school serviced a group of widely distributed hamlets, some of which were a very long way from the school. Now that these students are boarding at Niulangdang Primary and Cikai Primary, they no longer have to cover this distance on a daily basis. He also stated that prior to consolidation, the school's performance had been below average and there were not enough teachers.

Problems Associated with Consolidation

Nevertheless, consolidation has created a new set of challenges for rural communities and schools. The consolidation policy is having a serious impact on Gongshan's social fabric, and many parents fear that it is failing to adequately provide for their children's needs. Two main consequences are the demolition of an important training bridge between rural communities and the formal Chinese language–based education system by the closure of small village-based schools, and the fact that primary school-aged children now board at a central primary school, shifting many parental duties and responsibilities to teachers.

Transition to Schooling

Although village-based schools often lacked sufficient support and staffing to adequately provide for the needs of local children, these schools served as a bridge between rural communities and the formal Chinese language–based education system for preprimary and grade one and two students. In Gongshan, non-village-based primary schools use standard Chinese for instruction. However, most children have little or no exposure to standard Chinese until they begin primary school. This is because ethnic minority languages are the ordinary means of communication within Gongshan's rural communities. Traditionally, to compensate for this, teachers at village-based schools used both the local language and standard Chinese during their teaching. For instance, teachers used the local language to introduce new words in standard Chinese. Bilingual teaching in village-based schools made the transition to primary school much easier for ethnic minority children.

Village-based schools also provided an opportunity for preprimary-aged children to sit in on classes and to gain exposure to standard Chinese and the formal teaching environment. According to the former Ali Primary teacher, prior to consolidation, it had been normal practice for parents in Menke and Ali hamlets to send their four- to six-year-olds to Ali's single-teacher school. In the 2004–05 school year, the school consisted of seven informal students (aged four to six) and six formal students (of primary school age) (field notes, December 22, 2006). After a large number of village-based schools were closed, many of Gongshan's rural students no longer had this opportunity. Ali Primary's former teacher, now working at Manzi Primary, commented that seven- to eight-year-olds now start schooling without any exposure to standard Chinese or formal education, and teaching grade one and two students is now particularly difficult: "They don't even know how to use pencils. We have to teach them how to use them. They don't speak any standard Chinese" (ibid.).

Student Care

Interviewees also suggested that in some cases, parents feel a strong sense of unease at having their very young children living away from home. A teacher working at one of the remaining village-based schools for grade one students commented: "Parents feel that the school [Niulangdang] is very far away and that it is difficult [kelian] for their children. Being at school is not like being at home. The food at school is very basic. The children are very small, and the parents can't quit worrying [bu fang xin]. Students also feel quite lonely at Niulangdang. They can't speak in-depth with their teachers about their problems. The students also aren't receiving a sufficient diet at the school" (field notes, December 13, 2006). A retired teacher discussed his concerns about consolidation, particularly the perceived inability of the Niulangdang boarding school to substitute for effective parenting and nutrition provided in the home:

> I'm worried that the diet the students receive at the [Niulangdang] school may affect their development. Students [also] don't wash properly at Niulangdang [referring mainly to grades two to three]. They wash once a month when they go home. They come home with nits in their hair. [At school] they wash their faces, but not their hair or bodies. . . . Students also don't know how to wipe their bottoms properly, and some of them don't wipe their bottoms at all. They also don't have toilet paper, and use torn-up paper [from newspapers]. . . . The students aren't getting enough nutrition in their diet [at the school]. (Ibid.)

These comments were based partly on a visit we had made together to Niulangdang Primary the day before, during which an administrator and other teachers highlighted problems the school was having regarding the current funding arrangements.

At the time of our visit to Niulangdang, in December 2006, 205 students were living at the school (field notes, December 12, 2006). The school received ¥45 per month per student from the government to cover the students' boarding expenses. Most of this money was used to buy food. Table 1 illustrates how this ¥45 was being divided.

According to the administrator and his teachers, after they bought rice and wood for the students, there were only 3 to 4 *mao* left over per student per day to purchase oil, salt, MSG, vegetables, and meat for the students' diet.[11] As a result, meals consisted of one bowl of rice and one bowl of vegetable soup. Students were eating meat only once a week, although this would have been similar to the quantity they ate at home. One of the teachers stated that 3 to 4 *mao* per day was not enough to provide for the students' needs.

The administrator outlined some of the other problems the school was having regarding the consolidation: students living a long way from the school were paying a large sum of money to travel to and from school on their visits home; there was an increased workload for teachers and an absence of demarcation between their private and working lives; and parents did not feel at ease because their children were living far from home.

TABLE 1. Division of Students' Boarding Expenses
Costs are per student, per month

Rice (25 *jin*, or 12.5 kilograms)	¥31.25
Food (oil, salt, MSG, vegetables and meat)	¥11.15
Firewood	¥2.6
Total	¥45.0

This table shows the division of students' boarding expenses at Niulangdang Primary School. The ¥45.0 was calculated to be spent over twenty-six days because students return home for several days each month (field notes, December 12, 2006).

The administrator informed us that four students had recently dropped out of school, one reason being that their parents did not feel comfortable about their children living so far away. One of these students had since returned. Commenting on the lack of appropriate boundaries between teachers' private and working lives, the administrator stated: "The students and teachers live side by side. This is bad for the teachers. There is no separation from the students" (ibid.). He also noted that teachers were using their own wages to cover the cost of medicine for any students who fell ill.

A Cikai Primary School administrator raised the same issue of increased teacher burden following the consolidation. Cikai Primary is the main feeder school for Gongshan High School. The school is in the middle of the county town, just below Gongshan High School. Following consolidation, the number of students boarding at the school has increased significantly.

Prior to consolidation, the school had approximately five hundred students. This included approximately eighty specially selected minority students from across the county who boarded on campus. The rest of the students were from the county town and lived off campus. Following consolidation, the number of students boarding on campus has increased to approximately 270 and the total student population is now about 765. Most of these boarders are in grades four and six, although a small number of grade four students who could not be accommodated at Niulangdang Primary also board on campus. As with Niulangdang Primary, Cikai Primary was at the time of research receiving ¥45 per month per

FIG. 3.4. Cikai Primary School (September 2006).

student from government for students living on campus. The students in the special nationality classes are able to further supplement their diet and income by growing vegetables on land allocated to them by the school.

The administrator explained that teachers are suffering from greater workloads following the consolidation because "students also need to be supervised outside of class." She stated: "Teachers are working twice as hard as they did before and are under more pressure" (field notes, December 13, 2006). She acknowledged that the government had invested a large amount of money in the program, but indicated that the funds are insufficient to cover the school's needs.

This funding shortfall has translated into the school and its teachers taking on care and responsibilities outside their official realm. Echoing the concerns of the Niulangdang administrator, the Cikai administrator noted that teachers often pay for students' medical fees out of their own pockets because neither the school nor the students' parents have any money.

The transition to a more centralized schooling system will create challenges for Gongshan's primary school–aged population in the short term. Nevertheless, over the long term, the new system will enable efficient utilization of resources, providing Gongshan children with a uniform education that will better prepare them for the transition to high school than the old local schools did. Crucially, compared to poorly resourced village-based schools, the new boarding schools associated with the consolidation provide governing authorities with a more controlled space for acting upon the conduct and aspirations of the school-aged population. Children will spend considerably more time under the gaze and influence of the state and less time under the influence of their parents in their home environment. To this end, I will shine light on the "hidden curricula" that Gongshan children will be increasingly exposed to under these education reforms.

HIDDEN CURRICULA

In China, school grounds are an important site for the potential "capture," measurement, and cultivation of the child subject. The child subject enters a new physical and psychological space in which knowledge is transmitted through the prism of the Chinese Party-state's uniform educational apparatus and political ideology with the goal of producing patriotic, high-quality, and productive citizens. Schoolyard activities play a particularly important role in instilling discipline within students in China. Fig. 3.5 shows children lined up in rows in the school courtyard, taking part in a series of exercise drills. After completing the drills, these students cleaned their classrooms and the school grounds. The teachers and principal closely scrutinized the students while they undertook these activities. The conduct promoted through these activities is reinforced through textbook lessons that remind students to keep their classroom, bedrooms, and the greater environment clean and tidy.

In China, textbooks and additional media, among other things, devalue rural livelihoods by conflating modernity with cleanliness, hygiene, and urban identity (Yan 2003b: 587). As a consequence, children in rural areas such as Gongshan learn that they are dirty, poor, backward, and of low quality; further, they are portrayed as being of less value to the nation than children living in modern urban environments such as Shenzhen and Shanghai. Fig. 3.7 shows two pages from the textbook *Moral Character and Life* (Pinde yu shenghuo) (Chen 2005: 44–45), used in a grade one

FIG. 3.5. Primary school children take part in exercise drills in the courtyard of one of Gongshan's schools (September 2006).

FIG. 3.6. Primary school children clean up the school grounds under the supervision of their teachers and principal (September 2006).

FIG. 3.7. Student textbook: *Moral Character and Life* (Pinde yu shenghuo) (Chen 2005: 44–45).

morality class. Students study this textbook for two periods each week in semester one. This section of the book is called "I am very clean and tidy" (*Wo hen zhengjie*). On the left page, a small rabbit named Beibei asks the student: "Look at the mirror. Are you clean and tidy?" A cartoon of five very clean and tidy children can be seen looking at their clean and tidy reflections in a mirror. On the right page, Beibei then asks: "How can you become a clean and tidy child?" Below Beibei are a series of cartoons depicting a young girl brushing her teeth and washing her face, hands, and feet. The student is told that these activities should be carried out every day. To Beibei's right, another series of cartoons depicts a young boy having his hair cut, showering, changing his clothes, and clipping his fingernails. The student is told that these activities should be carried out regularly.

For the vast majority of Gongshan's children, these are unrealistic depictions of appropriate hygiene. Most houses are wooden huts with one to three rooms. Students certainly do not have access to showers, and they have very few clothes. Some villages still do not have running water. It is not uncommon for some children to never change out of the same set of

FIG. 3.8. Student textbook: *The Ten Things Primary School Children Should Know about National Conditions* (Xiaoxuesheng guoqing shi zhidao) (Wu and Wang 1995: 70–71).

clothes. These images simultaneously present children with the modern ideal and remind them that they are much poorer and less developed than the children depicted in the cartoon, each of whom has access to free-flowing water in a clean sink, clean sets of clothes, and a shower.

Fig. 3.8 shows the last two pages from a 1995 primary school textbook designed for grade six students that teachers still used as a study aid in Gongshan in 2007. The text, *The Ten Things Primary School Children Should Know about National Conditions* (Xiaoxuesheng guoqing shi zhidao), explicitly informs rural students living in places such as Gongshan that they are "poor and backward" as compared to students living in modern urban environments such as Shanghai and Shenzhen (Wu and Wang 1995: 70–71).

For instance, in the top right corner of the left page is a color photograph of a modern school courtyard. A group of children in brightly colored uniforms can be seen sitting and playing around a pond in the center of the courtyard. Juxtaposed against this image is a black-and-white photograph of a rural classroom that is typical of the classrooms found in Gongshan's village-based schools: students are sitting in a dimly lit, unpainted room where a teacher is writing on a blackboard attached to a bamboo screen. The text accompanying these two photographs informs students: "Even though the country wants to build large numbers of new school buildings every year, in some poor, backward areas some students still attend class in simple and crude classrooms." At the bottom of the right page is a picture captioned "Shenzhen Special Economic Zone's New Appearance," showing a modern metropolis with tall apartment buildings and an ordered urban grid. This image would be quite alien to many rural children who had spent all of their lives in unindustrialized rural environments such as Gongshan. The last sentence of the body of text above this photograph informs students: "The motherland's hope and future rest on our shoulders. Classmates, study hard!"

These texts conflate modernity with urban identity, and in so doing, remind the children of Gongshan that their rural lives are the antithesis of modernity: valued, high-quality members of the Chinese population do not engage in unproductive rural work in poor, backward rural environments such as Gongshan. High-quality human subjects are well educated and productive. Moreover, they live in modern, ordered urban environments, such as Shanghai and Shenzhen.

These texts are intended to indirectly act upon the dreams and aspirations of Chinese children, but they also offer a false promise to most rural children. While Shanghai and Shenzhen are powerful psychological attractions for Chinese rural youth seeking escape from a monotonous and insular rural life, their dreams and aspirations are often dashed once they begin work on the production lines of urban factories.

Out-of-class activities such as ceremonies also play an important role in shaping student conduct and patriotism (see Thøgersen 2002: 223–26). In June 2005, I was invited to attend a National Children's Day ceremony at a primary school in Gongshan (field notes, June 1, 2005). The ceremony took place on the school's basketball court. The students sat on rows of benches in front of a group of about twenty local exemplars: current and retired government officials, work unit leaders, and senior army officers, who all sat at one end of the court below a large red banner declaring, "Celebrating the June 1 Meeting" (see fig. 3.9). The students' parents and other villagers stood at the opposite end of the court, behind the students. Sitting toward the front of the student group was a group of five young army officers from the local barracks.

FIG. 3.9. Local exemplars deliver speeches to students at a National Children's Day ceremony at a Gongshan primary school (June 2005).

FIG. 3.10. Young Pioneers pledge their allegiance to the CCP at a Gongshan primary school on National Children's Day (June 2005).

FIG. 3.11. Satellite television dish in Gongshan (September 2006).

FIG. 3.12. A family watches a science-based documentary on China Central Television Four that is now accessible through the new satellite dish (January 2007).

The official ceremony began with a group of about twenty Young Pioneer members swearing a pledge to the CCP (see fig. 3.10). The students pledged "to wholeheartedly comply with the Communist Party's instruction, study hard, work hard, labor hard, prepare for the Communist cause, and contribute all my strength." The Young Pioneers is operated by the CCP via the school system and caters to children between the ages of seven and fourteen. The organization is a very explicit technique to integrate the students into the CCP and its doctrines and to inculcate discipline among the student body.

The Young Pioneers ceremony was followed by a series of speeches by the exemplars that placed strong emphasis on the critical role of education in developing the local people. Students received the message that if they studied hard, were disciplined, and obeyed the Communist cause, then they could succeed and emulate the exemplars sitting before them.

Following the speeches, students were awarded prizes for their educational achievement. Several exemplars were also presented with plaques in recognition of their contributions to education. These events were followed by several hours of student singing and dancing performances, as well as a comedy skit performed by the group of young army officers.

Gongshan villagers are now also increasingly engaged with China's mediascape via satellite television (see figs. 3.11 and 3.12). This particular hamlet started receiving Chinese satellite reception in 2006 after residents pooled their finances and purchased a government-subsidized satellite dish. Like modern schooling, the images and messages received via television contribute to the collapse of spatial and temporal boundaries between Gongshan and the world beyond the county border, and they remind local youth that they are not living up to the standards expected of a modern Chinese citizen.

IMPLEMENTATION AND ENFORCEMENT OF FREE NINE-YEAR COMPULSORY EDUCATION POLICY

Gongshan began implementing free nine-year compulsory education in 2006. Apart from abolishing tuition fees, boarding fees have been waived, children boarding at school are now provided with living subsidies, and children from poor households are provided with free textbooks. Despite considerable community resistance and continued high dropout rates during the 2006–07 school year, provincial-level officials inspected and approved Gongshan's compliance with nine-year compulsory education in October 2007. According to a senior official at the Gongshan Education Bureau, junior high schools and primary schools must maintain attendance rates of 97 percent and 98 percent, respectively, to continue to comply with compulsory education policy (field notes, January 28, 2008).

The case studies of Gongshan High School and a vocational school for dropouts illustrate the challenges associated with implementing and enforcing nine-year compulsory education in Gongshan. Achieving compliance is not a neat and precise process, and it requires an array of contingent strategies. Even though Gongshan officially complied with the compulsory education policy in 2007, this does not mean that all of the children drawn back into the education system in 2006 and 2007 received a full and effective education. There was a significant disparity between national development policies and the social terrain upon which those policies were implemented, and there were hazards associated with rapidly imposing a strict educational regime upon a population that has historically regarded formal education as offering limited utility. The Chinese Party-state bureaucratic apparatus has been able, however, to detect and respond to resistance at the local level, while local-level governments have used innovative strategies to manage unrealistic policies implemented from above.

Gongshan High School

Gongshan High School is composed of both a junior high school (grades seven to nine) and a senior high school (grades ten to twelve), with the former the target of the free compulsory education policy. When the policy was first implemented in Gongshan in 2006, the school authorities faced a range of challenges in ensuring compliance. One of the key challenges was to draw students back into the school system and prevent them from dropping out. At the beginning of the 2006 school year, Gongshan High School had a junior high school population of approximately 580 students. By January 2007, this number had dropped to about 466: nearly one-fifth had dropped out in fewer than six months. Among the dropouts, all but one were from Gongshan's rural areas.

A school administrator provided examples of the problems associated with keeping students in the school system. He stated: "One teacher has been to one household fourteen times to try to convince the student to come back." The student still had not returned to school at the time of our interview. Furthermore, "Another student says that they can't understand anything in class and refuses to come back." He also revealed that the school knew little about the circumstances of many of the students who had dropped out: "We don't know where some of the students have gone. They may have been sold [into prostitution or marriage] or may have gone to Burma. We don't know" (field notes, December 13, 2006). He said that two female dropouts had run away to Fugong, the county directly south of Gongshan. Both students were brought back by police, but they immediately ran away again. By January 2007, only eleven out of more than one hundred dropouts had returned to Gongshan High School. The administrator estimated that twenty out of the thirty students from Dulongjiang township who had dropped out of Gongshan High School were attending high school back in Dulongjiang, while around eight remained out of school entirely.

The administrator outlined some of the main reasons why students dropped out, among which was the inability of rural primary schools to properly prepare ethnic minority students for the transition to secondary school. For example, eighty of the 2006–07 grade one junior high school students achieved only seventy points in their final primary school exams. Students are expected to achieve at least three hundred points before entering junior high school. This meant that among the grade one junior high school population of around 210 students, nearly 40 percent had educational levels well below those required for this level of schooling. Some of these students actually had the equivalent of grade three primary school educational levels. According to the administrator, about sixty students had language problems and did not understand what the teachers were saying in class: "They attend class but don't understand. They don't do their homework. They have no interest in school" (ibid.). The information provided by the senior administrator about low educational levels among a large proportion of high school students underscores the frustrations many rural students must experience at school. In a follow-up interview, he expressed sympathy for the students in this predicament: "[They] don't understand what's being said. For them it's like being in jail; of course they don't want to be here!" (field notes, January 19, 2007).

Another reason for the high number of dropouts was student isolation from their home villages. This problem was especially acute for students from Dulongjiang township, thirty of whom were among the recent cohort of dropouts. Students from Dulongjiang in particular do not like living in the county town, partly because during the Chinese New Year winter break the road to Dulongjiang becomes snowed in and they are unable to return home to see their families.

However, these structural factors were not the only explanation provided by local educators for the high number of dropouts. Reflecting official perceptions that the Gongshan population is inherently backward and of low quality, local educators conflated the high dropout rate and poor educational outcomes with the psychological and social attributes of the Gongshan population. For example, the administrator and two other teachers isolated "poor parenting" as a major cause for the high number of dropouts. The administrator explained that some of the students have "psychological problems" because they do not receive proper care at home: "Their parents are irresponsible and gamble and drink and don't pay attention to their children's schooling" (field notes, December 13, 2006). Similarly, the two teachers, both of whom were from outside Nujiang, attributed much of the blame for poor educational outcomes to the behavior of local parents:

Teacher One: One of the biggest problems here is the money wasted on alcohol. I've been to a student's house to speak to his parents about their son. As soon as I entered the house, they encouraged me to drink. But I refused. Because I refused, the father would not talk to me and just sat there staring. He didn't seem to care about his son. He just wanted to drink. . . . The education level of the parents is also very low. A lot of parents don't even know their children's birth dates. . . . The parents are really bad. You can't rely on parents to look out for their children's interests. The parents don't care about their children's education. The parents don't watch television or listen to radio and don't know anything of the outside world. The students themselves would rather be in the mountains raising cows and goats and doing farmwork. (Field notes, December 7, 2006)

Teacher Two: A teacher from Bingzhongluo went to visit the parents of one of his students. When he entered the student's house, the parents didn't even offer him a cup of tea. They sat drinking alcohol and ate and offered him nothing. He couldn't believe their behavior. He'd come a long way to speak to them about their child's education, and they didn't even seem to care. Their quality [*suzhi*] is very low. (Ibid.)

One of the teachers also told the story of a student whom he had managed to stop from dropping out of school. The student's father tried to pressure the student to discontinue his studies so he could start earning money on the family farm instead. The father said that if the son stayed in school, he would use up the family's money.

During my interview with these two teachers, it became apparent that they shared a degree of contempt for the local ethnic minority population. For instance, Teacher One emphasized the amount of financial support the local farmers, particularly the Dulong nationality, received from the central government as compared to the rest of the population. He suggested that this government support has engendered community dependence upon government:

The local farmers receive a lot of finance and subsidies from the central government. They don't need to work. The Dulong population is only six thousand people, and the government wants to protect them. Therefore they give them a lot of support. They give them cows, goats, etc. . . . [But] the locals are very lazy. If locals are employed, they work for a couple of days, then demand to be paid. They then use that money to buy alcohol. Then they don't return to work. The Dulong people were given some goats to raise as part of a poverty alleviation program. But they ended up eating them instead. (Ibid.)

Two Gongshan High School Dropouts

The stories of students who had recently dropped out of school provide a different view. Contrary to some of the teachers' statements, the decision to drop out is often made for very rational and practical reasons.

Zhang

Zhang is sixteen and Lisu and lives in a hamlet that is a thirty-minute walk north of the county town, along the road to Pengdang and Bingzhongluo townships. When I first visited Zhang, in November 2006, she was living in a small hut by the roadside with her parents, brother, and two grandparents. Her father makes ¥5,000 to ¥6,000 per year by collecting and selling recyclable glass bottles around the county town.

In August 2006, Zhang dropped out of school to go with a number of other young women from her hamlet to undertake employment in Fujian as part of a labor export program. However, the work did not prove to be as financially lucrative as promised, and most of them returned to Gongshan in October 2006.

When I visited her house again in December, she still had not returned to school, nor had she found any local work. Zhang said that she was legally required to return to school due to the enforcement of the nine-year compulsory education policy, but she was still not sure if she would go back. Her mother explained to me that a group of officials, including a county education department official, the village committee leader, and Zhang's class leader, had visited the house three or four times and yelled at her and her husband, demanding that they send Zhang back to school. The mother appeared to be very dissatisfied with the school environment Zhang had been exposed to, stating: "The education here is very bad. The management is also very bad" (field notes, December 23, 2006). Nevertheless, she told me that if Zhang did not return to school, they would be fined ¥500.

When I returned to Zhang's house, in January 2007, she was not at home. Her mother explained that she had returned to Fujian to work and would not be returning to Gongshan for three years. I was quite surprised, as in previous interviews Zhang had told me that the conditions she had experienced during her previous migration experience to Fujian had not been particularly good: she felt that she had been tricked by the boss, and she had earned far less money than she originally had been promised.

Zhang's mother asked me to stay for dinner, and not long after I sat down, Zhang's father returned home. This was the first time I had met him, and our conversation revealed that Zhang's original decision to drop out of school and travel to Fujian to work, and her recent decision to return there, was actually made in response to quite desperate conditions within her household.

The father told me that the household's economic situation was very difficult. Zhang's mother and brother were both ill, and Zhang had gone out to work to make money to help pay for their medical costs.

In September 2006, the family received ¥4,000 in poverty alleviation funds from the civil affairs bureau because of their difficult circumstances, and the following month they received an additional ¥1,500 from an insurance company for the brother's illness. All of these funds were immediately used to pay medical fees. The father also paid ¥300 of his own money toward medical costs, and the local village committee had given his wife ¥200 for Chinese New Year because of her circumstances. The mother's illness would cost over ¥10,000 to treat at a hospital in Liuku. The money Zhang makes in Fujian would be used to pay for this treatment, and the main reason Zhang had gone out to work the previous year was to make money to pay for her mother's medical expenses.

He explained that after Chinese New Year the family would borrow money from the bank and go to Liuku, the prefectural seat, for the mother's treatment. They would use the money Zhang sent back to repay the bank.

I questioned the father about the compulsory education policy and whether officials had recently returned to try to force Zhang back to school. He explained that the village leader and secretary, as well as township officials, had visited the household. But after learning why Zhang had to go out to work, the township and village governments had decided not to force her back to school. He said that Zhang had been in tears as she explained the situation.

According to Zhang's father, the local village committee ultimately sympathized with her case, and before she left for Fujian, she was provided with a letter of introduction (*jieshao xin*) from her village committee, allowing her to leave the prefecture without any problems. Being provided with this letter was quite unusual (and probably technically illegal) because Zhang was officially required to return to school in compliance with the compulsory education policy. According to the father, without this letter, his daughter would have had trouble crossing the prefecture border check near Liuku (field notes, January 22, 2007).

Zhang's situation provides an important insight into the other side of the compulsory education policy story. Her dropping out of school appears to be a rational response to desperate financial circumstances within her immediate family. Zhang's case demonstrates that even when education is free, it can actually be a burden for rural families experiencing a financial crisis. This is the opportunity cost of education: it is often important in rural farming areas, and it is rarely (if ever) calculated when development planners examine how to deal with poor rural people's access to educational opportunity.

Wang

The experience of a dropout named Wang provides a further illustration of the complex and often rational reasons behind a student's decision to leave school. Wang is seventeen and Lisu. He dropped out of grade three (junior high school) at Gongshan High School in September 2006 after attending just two to three weeks of the new school year. During my interview with Wang's parents, his mother explained that her son's school results actually had been very good prior to his leaving school and that at home he was well behaved.

His mother was particularly vocal in expressing her dissatisfaction about the way her son had been treated by the school. She explained that after he dropped out the first time, two teachers came to the house and took him back to school. Once he was back at the school, the teachers berated and bullied him for a whole day. He then immediately dropped out again and came back home. He had not returned to school since. She told me that the teachers were always shouting at students, whether they had dropped out of school or not, and that they seemed to show little concern for the students' well-being: "Even if the students are sick, they don't pay attention to them" (field notes, December 21, 2006). When I asked her why the teachers shouted at the students, she replied that "[the teachers'] temperament [*piqi*] isn't good."

The parents then explained that fifteen other students from Wang's class of fifty-three had also dropped out. I asked why so many students had dropped out. Their explanation was that the "school's management wasn't good." They said that the richer students from the county town would get drunk and then intimidate other students, such as their son. The school was unable to control these rich students, who were not afraid of the teachers. There was another, more serious indication of violence at the school: earlier that month a student had been stabbed in the neck with a knife by another student.

A degree of peer pressure may also have influenced their son's decision to drop out, as three of Wang's good friends from a nearby hamlet and in the same class had also left. Wang's father said that the three good friends were among the four to six classmates who all dropped out with him at the same time. During my conversation with his parents, Wang was inside their house listening to dance music with another young friend who had also dropped out of school.

I asked how they had felt when their son dropped out. The mother replied that she was "very sad and cried." She said she cried "because his results were very good, but he dropped out."

These parents said that they hoped their son could still go on to senior high school and university: "We hope he can go back to school, but he doesn't agree. Three weeks ago we yelled at him to go back to school, but he hasn't. If he stays at home too long, he'll get too used to having fun at home and not studying" (ibid.).

The father explained that two teachers had come together twice to speak to them and their son. These teachers told the parents that their son's school results were good and that he should continue studying. The Cikai township leader had also come to their house three times to "yell" at the son to try to encourage him to return to school.

My research assistant indicated that the dropout rate in Wang's hamlet was particularly high. I asked the father why this was so. Initially he said it was because the school was a long way from the hamlet. He then went on to tell me that their hamlet had never had a member attain a highly coveted appointment to the local government bureaucracy and that therefore there were no local role models for young people like his son.

The information presented by this family provides a more nuanced account of why some students drop out. Although the teachers I spoke with essentially blamed parents for students dropping out, saying that they were lazy and did not care about their children's education, the story provided by this family suggests that this is not always the case and that the reasons for dropping out can be far more complex. The parents also appeared to be quite torn regarding their son's predicament. While they were upset and angry at him for dropping out, they also expressed anger at the school for not providing an appropriate learning environment for him.

The family clearly placed high value upon formal education, even though their child was not complying with the compulsory education policy.

The Campaign to Return Dropouts to School

Despite the high degree of initial resistance to strict enforcement of the compulsory education policy, local authorities eventually succeed in returning most dropouts to school. These authorities employ an array of strategies to ensure compliance. While a high degree of coercion is required in some cases, it also appears that local parents increasingly recognize the value of nine-year compulsory education and autonomously comply with the policy guidelines.

I interviewed a senior official at the Gongshan Education Bureau on my follow-up field trip in January 2008. She outlined the techniques employed by the county government and the Gongshan Education Bureau to ensure compliance with the compulsory education policy. First, the Gongshan government undertook wide-scale propaganda campaigns during the implementation process that emphasized that it was parents' responsibility to keep their children in school. According to the senior official, the campaign contributed to engendering a change in parents' attitude toward the value of education for their children. A key feature of the campaign was to place responsibility on parents to keep their children in school. She explained: "Parents have a responsibility [zhize] and obligation [yiwu] to ensure their children attend school" (field notes, January 28, 2008).

However, relying upon the self-governance of the local population was not enough to ensure compliance with compulsory education. Consequently, local governing authorities also employed coercive strategies to ensure compliance. One of the most important strategies was the detection and reporting of dropouts. According to the senior official, leading up to the scheduled official inspection in October 2007, schools had to report nonattendance on a daily basis. Follow-up inspection reports would be made on a weekly basis. Schools reported nonattendance to the township governments. Township governments reported nonattending students to their respective village committees. Village committees then coordinated with hamlet leaders to visit the households of dropouts. According to the official, the Gongshan Education Bureau does not fine households that do not comply. This is only because the majority of households are very poor and do not have the money to pay fines. Nevertheless, she explained that local businesses that are found employing people below the age of sixteen face fines enforced through the Gongshan County Business Bureau (ibid.). This coercive device is not unique to Gongshan and has been applied in other parts of China to ensure compliance with compulsory education policy (see Thøgersen 2002: 214).

While the Gongshan Education Bureau does not impose fines directly upon households to ensure compliance with compulsory education, it does have other, less direct coercive devices at its disposal. A local hamlet leader explained:

> The majority of households support the compulsory education policy. For the small number of households that don't support the policy, we can employ certain threats to ensure that they comply. For example, if government or NGO poverty alleviation projects are implemented, they will be the last to receive support. For example, the government recently provided the village with free sheets of roofing [*shimianwa*]. Families not complying with compulsory education would be the last to receive free roofing. The punishments are similar to family planning: if households don't comply, then they'll receive fewer poverty alleviation benefits from government. (Field notes, January 26, 2008)

Initially, the campaign appears to have had mixed success and to have placed major stress upon officials, teachers, students, and parents. Even though the vast majority of school dropouts were eventually returned to school, it is unlikely that schooling will provide them with substantial long-term educational benefits. Commenting on the predicament of these students, my research assistant stated: "While they may have physically returned to school, their hearts are not there" (*Ren zai na ge difang, xin bu zai na ge difang*) (ibid.). One of the main reasons for the high number of dropouts in Gongshan is the overall failure of the school system to effectively prepare students for the transition to high school. Nonetheless, the recent consolidation of the primary school system should ameliorate this situation for future cohorts of students entering high school.

Special Vocational Schools for Dropouts

The creation of three special vocational schools (*zhiye xuexiao*) providing vocational and political education to long-term dropouts was another contingent response by local governing authorities to the strict enforcement of the nine-year compulsory education policy in Gongshan. From late 2006 onward, Gongshan teenagers who had not attended school for more than one year and who fell within the age range of the compulsory education policy were rounded up by village committee officials and taken to the special vocational schools. A head teacher from one of the schools described this process as "casting out a net and concentrating the fish" (*Biandi sawang, zhongdian laoyu*) (field notes, January 24, 2007). From the outside, these schools appeared to be strategic sites for cultivating and integrating members of the population who had fallen outside the formal education system and the reach of the state apparatus. However, upon closer inspection, the reality was somewhat different. In fact, the schools were established by the local governing authorities as a short-term practical measure to ensure compliance with the compulsory education policy and to meet bureaucratic quotas, rather than as a genuine long-term strategy to provide full and effective education for teenage dropouts. Most of the students who attended the schools were awarded the equivalent of a junior high school "leaving" certificate. However, based upon the very short length of time the students ultimately spent at the schools, as well as the conduct of the teachers charged with delivering education, it was unlikely that the schools provided students with an effective education.

On January 24, 2007, I visited the Cikai Township Vocational School, which had officially opened a month earlier. At the time of my visit, the school had ninety-three students. The school was set up by the Gongshan Education Bureau and Cikai township government, with the latter taking responsibility for managing the school.

The school's students met official criteria: (1) they were between fourteen and seventeen years of age (although I met one student who claimed he was thirteen and another who claimed he was eighteen); and (2) they had either dropped out of school before the end of grade two junior high school or had never attended school. The student population was divided into two classes of fifty-eight and thirty-five students, respectively, although the curriculum for each class was the same. The students at this particular school were all drawn from Cikai township and came from the Lisu, Dulong, Nu, Tibetan, and Han ethnic groups. Students were not required to pay any tuition, and all of their food was provided by the school. A quilt (bedding) was the only item the students were required to supply themselves. The students were brought to the school by officials from their respective village committees. During our discussion, the head teacher explained that in two days' time (the official end of the school semester), the same village committee officials would return to the school to take the students back to their villages. Students appeared to be unaware of this particular tactic, and it was most likely put in place to prevent them from running away once the semester finished.

All of the students lived in dormitories in former classroom buildings. They were strictly forbidden to return home while studying at the school. The boys' and girls' dormitories were segregated. There were also two officers from the police station living on campus to prevent the students from running away and to stop outsiders from entering the school grounds.

On the surface, the school served as an ideological and vocational training ground for undereducated and politically nonintegrated teenagers. The head teacher explained that one of the school's main goals was to increase the students' *suzhi*. Referring to the students, he stated: "They are society's garbage. The school provides them with an opportunity to change that." At another point during our conversation, he stated: "These students don't have any refinement [*wenhua*]. From a young age they drank, smoked, and got into fights" (ibid.). He said that one of the school's key responsibilities was to reacquaint the students with society (*chongxin renshi shehui*). Regimentation appeared to be an important part of the school curriculum.

While one of the stated goals of this school was to provide basic vocational and language skills for undereducated teenagers, it also served to instill social and political conformity among the student body. Because none of the students attending the school had undertaken or completed a formal education, they also had not received the social and political education normally instilled via China's national school curriculum. When the head teacher outlined the details of the school curriculum, the first area he listed was political education. Later in the interview, when he was discussing the content of political education, he told me: "We are a border area; it's important to have unity among the nationalities" (ibid.).

The school's curriculum was taught in three languages—standard Chinese, the local dialect (*fangyan*), and Lisu—and it covered the following areas: (1) political education; (2) farming practices and skills, including "scientific farming techniques"; (3) Chinese medicine, including knowledge about the economic value and health properties of local medicinal plants; (4) tourism; (5) language, with an emphasis on practical Chinese language terms (e.g., "contract" [*hetong*]); (6) mathematics; (7) local music; (8) art/painting; (9) sports; (10) basic army training; and (11) safety. The head teacher also emphasized that a major part of the school's role was teaching the students appropriate etiquette (*limao*). Alongside the school's two permanent teachers, specialists from different government work units also visited the school to teach in specific areas. On the day I visited, an agricultural specialist was at the school to deliver lessons.

The students finished their exams on the day I visited and would return home for a month of Chinese New Year holidays in two days. The head teacher said the program would continue until July 2007. Some of the students I spoke with appeared to be under the impression that they had now finished the program. But based upon what the head teacher said, it appeared that all of the students would be continuing the program the following semester. After the holidays, some students would undertake just two more one-month training programs. After completing these programs, they would receive a junior high school vocational leaving certificate (Zhiye Chuzhong Zige), which is technically equivalent to a junior high school leaving certificate (Chuzhong Zige).

Other students, considered by their teachers to have greater ability and potential than their peers, would be encouraged to return to formal schooling to complete their education. The head teacher explained that students under seventeen years of age who had dropped out of junior high school in either grade one or two had the opportunity to formally complete their junior high school studies in full at Gongshan High School, their former school. He stated: "Some students asked me if they could join the army if they continue their studies. I said, 'Yes, you can, and you can protect the country'" (ibid.).

The junior high school leaving qualification awarded via the school potentially offered very practical economic benefits for students. According to the head teacher, students who received graduation certificates would be able to use it to apply for "labor export programs, local work, and work in tourism." He also told me: "We tell the students that although this is a poor place, it has beautiful scenery and attractive folk culture [*Shan qing shui xiu, min feng chun pu*], and it isn't polluted. Therefore, people want to come here for travel. If the students have the right skills, they can take advantage of it. We also tell them that outsiders are coming here and becoming rich, while we are still poor" (ibid.). There is a degree of veracity to these comments. The Nujiang and Gongshan governments have identified tourism as one of several avenues for developing the economy in the years ahead (see fig. I.2). The ability to speak standard Chinese will be a particularly important skill for gaining employment in any tourism-related work assignments.

Contrary to outward appearances, the quality of teaching at the vocational schools was clearly not a priority of the local governing authorities. The head teacher and other male teachers I met during my visit appeared to be particularly poor role models for the students. For example, when I arrived at the school, I found the head teacher and two other male teachers drinking rice wine and playing drinking games in the staff room. They also poured some beer for me when I sat down with them. Because I was in a school environment and carrying out a formal interview, I said that I would prefer not to drink. The head teacher poured my beer anyway and said: "Have a little bit; this is nationality culture" (ibid.). This took place in full view of students who were walking in and out of the room.

The head teachers asked one of the students to take me for a tour of the school. When I returned to the staff room approximately twenty minutes later, one of the teachers proudly exclaimed: "Look, we finished the bottle [of rice wine] while you were away." The head teacher appeared to be conscious that drinking in front of the students on school grounds was officially frowned upon, telling me that they did not drink during the semester. He told me the reason they were drinking on the day I visited was that the students had just finished their exams. However, based on my experiences at many other local schools, drinking in front of students during school hours is common practice.

After my visit to the school, the head teacher and I walked together to the main road in order to catch a taxi back to the county town. During our walk, he told me, in a rather inebriated state, that "the ethnic minorities drink, are lazy, and sleep. We try to inspire them" (ibid.). The head teacher was a member of the Bai ethnic minority group.

By the time of my follow-up fieldwork trip to Gongshan, in January 2008, the vocational school had been closed down. As discussed earlier, it would appear that the schools were created by local governing authorities as a short-term, stop-gap measure that enabled them to comply with the nationally mandated compulsory education policy, rather than as a genuine attempt on their part to provide a comprehensive education for teenagers who had fallen out of the school system. Many of the dropouts who were drawn into the schools had been absent from the formal school system for a long period of time and had low literacy levels. Thus, it would have been difficult to place them directly back into a mainstream educational environment such as Gongshan High School. By placing dropouts within these special schools, the local authorities were able to demonstrate compliance with the compulsory education policy, even though many of the students who attended these schools ultimately received a very limited education.

SPECIAL NATIONALITY CLASS

Gongshan's education system also plays a central role in selecting and cultivating future ethnic minority government officials and leaders, for work in both local and higher levels of government. Because Gongshan is an official autonomous county of the Dulong and Nu ethnic groups, a large proportion of local government officials must be drawn from these same ethnic groups. As the administrator at Cikai Primary School explained: "The county leader must be either Nu or Dulong, and we need to cultivate [*peiyang*] them from an early age" (field notes, January 22, 2007). In line with central government policy, both Cikai Primary School and Gongshan High School have a separate nationality class (*minzu ban*) designed to cultivate future nationality officials (*peiyang minzu ganbu*). The vast majority of students selected for these classes are Dulong or Nu, with a small number of Lisu and Tibetan students also selected to reflect Gongshan's ethnic diversity. Also, at the end of grade six primary school, a very small group of high-performing students is selected for transfer to a special ethnic minority high school in Kunming to complete their schooling.

In Gongshan, the streaming of students into special nationality classes begins at the end of grade four. Teachers from Cikai Primary visit rural schools across the county to identify academic high achievers. Suitable candidates transfer to Cikai Primary's nationality class for grades five and six. In 2006, these classes consisted of approximately thirty-five students each. The academic performance of the students in these classes is comparatively high: in the 2005–06 school year, one of Cikai Primary's nationality classes was the top class in the county. Because Cikai Primary is the best primary school in the county, students selected for these classes receive a higher-quality education than they would have received in their home townships.

At Gongshan High School, grades one to three of junior high school each have a special nationality class. In 2006, these classes were composed of approximately fifty students each. Most of the students from the special nationality class at Cikai Primary are accepted into the special nationality class at Gongshan High School. As noted, the top students from Cikai Primary transfer to a special ethnic minority high school in Kunming.

Students selected for the nationality classes are taught by the schools' best teachers and receive superior levels of teaching compared to other students. They are also allocated land on the school grounds that they can use to grow vegetables to subsidize their living expenses.

CONCLUSION

The reform of the school system in an ethnic minority community reflects the broader governance strategy of the current Chinese Party-state. China's transition from a socialist command economy to a more open and market-based economy has weakened the Party-state's influence over many aspects of society. With the proliferation of mass media, the Internet, and overseas education and travel, the Chinese population is exposed to a range of ideas and opinions that have not been subjected to the strict political filters of China's governing authorities. While these authorities maintain a tight grip over national media and deploy significant resources to police the boundaries within which public discussion takes place, their capacity to influence the views and opinions of the Chinese population has declined dramatically over the past three decades. In this milieu, the formal education system remains a strategic and enduring site to shape the values and dispositions of the Chinese population. The education of ethnic minorities is a particular concern of China's governing authorities. China's rapid economic development has created significant social and economic disparity between the coastal regions and the western peripheral regions where the ethnic minority population is concentrated; today standards of living and educational outcomes among the ethnic minority population are lower compared to most of the majority Han population. This disparity has heightened Chinese leaders' concerns about social stability and national unity. This has in turn precipitated a series of large-scale developmental campaigns for western China. The implementation and strict enforcement of nine-year compulsory education and the consolidation of the school system are key manifestations of these campaigns.

While I have shown clear evidence of the capacity of local governing authorities and the community to resist and, in some cases, to circumvent education reforms imposed from above, in the long term the central government's strategies will succeed in drawing the vast majority of the school-aged population into the formal education system. Although the reform era has witnessed the retreat of the state from many aspects of Chinese society, the people of Gongshan actually experience it as an intensification of the state's influence over their lives and a closer integration into the Chinese Party-state.

4
MIGRATION FROM THE MARGINS

Increasing Outward Migration for Work

Export one person and pull one household out of poverty. Export a team of people and pull an entire region forward. [*Shuchu yi ren, tuopin yi hu, shuchu yi pi, daidong yi fang.*]

—Quoted in Yang Yuhua, *Nujiang News*, October 26, 2006

The move was not only in space, but in time and mind as well.

—Weber 2007 (1976): 218

The treacherous road that connects the Gongshan county town with Dulongjiang, Gongshan's poorest and most isolated township, was completed only in 1999 and at significant cost: approximately ¥120 million. Prior to the road's construction, Dulongjiang was very difficult to access and could be reached only by trekking for two to three days along dangerous mountain paths. According to the Nujiang Prefecture Labor and Social Guarantee Bureau (Nujiang Zhou Laodong He Shehui Baozhang Ju) (2008), in September 2008, nineteen farmers from Dulongjiang were among a group of twenty-one Gongshan farmers who participated in a formal labor export (*laowu shuchu*) program to Dongguan City, Guangdong Province. This appears to have been one of the first reported cases of labor export from Dulongjiang.

One mode of labor export in China involves rural governments actively organizing the export of teams of surplus rural workers to off-farm work assignments in urban and other rural areas. Dongguan is one of the biggest economic success stories of China's reform era. As one of China's largest centers for manufacturing, it is a key destination for rural migrants seeking better work and income opportunities in China's coastal region. These migrants generally take up low-skilled production-line work in highly regimented factory environments, very different from the work of Dulongjiang's subsistence farmers. The new road is not only improving the transportation of goods and services into and out of Dulongjiang; in conjunction with education, land reform, and labor programs, it is also facilitating the insertion of Dulongjiang's surplus rural labor into the coastal, low-skilled industrial work regimes that sustain China's economy.

Temporary rural-to-urban migration for work has been a defining feature of China's reform era. China's rapid economic development has been fueled largely by the tens of millions of surplus rural workers who migrate to urban areas each year to undertake low-skilled industrial work. Importantly, these workers have not only helped to stimulate urban industrial expansion; they have also contributed to the social and economic transformation of China's rural hinterlands (Murphy 2002). Nevertheless, until recently, the Gongshan population has been excluded from the outward migration phenomenon. Obstacles included poorly developed transport and communication infrastructure and low levels of education and fluency in standard Chinese among Gongshan's ethnic minority population. The subsistence-based livelihoods of Gongshan's local population also presented a major obstacle to outward migration.

This situation is beginning to change. The example of the nineteen Dulongjiang farmers who temporarily migrated to Dongguan suggests that local livelihoods are becoming increasingly defined by external economic forces associated with the encroaching market economy. As the opening epigraph from the *Nujiang News* (Nujiang bao) illustrates, in recent years, the Gongshan and Nujiang governments have identified outward migration for work via labor export as a key vehicle for developing the local economy. These governing authorities argue that labor export will raise rural incomes, improve the skill set and psychological disposition of the local population, and contribute to the development of the local economy. In other parts of rural China, the financial remittances made by urban-based rural migrants have become critically important to the development of local rural economies. In this regard, labor export has been recognized as a factor that will contribute to resolving the "Nuji-ang issue." While labor export participation rates were very low at the beginning of the 2000s, participation has expanded in recent years. Participation rates will increase even further in the next five to ten years as government development programs, such as strict enforcement of free nine-year compulsory education, expand the proportion of the population that is eligible for labor export. Labor export also presents local governing authorities with an enticing mechanism for dealing with the significant population displacement that will result from dam construction along the Nu River.

Increasing outward migration from communities such as Gongshan represents the culmination of a much larger social engineering project of China's central governing authorities, to which the schooling programs also contribute: the transformation of so-called low-quality, unproductive subsistence farmers into higher-quality, productive industrial workers who can contribute to the development of the national economy. The everyday reality of migration, however, will present new and complex challenges for the Gongshan population. Rural-to-urban migration promises rural youth an opportunity to "see the outside world," improve their skills and knowledge, and alleviate household poverty. However, the dreams and aspirations of these young people are often dashed by the realities of exploitative urban work regimes that are premised upon the devaluation of rural life.

CHINA'S RURAL MIGRANTS

During the reform era, the increased flow of economic migrants within and among China's provinces has been a major economic and social phenomenon. This relatively free flow of surplus rural labor has provided state and nonstate enterprises with an abundant source of cheap, flexible labor and has been a key factor behind China's highly successful manufacturing economy. Furthermore, both central and local governments regard migration as a strategic mechanism for raising the overall skill level and *suzhi* of the rural population and for stimulating development in otherwise economically underdeveloped rural areas (Murphy 2002).

According to one official estimate, by 2010 the total rural migrant population had reached 160 million (Xinhua News Agency, March 1, 2011). These rural migrants make up the majority of a larger demographic group officially known as the "mobile population" (*liudong renkou*). By 2010, the size of this mobile population had reached an estimated 221 million, whereas in 1993 this group had numbered 80 million (ibid.; Sun 2000).[1]

The mobile population is, as noted, a phenomenon of the reform era. During the Maoist era (1949–76), particularly after the establishment of the household registration (*hukou*) system in 1958, internal population mobility was severely restricted through rigorously enforced central government policy. Any movements that took place during the Maoist era were generally enforced by the state. In contrast, the large population movements of the reform era have been largely voluntary. That is, individual households have decided that there are better work and income opportunities in urban areas. There are many factors that motivate rural residents to move; they can be broadly summarized as "push" and "pull" factors. Push factors include high unemployment, poor income opportunities, excessive fees and taxes, government appropriation of agricultural land for local development, the implementation of conservation programs such as the Sloping Land Conversion Program in rural areas, and the desire, particularly among young people, to see the world outside the farm. Pull factors include the increasing autonomy of urban firms, the partial dismantling of household registration and grain-rationing systems, and the growing economic and employment opportunities in towns and cities, particularly along China's coast.

During the Maoist era, the household registration policy virtually eliminated voluntary rural-to-urban migration.[2] Household registration is assigned at birth. Those living in rural areas are assigned rural registration, while those in cities are assigned urban registration. Registration traditionally has been very difficult to change, and rural migrants were unable to survive in the city without urban registration. A strict state-controlled rationing regime, the "fixed labor system" (which virtually guaranteed state employment for all urbanites and urbanites only), and an absence of open food markets (food was procured by work unit–issued ration tickets) meant that only those with urban registration were able to access state-allocated work, housing, medical care, education, and food. Rural communities were expected to be self-sufficient.

However, during the reform era, this situation changed. Two key changes meant that rural migrants could find work in urban areas and purchase the goods needed for daily sustenance, even if they were unable to acquire urban registration and its associated fringe benefits. These changes were the emergence of produce markets at which farmers could sell surplus produce, and changes to urban labor allocation.

In 1986, the State Council introduced a new contract labor system, issuing regulations that allowed urban firms to be responsible for whom they hired. This brought an end to China's long-standing fixed labor system (Lei 2001: 484–85). The new system was intended to end the historically inefficient "iron rice bowl" system and to create greater efficiency in state industry. By the mid-1990s, state managers had attained close to full autonomy regarding the employment of workers (ibid.).

These changes to state labor allocation presented employers with a new and lucrative source of cheap labor: rural migrants wanting to enter the urban job market. Rural migrants were far cheaper to employ than urban residents. Their rural household registration meant that they were not entitled to the same fringe benefits historically received by urban employees (Solinger 1999: 199). Understandably, managers from the state-owned, private, and emerging foreign sectors were keen to employ rural migrants. During the 1990s, the private sector became a significant employer of rural migrants, particularly in the boom areas along the coast (Cheng 1996: 1131). Foreign-owned companies and joint ventures in particular have been major employers of rural migrants.

China's phenomenal economic growth over the past three and a half decades has been enabled largely by the cheap, abundant, and flexible labor provided by China's rural population. As indicated, surplus rural workers are an attractive source of labor for urban employers because they are paid significantly lower wages and are allocated fewer fringe benefits than urban employees. Although rural migrant workers earn much less than their urban counterparts, they still tend to earn more than they would if they were engaged in farmwork.

The governments of poor rural areas also play a decisive role in facilitating rural-to-urban migration. Temporary rural migration to prosperous urban areas such as Shanghai and Shenzhen is actively promoted by governments at all levels as an instrument for alleviating household poverty, unleashing economic development, and raising the *suzhi* of the population in rural areas (Murphy 2002; Yan 2003a).[3] Indeed, in response to inadequate education provision in rural China, "prosperous and bustling cities are seen as a 'comprehensive social university' [*shehui zonghe daxue*] in which millions of peasants can go to develop their *suzhi* at no cost to the state" (Yan 2003a: 501). The recent decision to provide free nine-year compulsory education in rural China suggests an adjustment to this equation, namely, the cultivation of a new generation of enhanced rural migrant workers for China's urban work regimes.

Paradoxically, whereas school-based texts, as well as official and popular population-quality narratives, represent urban China as a place where rural people can raise their quality and achieve upward social and economic mobility, rural-to-urban migration is premised to a large degree upon the devaluation of rural people (Anagnost 2004). The reality of urban life for the majority of rural migrant workers is characterized by social discrimination, anxiety, and economic exploitation (Gaetano and Jacka 2004; Pun 2005). Even when physically displaced from rural China, migrants are still regarded as low-quality subjects. Rural migrants take the jobs deemed undesirable by urbanites and are not accorded equal social status.

We would expect the experience of ethnic minority migrants to be even more difficult. China's ethnic minorities are among the most devalued members of Chinese society, with official narratives continuing to present them as less advanced and of lower quality than the Han population.[4] Ethnic minority rural migrants are also likely to come from more economically disadvantaged areas of the country and to have lower levels of education than do Han rural migrants. Here a case study undertaken in 2007 of the migration experience of Yi rural migrants who temporarily traveled to work assignments both within and beyond their native Sichuan adds some much-needed texture to our understanding of the experience of ethnic minority rural migrants (Monteil and Vermander n.d.). The Yi migrants involved in the study were generally undertaking menial, comparatively low-paid work assignments. Nevertheless, they did not perceive themselves to be discriminated against while temporarily living and working in an urban context. Furthermore, they often held a positive view of the Han people with whom they engaged.

The Impacts of Rural-to-Urban Migration on Migrant-Sending Areas

The mobile population has had a dramatic effect on China's social and economic landscape, not only providing urban industry with a continuing source of cheap, flexible labor, but also helping to raise income levels and stimulate economic activity in rural areas. Official labor export programs constitute a core element of the rural-to-urban migration phenomenon. Labor export is particularly valued by poor inland areas, where it has at times been identified as the main vehicle for local economic development (Lei 2005: 360).

Migration is not solely an economic phenomenon, and research from other parts of rural China provides some indicators of how Gongshan's social fabric may be affected by increasing rural-to-urban migration in the years ahead (see Lee 1998; Murphy 2002; Gaetano 2004).[5] For example, some evidence suggests that a transforming rural *habitus* also affects the decision to migrate.[6] That is to say, migration has altered the rural social environment and has contributed to instilling a new set of values and dispositions among the population: "The culture of migration means that children grow up expecting to spend part of their lives in the cities, and young villagers who do not migrate are derided by their peers for being unadventurous and without ability" (Murphy 2002: 21).[7] In a similar vein, the romanticized stories of urban life told by fellow villagers returning from Shenzhen in the 1990s powerfully influenced the desires of younger cohorts of women to temporarily migrate to southern China (Lee 1998: 81). Factory work in Shenzhen not only promised rural youth high wages; it also offered them "an expanded horizon of modernity" whereby they had the opportunity to enjoy reprieve from familial obligations in a clean, modern, and exciting urban environment that was the antithesis of rural life (ibid.: 8). Even though young female migrants were subject to a high degree of discrimination in Shenzhen's factory-based work regimes, factory life still offered an attractive alternative to a life of rural idleness and boredom (ibid.).

However, much of the literature on migration focuses on the experience of Han rural migrants and Han migrant-sending areas. The realities for ethnic minority migrants who return to their community following a migration experience can be somewhat different. The case study of the outward migration experience of Yi farmers from Liangshan Prefecture in Sichuan suggests that the skills and knowledge attained through migration were not always transferable back to migrants' native rural context, and that migration served primarily as a means to see the outside world and satisfy short-term needs rather than as a long-term strategy to ensure future economic prosperity. A notable exception to this trend was parents or relatives who migrated so they could earn money to pay the education costs of children and relatives back home (Monteil and Vermander n.d.). One possible explanation for this is that ethnic minorities tend to live in more remote, mountainous areas of the country, areas that are less enmeshed in the broader industrial economy and have lower demand for nonagricultural skills and knowledge. Thus, when an ethnic minority migrant returns to a rural context, the skills and knowledge attained during the outward migration experience would tend to offer less utility to him or her than they would to a Han migrant.

THE STORY OF OUTWARD MIGRATION FOR WORK IN GONGSHAN: OLD BARRIERS AND NEW GATEWAYS

In recent years, temporary migration for work out of Gongshan has expanded, and the county is now at the precipice of a significant transformation, wherein a much higher proportion of the local population will engage in temporary outward migration for work.

Old Barriers

Although rural-to-urban migration has been a major phenomenon of the reform era, temporary outward migration for work from Gongshan has been very limited.[8] Gongshan was relatively cut off from the rest of the economy, and community members had no external benchmarks against which to measure their own standards of living. Indeed, even in 2006, it was not uncommon to meet people who had not traveled beyond Gongshan's county border. Most of the population have lived as subsistence farmers, relying on local natural resources for survival. There have been limited reasons to undertake travel.

Transport costs for travel out of Nujiang is one of the main barriers to potential migrants. The cost of travel from Gongshan to a major migrant-receiving area is at least ¥500.[9] This is a major financial expense in an area where the 2008 average rural per capita cash income was only ¥1,064. A recently returned female migrant informed me that she had paid a total of approximately ¥1,400—equivalent to more than 130 percent of Gongshan's rural per capita cash income—for the return journey to Gongshan from Jiangsu Province (in China's east). She was able to pay these expenses with money given to her by her father (field notes, October 3, 2006).

Interviews conducted with local farmers in 2005–06 suggest that a more significant factor affecting their decision to migrate out of Nujiang for work, as well as to engage in local off-farm work, is the way that they have been treated by former employers both within and outside Gongshan. These farmers reported that they often were not paid by employers after engaging in off-farm activities such as working on road-building teams. According to their accounts, it was common practice for local contracts to be awarded to outside construction contractors. Once the contract was completed, however, the contractor would often flee Gongshan without paying the workers. Informants also said that they knew of people who had suffered a similar fate outside Nujiang. A local farmer remarked: "It's not easy for us to go out. It seems like all of the bosses [outside] are cheats [*pianren*]. It's pretty much the same in the county town. The bosses that come in from outside are cheats" (ibid.). These experiences appeared to play a powerful role in shaping local attitudes toward outward migration for work, even among those people not engaged in outward migration. A local village leader explained: "Some people go out to work, but they come back without being paid. The boss didn't pay them. This is why [other] people don't go out to work" (ibid.).

These experiences also demonstrate the financial risks associated with outward migration for work for members of the local population. If farmers go unpaid after engaging in work either within or outside Gongshan, they forego income that could have been earned by undertaking other activities, such as farming. Furthermore, the migration experience is a considerable financial loss if farmers go unpaid after engaging in off-farm work but have also paid for transport costs out of Gongshan or Nujiang. Local work activities might not be very lucrative, but they are low cost and low risk. Many of Gongshan's subsistence-based rural households have very low, unstable cash incomes; they are therefore unable to risk absorbing a large financial loss. In this regard, government-organized labor export programs are presented to the local population as a less risky method of migration. However, even these organized programs can expose Gongshan residents to a high degree of financial risk.

The greatest barriers to migration out of Gongshan are low educational levels and the inability to converse fluently in standard Chinese. The literacy rate among the local rural adult population is low; in some villagers visited by the author, few, if any, of the local farmers spoke standard Chinese. Without standard Chinese, finding and successfully engaging in off-farm work are virtually impossible, particularly outside Gongshan.

New Gateways

The Nujiang and Gongshan governments have recently identified temporary rural-to-urban migration as a means to alleviate household poverty, unleash economic development, and socially reengineer the local population. Local governing authorities in Nujiang and Gongshan are encouraging farmers to reduce their dependence on subsistence agriculture and to actively engage with the off-farm work economy. A 2006 household survey suggests that most parents recognize the utility of education, particularly its role in improving their children's prospects in the off-farm work market.[10] These parents identified education and the ability to converse in standard Chinese as important prerequisites for engaging in off-farm work. Education was viewed as a platform for not only accessing better off-farm work opportunities, such as entry into the comparatively well-paid local public service, but also for performing the day-to-day practical tasks associated with the commercial economy, such as calculating business transactions and reading signs and advertisements.

The SLCP is another factor affecting labor mobility in Gongshan. While 83 percent of Gongshan's population is officially classified as engaging in agriculture, the amount of household labor actually allocated to agricultural production declined dramatically following the implementation of the SLCP in 2002.

Recent improvements to transport and communication infrastructure also facilitate labor mobility out of Gongshan. The central government has invested heavily in transport and communication infrastructure in Gongshan, as exemplified by the Dulongjiang Road, which was not built until 1999 but now connects Dulongjiang to the rest of the county, and to China.

In recent years, several new labor-oriented government development programs have provided a formal vehicle for migration out of Gongshan. Labor export and "work-study" are prominent among these programs.

Labor Export Programs

Nujiang Prefecture's Eleventh Five-Year Plan for Economic and Social Development, published in the *Nujiang News* (cited in He Daguang, January 24, 2006), states: "By 2010 one quarter of the prefecture's rural labor force will be engaging in labor export programs . . . this will contribute to the promotion of rural enterprises [*daidong xiangzhen qiye*] and the development of small towns [in Nujiang]." Labor export has been highlighted as a key driver for resolving the "Nujiang issue" (He Shizhong, July 4, 2007). At the same time, labor export is a major component of a larger social engineering policy known as rural labor transfer (*nongcun laodongli zhuanyi*). As the name suggests, rural labor transfer involves shifting surplus rural labor into off-farm work. This transfer can take place locally or can involve temporary migration to work assignments in other provinces and countries. It offers significant financial incentives. For example, information provided by officials at the Gongshan County Labor Bureau (Gongshan Xian Renshi Laodong Ju) indicated that local farmers participating in a 2006 labor export program to Shenzhen were earning more than ¥900 per month (field notes, October 9, 2006), which was roughly equivalent to what they would have normally earned over an entire year back in Gongshan.

Gongshan's rural labor transfer participation rate is gradually increasing, according to official policy documents and anecdotal accounts. However, participation is advancing from a very low base due to relatively low levels of literacy and capacity to converse in standard Chinese. It is difficult to verify an accurate figure for the total number of Gongshan residents currently taking part in rural labor transfer programs, including labor export. What is clear is that the participation rate is significantly lower in Gongshan than in Nujiang's other three counties, Fugong, Lanping, and Lushui. According to the Gongshan County Labor Bureau (ibid.), they have been organizing teams of Gongshan farmers for local off-farm work assignments since at least 1998. Participation rates in labor export programs have been increasing steadily since 2004. In that year, the Gongshan County Labor Bureau assisted with the export of more than twenty farmers to work assignments beyond the prefectural border. Official statistics published in the *Nujiang News* suggest that at least 469 Gongshan residents took part in formal rural labor transfer programs in 2006, although it is unclear how many of these farmers were exported to work assignments outside Gongshan (Yang Yuhua, October 26, 2006). In April 2007, an article in the *Nujiang News* described how a rural migrant working in a factory in Fujian transferred ¥500 back to his hometown relatives in Puladi township so they would have money for Chinese New Year celebrations (Yang Yuhua, April 2, 2007). Puladi is one of the five townships that constitute Gongshan, and the rural migrant was one of fifty-six villagers whom the Puladi township government had sent to a Fujian factory as part of a formal labor export program. According to the article, the Puladi township government has identified labor export to provinces such as Fujian as an avenue for raising local household incomes. According to officials at the Gongshan County Labor Bureau, in 2007 they assisted with the export of 142 locals to workplaces in Fujian, Guangdong, Kunming, and Shenzhen.

An official report published by the Gongshan Agricultural Bureau (Gongshan Xian Nongye Ju) (2009) indicates that in 2008 Gongshan organized the export of 1,624 people, which represented 54 percent of the target set for that year. Of these, 199 were working outside Yunnan (*sheng-wai shuchu*) and 254 were working in other areas of Yunnan (*shengnei shuchu*), while 1,171 were transferred to off-farm work assignments within their home township (*kuaxiang shuchu*). These figures do not account for migration that has taken place outside official channels.

An official from the Gongshan County Labor Bureau outlined the following selection criteria that applicants were required to meet in order to be accepted into labor export programs: they had to (1) hold a junior high school diploma; (2) pass a health examination; and (3) be between eighteen and twenty-five years of age. Official compliance with these criteria was not always rigorously enforced, and the same official indicated that some of the labor export program participants had completed only a primary school education. Nevertheless, the official emphasized that literacy

FIG. 4.1. A government propaganda banner hanging outside a bus station in Liuku reads: "Go out to work and improve your skills, return to your village and start a business." The Nujiang government regards rural-to-urban migration as a strategic vehicle for nurturing human talent that will eventually return to Nujiang to help stimulate the local economy. Until 2007, this bus station was a major hub for temporary migration into and out of Nujiang (November 2006).

and the ability to speak standard Chinese were still essential prerequisites for engaging in labor export and that participants still had to satisfy these selection criteria to gain acceptance into the programs (field interview, October 9, 2006).

While the proportion of Gongshan residents currently taking part in outward migration for work is still low, it is likely to grow significantly in the coming years as increased high school retention rates expand the pool of residents eligible for labor export programs.

In Nujiang, government-organized labor export is as much about social engineering as it is about economics. Aside from generating higher incomes, the governing authorities clearly want to foster values such as competition and self-discipline among the rural population.[11] These values are regarded as essential attributes for successful engagement with China's increasingly marketized economy, as demonstrated by a 2006

Nujiang News article, "Labor Export Becomes a Bright New Platform for Increasing the Income of the Prefecture's Rural Population" (Yang Yuhua, October 26, 2006): "Exporting rural labor will not only move more of the prefecture's surplus rural labor into employment, increase rural incomes, and speed up poverty alleviation; it will raise the quality of rural migrants, expand their minds, and change their outlook." Furthermore, according to a Nujiang government draft discussion paper, the export of rural labor out of Nujiang is "a way of increasing farmer income, promoting local economic development, [and] maintaining social stability ... [and is] a major scheme for creating a harmonious society" (Anonymous 2006: 1).[12] This paper outlines some of the principles that personnel should adhere to when implementing the scheme among the local population: "Promote a change of thinking, establish a new career-minded consciousness [*shuli xin de zeye yishi*], strengthen the concept of the market [*qianghua shichang guannian*], [and] nurture a hardworking spirit [*peiyang chiku naidong jingshen*]." This last principle is significant in the context of Nujiang's largely ethnic minority population. Among China's majority Han population's stereotypes about the ethnic minority population is the belief that ethnic minority people are lazy and unproductive. To this end, labor export is seen by governing authorities as another means to remedy these perceived negative traits.

Official statements such as this do not account for the trauma and dislocation often associated with rural-to-urban migration. For example, one of its consequences is that one or both parents are away from the rural family home for an extended period of time, leaving children in the care of a single parent or grandparents. This can place tremendous physical and psychological strain on household members who remain in the countryside. Women who stay behind often suffer the greatest burden, having to single-handedly manage farmwork, raise children, and care for the husband's parents.

Several high-profile local government officials have made public comments that reflect the new expectations projected upon the Nujiang population. These comments imply that local parents and government officials increasingly recognize the utility of education and its role in improving population quality and improving off-farm employment prospects. Yang Yunhui, a *China Education News* (Zhongguo jiaoyu bao) journalist, asked a Dulongjiang township official: "Why must compulsory education be

FIG. 4.2. Government propaganda on a building in Lushui County reads: "Illiterate migrants who go out seeking money end up working in exhausting conditions and return home empty-handed." Such slogans actively encourage potential rural migrants to improve their educational levels before undertaking outward migration for work. This building is located along the road that connects Gongshan and Liuku and would be visible to Gongshan migrants leaving Nujiang to participate in off-farm work—of course, illiterate migrants would not be able to read the sign (September 2006).

introduced?" The official replied: "The Dulong ethnic minority group is one of China's fifty-six ethnic groups. If the Dulong do not develop, do not increase their quality, then we will trail further behind other ethnic minority groups" (Yang, July 9, 2007). Similarly, Wang Lixin, Dulongjiang township leader, states: "If children do not study, then when they go to work for a boss in the future, they will earn less money. The Dulong people believe this; thereupon they have brought their children to school" (ibid.). These comments gesture toward the transformation of local life in Gongshan. Local farmers are no longer regarded by officials as subsistence farmers reliant on government subsidies and cut off from the broader economy. Rather, they are increasingly regarded as "autonomous," "neoliberal" subjects, expected to respond and adapt to the value system that underpins this economy. Central to this system is the privileging of formal Chinese language–based education and nonagricultural skills and knowledge and the devaluing of agricultural livelihoods, with the traditional subsistence-based agricultural livelihoods of ethnic minority people living in marginal mountainous areas such as Nujiang being particularly devalued. Of course, not all Dulong parents subscribe to this value system, but the Nujiang and Gongshan governments are very keen to push the local population away from traditional agricultural livelihoods and toward off-farm work, and they recognize that out-migration both requires and will instill a new value system.

The Work-Study Poverty Alleviation Program

A new migration initiative, the Work-Study Poverty Alleviation Program (Gongxue Fupin Xingdong), was launched in the late 2000s. This program runs parallel to the labor export program. Rather than simply exporting surplus rural labor to urban-based job assignments, the new Beijing-based program is designed to augment the vocational skills of participants while they undertake urban-based work assignments. A Gongshan County Labor Bureau official described the program as a "vocational qualification expansion project" (*zige kaifa de yi ge xiangmu*) (field notes, January 23, 2008). Upon graduation, students are awarded two qualifications: a National Adult Education Graduation Certificate (Guojia Chengren Xueli de Biye Zhengshu) and a National Vocational Qualification Certificate (Guojia Zhiye Zige Zhengshu). According to the program flyer, these qualifications will greatly improve participants' competitiveness in the rural migrant employment market in urban areas. There is some legitimacy to these claims: the technical qualifications attained through the program will reduce the likelihood of rural migrants from areas such as Gongshan working in the very low-skilled, and particularly exploitative, work assignments at the lowest end of the off-farm work market.

According to the Gongshan County Labor Bureau, those accepted into the program study for three to four years at the Beijing Western-Region High-Level Vocational Institute (Beijing Xibu Gaoji Zhiye Xueyuan). Although students do not pay any fees, they are required to work while they study (as is indicated by the program's name). Following graduation, they can seek full-time work in Beijing based upon the recommendation (*tuijian jiuye*) of the institute.

In September 2007, the Gongshan County Labor Bureau sent eighty-five students to the institute. Students were between sixteen and twenty-five years. Prior to commencing the program, some of the students had graduated from senior high school, whereas others had only graduated from junior high school. An official from the Gongshan County Labor Bureau explained that young people from Gongshan are taking part in the program because their parents cannot afford to pay their higher education costs. The flyer highlights the program's goals: "Poor students who participate in this program will (1) learn what society requires of them; (2) find their position within society; (3) learn how to apply their knowledge; and (4) become human talent that fully meets the requirements of society. Once they receive their work-study qualifications, they will be much more competitive in the job market. Upon their graduation, their organizing work unit will allocate them a work position or assist them in starting their own business back in their village" (Yunnan Representative Office of the China Work-Study Agency n.d.).

Here we see further evidence of the social engineering agenda underpinning the central government's developmental goals for western China and ethnic minorities. Like educational programs, this program is designed to transform "lazy," "backward," "unproductive," and "low-quality" ethnic minority farmers into human talent useful to the development of the national economy. The program is intended to instill a particular set of dispositions among participants. These include competitiveness and greater self-awareness of the role they are expected to play in developing the national economy. Simultaneously, programs such as this are deeply implicated in the devaluing of rural livelihoods, reminding participants that valued members of the national economy are competitive and productive and undertake work in the off-farm sector.

STORIES BEHIND MIGRATION

I met several young people in Gongshan who had participated in outward migration for work. Some had joined officially organized labor export programs; others were involved in unofficial chain migration with relatives. Their experiences underscore the financial hazards, social dislocation, and discrimination sometimes associated with outward migration from Gongshan. At the same time, migration provides Gongshan youth with unprecedented levels of agency to achieve specific personal and family goals, such as paying for family medical expenses, attaining higher educational qualifications, building a more comfortable house, and improving marriage prospects.[13] The experience of two young women, Chen and Zhang, provides insight into the motivations of those who decide to migrate out of Gongshan for work.

Chen

In October 2006, Chen was twenty-six years old and had recently returned from an outward migration for work experience to China's coastal regions. She had not participated in a formal labor export program (field notes, October 3, 2006). She had completed only four years of primary school and described herself as "illiterate" (*wenmang*). She was the only person in her village of ninety-eight people who had engaged in outward migration for work in recent years. In March 2006, she traveled to Jiangsu with a number of other locals, including her cousin, to work in a bag-making factory. She was able to find work in this factory because another cousin already worked there.

However, after six months, in September 2006, Chen and the cousin with whom she had left Gongshan returned to their homes because the ¥600 per month salary they were earning in the factory was too low. She spent all of this salary on living expenses while she was living in Jiangsu, and she returned to Gongshan without any money. Chen appeared to be quite ambivalent about her outward migration experience. On the one hand, she had felt the salary she was earning was too low and so she decided to return to Gongshan. On the other hand, she said that if she had the opportunity to again migrate out for work, she would do so as long as she had friends to go with her. The opportunity to earn a higher income appeared to be the main motivation behind her decision to migrate out and work. Her impression of the "outside" as compared to Nujiang was that "outside is better. There are no factories here [in Nujiang]. We can work in the factories [outside Nujiang] and make money" (ibid.).

Chen was very reluctant to speak about her outward migration experience. She was still unmarried, and it appeared that her family had pressured her to return to Gongshan. Nevertheless, this example demonstrates that although low educational levels and poverty generally act as significant barriers to outward migration for work, this is not always the case. China's migration phenomenon is not a uniform process, and it is therefore problematic to predict migration patterns based on educational level, ethnic minority status, or household income alone. Chen was from a very poor household and was illiterate, yet she was still able to engage in a cross-country migratory network. However, a key factor distinguishing her from most other members of her village was that she had a relative already working in a factory who was able to hook her into a migratory network. Without this connection, it is highly unlikely that she would have been able to migrate out of Gongshan for work. At the same time, Chen's migration experience was relatively unsuccessful, for she returned home in fewer than six months. Her low level of education would have placed her at the bottom end of the labor market, where working conditions and wages are low and insecure. If she had had a higher level of education, her outward migration experience might have been more successful.

Zhang

We encountered Zhang earlier, in chapter 3, as she headed back out to Fujian for work and in so doing circumvented the strictly enforced compulsory education program. Her first outward migration experience was in August 2006 when she left Gongshan with thirty-three other young people to undertake employment in Fujian as part of an official labor export program organized by the Puladi township government. Zhang was one of seven young female migrant workers (*dagongmei*) who took part in this particular program. Their experience contrasts dramatically with the positive newspaper report cited earlier, which lauded labor export programs for providing "ready-cash" with which to celebrate the Chinese New Year.

Zhang took part in the labor export program to make money to pay for her family's mounting medical costs. However, the work in Fujian did not prove to be as financially lucrative as she and the other young women had been promised, and six of the seven returned to Gongshan in October 2006. Before they had left for Fujian, they had been told by government officials that they would receive ¥1,000 per month while working in the factory. Once they arrived, they realized that the piece rate they were being paid meant that they could earn only ¥192 per month. Moreover, although the company paid for transportation to Fujian, these costs were to come out of their pay once they started working. They also would have to pay their transport fees home themselves. Rent in the factory dorms was free. But food costs (¥60 per month) were to come out of their pay. Zhang described conditions in the factory: "In the dormitory we were only provided with a straw mat to sleep on. Even though we are from the countryside, we were not used to these living conditions. . . . Surveillance cameras were also used in the factory to monitor our movements into and out of the factory. We had very little freedom" (field notes, November 9, 2006). Zhang worked in the factory for only one week. She was not paid for the work. The women were told by the factory manager that they needed to work for two months before they could receive their salary. They were not allowed to take luggage or personal items with them when they left the factory outside work hours, in order to prevent them from absconding.

According to Zhang, when she and several other female members of the Gongshan cohort told the factory manager that they wanted to leave their jobs, the manager told them that it was not possible and refused to let them access their luggage. Their only recourse was to "steal" their luggage from their rooms and throw it over the factory wall. They then walked out of the factory and collected their luggage. Their families sent them money to pay for their travel costs back to Gongshan. Thus, for Zhang and her family, outward migration for work represented a significant financial loss. This outcome was completely at odds with the positive outcomes propagated by local government and newspaper reports.

Despite what appeared to be a very negative experience, Zhang still described Fujian as a "fun" place to visit. She felt it had provided her with an opportunity to "see the outside world" and experience a life quite different from the one she experienced in Gongshan, which she described as a "very backward" (*tai luohou*) place. She said she would strongly consider engaging in outward migration for work again (ibid.). Consistent with research findings from other parts of China on ethnic minority labor migration (Monteil and Vermander n.d.), she also held a positive view of the Han people she had met in Fujian, stating, "Fujian people, apart from the bosses, are very nice" (field notes, November 9, 2006).

Zhang's experience highlights the psychological tensions associated with rural subjectification in contemporary China. Her experience and comments reflect the assertion that "post-Mao development has robbed the countryside of its ability to serve as a locus for rural youth to construct a meaningful identity" (Yan 2003b: 579). The devaluing of rural China through official and popular narratives, and the concomitant failure to invest in infrastructure and public services during much of the reform era, has rendered places such as Gongshan as lacking and undesirable for young people. Zhang's comment above about the difficult living conditions in the factory revealed the instability and ambivalence she felt. She stated: "Even though we are from the countryside, we were not used to these living conditions," revealing both her internalization of the dominant narrative about rural China and her ability to place her own experience of rural life "above" that narrative. But ultimately her comments revealed that she valued urban life above rural life.

THE MOBILE POPULATION AND ITS IMPACTS ON ECONOMICALLY MARGINALIZED COMMUNITIES

The free flow of labor around China has been a boon for the Chinese manufacturing economy. It also has provided much-needed income for rural households and stimulated economic activity in otherwise economically underdeveloped rural areas. However, in economically marginalized areas, a much lesser-known phenomenon—the inward migration of business migrants and workers—can displace locals from markets and jobs. Gongshan's experience with inward migration has not been entirely positive.

Increased Competition for Locals

Since the creation of the nature reserve and the subsequent logging ban, selling vegetables in the Gongshan county town has become the main source of income for many farmers. However, during household surveys conducted by the author in 2005, many local farmers complained that in recent years it had become harder for them to sell their vegetables in the local market. This was because higher-quality and competitively priced vegetables from Nujiang's neighboring prefectures (Baoshan and Xiaguan) were being supplied to outside migrants who had established themselves in Gongshan's markets. Baoshan and Xiaguan have more fertile and productive land than Gongshan. When farmers were asked what it was like to sell their homegrown produce in the local market compared to five years ago, a common response was "It was better before. We can't compete with the outsiders who [now] come in and sell" (household surveys, July 2005).

High start-up costs and limited networks with businesses and relatives outside the prefecture appear to be preventing local farmers from taking advantage of Nujiang's gradual economic expansion. A survey conducted in Gongshan's main vegetable and meat market in October 2006 found that at least 72 percent of permanent market sellers were from outside Nujiang (market surveys, October 2006). While local farmers can sell their vegetables at temporary stalls within the market, high start-up and ongoing management costs prevent them from establishing permanent stalls.

New Opportunities for Outsiders with the Right Skills and Resources

When compared to business start-up costs in more economically developed areas of the country, those in Gongshan are much lower. This factor, combined with the relatively underdeveloped and "untapped" nature of the local economy, makes Gongshan an attractive destination for some outside business migrants. A family from Zhejiang (a wealthy province on China's east coast) runs a print shop on the county town's main street. By their own account, these migrants were attracted to Gongshan for the above-mentioned reasons, and their experience provides a useful insight into the motivations of outside migrants doing business in Gongshan. A member of the family explained why they had made the decision to migrate to Gongshan: "The people here are very backward. They don't understand this type of technology [printing]. In Zhejiang, this type of business is already very backward. You can't make money back there doing this type of business. . . . The people here don't have an economic mind [*jingji naozi*]. They are very lazy. If it wasn't for the 'mobile population,' this place wouldn't have developed. . . . You look, the government gives the people here so much!" (field notes, October 1, 2006).

FIG. 4.3. A team of migrant workers from Dali Prefecture constructs retaining walls along the main street of the Gongshan county town (December 2006).

The informant said that doing business in Gongshan was quite good— *"zheli hai keyi."* Like the female informant introduced in the previous section who had migrated to Jiangsu for work, this family's migratory experience demonstrates that in China migration is a nuanced and individual phenomenon. While for many locals Gongshan offers little in the way of work or business opportunities, there are attractive opportunities for those outside migrants who are able to offer the right niche skill or product.

Despite government efforts to move the local population away from agricultural work and toward off-farm work assignments, the local ethnic minority population still faces a high degree of discrimination in the local off-farm work environment, as is demonstrated by my interview with a construction team leader supervising a project in Gongshan in December 2006. The construction team, which was composed of fifty-six workers, including the team leader, was constructing a large retaining wall beside the road that dissects the county town (see fig. 4.3). The wall was intended to prevent landslides. All of the workers, including the team leader, were farmers who had temporarily migrated from Xiangyun County, Dali Prefecture. They arrived in Gongshan on November 1, 2006, and planned to stay until Chinese New Year (early 2007). According to the team leader, the workers were paid more than ¥20 per day, but the amount varied according to their positions. The team leader explained why he did not employ local farmers to undertake this type of work: "They are Lisu and Nu. They like drinking and don't work. If they are drunk and then work, they will fall over. You go to any of their houses and it's always the same. They're always drinking. Haven't you been to their houses [and seen for yourself]?" (field notes, December 6, 2006).

The team leader was not making a blanket claim about ethnic minorities, but was referring specifically to local ethnic minority groups. According to my research assistant, another reason bosses prefer to employ outsiders is that many of Gongshan's locals are Christian and rest on Sundays. If a boss wants a job finished quickly, he or she will expect workers to work seven days a week.[14]

CONCLUSION

Until quite recently, the Gongshan population was largely removed from the rural-to-urban migration phenomenon. Geographical isolation combined with low levels of education and proficiency in standard Chinese were formidable barriers to outward migration. Furthermore, livelihoods in Gongshan were defined largely by local conditions. The local population historically have subsisted via a combination of farming, hunting, small-scale logging, and collecting nontimber forest products, and were not as dependent upon the cash economy as rural communities in other parts of China were. As a consequence, outward migration for work was not a prominent feature of the local economy.

In recent years, the confluence of several wide-scale government programs and major improvements to transport and communication infrastructure has rendered outward migration for work an increasingly accessible option for Gongshan's farmers. These programs include labor export, the Sloping Land Conversion Program, free nine-year compulsory education, and the increased policing of the Gaoligongshan Nature Reserve. Underlying these programs is a broad social engineering agenda designed to shift the agricultural population away from agricultural work and to insert them within what governing authorities consider to be more productive off-farm work regimes. The labor export and work-study programs detailed in this chapter are regarded by governing authorities as particularly useful instruments for nurturing the psychological attributes and technical skills necessary for engaging with the expanding market economy. Paradoxically, even though these programs appear to be creating neoliberal subjects who will take increasing responsibility for developing their own capacities in an expanding market economy, they signal the local community's increasing dependence upon government.

CONCLUSION

Our older generation has no education, making life very hard for us.
We don't want our child to have the same difficulties. We're placing a
lot of hope in her.

—Gongshan farmer from Menke hamlet,
field notes, December 18, 2006

Prior to 2007, many of Menke's primary school–aged children were miss-
ing out on a full education. This was not because their parents did not
want their children to attend school; as the quote above suggests, many
of Menke's parents in fact placed great value upon education. The reason
was that when it rained or snowed, the steep, 1.3-kilometer dirt path connecting Menke with the local primary school became extremely slippery
and very dangerous to walk down, and parents did not allow their children to make the treacherous journey to and from school. Recognizing
the difficulties these children were facing in getting to and from school
and the impact it had upon their education, a local teacher and I initiated
the building of an all-weather concrete path to safely connect Menke with
the local primary school. The project was also a response to our perception that local governing authorities were providing inadequate access to
education for the local community. The Safe Path (Ping'an Lu) project
was made possible through funds donated by a Western Australian community organization as well as other members of the Western Australian
community. Later I initiated a project to fund university scholarships for
women from particularly disadvantaged ethnic minority households in
Gongshan. The first two recipients of these scholarships graduated from
universities in Kunming in July 2011. The path project embodies the theo-

retical threads woven through this book and gives practical context to the development programs directed at China's ethnic minorities.

The path project was initially perceived as a minor embarrassment for the local governing authorities, as it appeared to highlight their failure to provide adequate levels of infrastructure for the local population. In response, the local government made considerable efforts to ensure that it was involved and ultimately had symbolic ownership of the project. For example, upon completion of the project in 2007, a special opening cer- emony was organized by the local governing authorities. It was attended by senior government officials from both the Gongshan and the Nujiang governments. The Gongshan television station produced a special news story on the path and the opening ceremony for its daily *Gongshan News* (Gongshan Xinwen) broadcast, including separate recorded interviews with the hamlet leader and me. Through this highly choreographed news story, the path project became encapsulated in the "Build a New Social- ist Countryside" campaign. Indeed, the newsreader introduced the news story by stating: "Menke village has answered the Party's call to 'Build a New Socialist Countryside.'" The path was a symbol of the efforts that China's governing authorities were making to modernize rural China and to provide better social and economic outcomes for poor rural commu- nities such as Menke. Following the completion of the path, Menke was named a "model village" in acknowledgment of the sacrifice and hardship the villagers had endured as they worked without pay for several months to complete the path. In being named a model village, Menke became directly implicated in the population improvement program directed at Gongshan's ethnic minority population. The implicit message to the rest of the community was quite clear: "Gongshan's farmers are unproductive and engage in backward livelihoods that are holding back the develop- ment of the country. But if you are willing to work hard and comply with the opportunities, resources, and direction provided by government, you too can become productive, valued citizens."

To this end, my involvement in these projects inadvertently made me complicit in the state engineering project that has been the focus of this book: the socialization and political integration of China's ethnic minor- ity population into the Chinese Party-state. The path and the university scholarships were initiated to improve access to state education and work opportunities for children from disadvantaged households. However, another critical outcome of these projects is that they have drawn members of Gongshan's ethnic minority population further into the institutions and rationalities of the Chinese Party-state.

Since the late 1990s, major policy reforms in areas including agriculture and education, in conjunction with the rolling out of large-scale economic infrastructure such as roads and rail networks, have accelerated the collapse of time and space between peripheral ethnic minority communities and the market-driven industrialized economy concentrated in China's coastal areas. Reflecting Anthony Giddens's analysis of modernity, the movement of people and ideas is becoming more fluid, with livelihoods increasingly influenced by distant events and disembedded from their local context (Giddens 1990: 18–19; Giddens and Pierson 1998: 98). In once-peripheral rural communities such as Gongshan, this transformation has been marked by, among other things, an unprecedented proportion of the population being drawn into the state education system and the increased movement of surplus rural labor away from traditional subsistence-based livelihoods and toward off-farm work regimes, both locally and beyond the county border.

These changes are providing opportunities for many economically disadvantaged ethnic minority people to engage in off-farm work and improve their financial situation. They are also, for better or worse, further facilitating these people's integration into, and dependence upon, the Chinese Party-state. In line with Michel Foucault's notion of governmentality and his analysis of the ways in which modern nation-states are governed (1978, 1991), reforms such as the strict enforcement of compulsory education, the SLCP, and the increased penetration of state media reflect the increased governmentalization of ethnic minority communities, wherein the Chinese Party-state has an enhanced array of technologies at its disposable for influencing, and governing through, the desires and aspirations of the ethnic minority population.

As the epigraph above from a parent in Menke illustrates, many of Gongshan's parents are choosing to keep their children in school not as a response to active coercion by governing authorities, but because they genuinely believe it will improve their children's prospects of finding off-farm work and provide greater social and economic security in the long term. Paradoxically, just as choices such as this gesture toward providing a child with educational opportunities that will enable them to have greater individual autonomy and life choices upon completing school, they also reflect increased dependence upon the institutions and rationalities of the Chinese Party-state. Further, they reinforce the developmental agenda prescribed by China's governing authorities for the ethnic minority population, an agenda directed toward cultivating "high-quality," "patriotic," and "productive" citizens who will turn away from the "backward" and "environmentally destructive" subsistence-based rural livelihoods of their parents' generation and move into the off-farm work economy.

That said, the people and government of Gongshan have not been (and most likely never will be) completely acquiescent to the developmental agendas of the Chinese Party-state. The local governing authorities, for example, deftly circumvented the strict enforcement of the nine-year compulsory education policy. Even though official reporting indicated full compliance with the compulsory education policy, the makeshift vocational schools for dropouts created just prior to official inspection did little to advance the education of their students or to acquaint them with the rationalities and ideology of the Chinese Party-state, with many students appearing to return home soon after inspection. Government conservation programs directed at cutting off access to local forestry resources continue to be resisted by locals and outsiders. It is also critical to acknowledge that most of Gongshan's ethnic minority population has maintained a value system and livelihood structure quite distinct from that prescribed by governing authorities, despite living through more than six decades of highly interventionist CCP population improvement programs, many of which were overtly directed at breaking down traditional social structures and livelihood practices. Gongshan's ethnic minority people, whether Dulong, Lisu, Nu, or Tibetan, take great pride in their ethnic identity, history, and customs even as they continue to be subjected to demeaning official and popular narratives that portray them as being of low quality, lazy, and less advanced than the majority Han population. Although officially frowned upon, an enduring aspect of ethnic minority identity in Gongshan is Protestant and Catholic worship, a legacy of the missionaries who proselytized in northwestern Yunnan in the late nineteenth and early twentieth centuries. Churches, both legal and underground, are a prominent feature of contemporary Gongshan society.[1]

As Marshall Berman's epigraph in this book's introduction suggests, the experience of modernity brings with it both transformation and disintegration: on the one hand, it promises "adventure, power, joy, growth, transformation of ourselves and the world," and on the other, it "threatens to destroy everything we have, everything we know, everything we are" (1982: 15). This description is highly applicable to Gongshan, but with qualification: the experience of modernity in Gongshan has also been decidedly authoritarian. Gongshan's people have been subjected to an exceptionally paternalistic form of government intervention, or "authoritarian governmentality" (Dean 1999: 131–48), in the name of modernization and to remedy what governing authorities perceive to be backward and environmentally destructive livelihood practices, and local people have had little, if any, say in the development programs that are rapidly transforming their community.

An important question is what Gongshan would be like today—or in twenty years' time, for that matter—if it had not been subjected to this level of intervention. If the local population had been left to continue to practice their traditional livelihoods, had not been exposed to mainstream education, or had not been provided the opportunity to jump on the back of a truck and temporarily migrate to China's coastal regions for work, there is no doubt that social and economic conditions in Gongshan would be depressed, with food security a major concern for many households. Furthermore, if given the choice, it seems unlikely that the people of Gongshan would have opted out of the modernization process that has transformed their community. However, it is just as important to ask what a more inclusive development model might have achieved. National development policy that seeks to incorporate the diverse needs and desires of communities during both conception and implementation generally leads to more sustainable and equitable development outcomes for these communities. In contrast, Gongshan's people are governed under an authoritarian regime that offers limited space to openly discuss, challenge, and contribute to policy. While in the short term they have experienced vast improvements to their livelihoods, only time will tell if the current authoritarian approach to development results in genuinely sustainable and equitable outcomes for them and future generations.

Finally, increased government intervention is providing Gongshan's farmers with more choices and far greater opportunities than their parents' generation enjoyed. Over time, more of Gongshan's farmers will take up off-farm work, whether in Gongshan, Yunnan, or beyond. Nonetheless, they will not be competing on an equal basis in China's increasingly urbanized and market-oriented economy. Persistent structural inequalities will relegate Gongshan's farmers to the worst-paid off-farm jobs in the least-valued economic sectors. To this end, the greatest challenge for China's governing authorities in the coming decade will be to determine how the opportunities and economic spoils of three and a half decades of rapid economic growth and development can be more evenly distributed among its 1.3 billion people, including the people of Gongshan.

NOTES

1   Throughout this book, I use the term *Chinese Party-state,* as opposed to *Chinese nation-state,* to describe contemporary China. I use this term as a specific allu-sion to the imaginary single-party political fabric that the CCP has attempted to stretch across China's multiethnic territory since "Liberation" in 1949. In the Chi-nese Party-state, the CCP is the hegemonic form of the polity; the CCP not only dominates all aspects of government and political life, but also maintains consid-erable influence over the public sphere. Another unique element of the Chinese Party-state is the subservience of the People's Liberation Army to the CCP. I do use the term *nation-state* on several occasions throughout this book in reference to China. This distinction between the Party-state and the nation-state is important. However, the conflation of these terms is difficult to avoid. For example, in this introduction, I use western theories of modernity and the nation-state to examine the ways in which the Chinese Party-state is governed. Although these theories are relevant to our analysis, they do not account for the intricacies of the Chinese Party-state.

2   This era is referred to in Chinese as *gaige kaifang:* the era of "reform and opening up." The era is also described in English as the reform period or economic reform period. This book generally uses the term *reform era.*

3   In standard Chinese, the word *Nujiang* consists of two separate words: *nu,* mean-ing "angry," and *jiang,* meaning "river." However, the river's name actually derives from a Chinese phonetic interpretation of the local name for the river. In this case, the word *nu* derives from *Nong* (or *Anong*), the name of the people who originally occupied the northern reaches of the Nu River and from whom the river takes its name. The Anong are a subgroup of the Nu ethnic minority group (Sun and Liu 2009 [2005]: 1, 12–13). The word *Nujiang* is used interchangeably to describe both

Nujiang Prefecture and the Nu River. To avoid confusion, in this book *Nujiang* designates Nujiang Prefecture, and *Nu River* the river itself.

The Lisu are Nujiang's dominant ethnic group. In 2004, they composed approximately 51 percent of Nujiang's total population of 480,400 people (Foreign Affairs Office of the People's Government of the Nujiang Lisu Nationality Autonomous Prefecture 2006).

4   The Nu River is known as the Salween River upon entering Burma.

5   Despite their importance to the local rural economy, these types of transactions are not recorded in official government statistics.

6   The program is more accurately translated as "returning cultivated land to forest or grassland."

7   This tendency is not reserved to authoritarian governments such as China's. In his article "The Liberal Government of Unfreedom," Australian political scientist Barry Hindess (2001) delineates the contours of liberal political reason and its application to western societies such as Australia's. He notes that although western liberal democracy hinges on the autonomous actions of self-governing members of the population, western governments also recognize that certain sections of the population do not have the same capacity for self-improvement and therefore require more intervention and direction from government (see also Dean 1999: 131–48).

8   Maintaining unity and stability in these border areas, where local communities often share strong cultural and kinship ties with communities in neighboring countries, is of particular concern to both central and local governing authorities. Consequently, local officials are generally wary of outsiders, particularly foreign journalists, missionaries, nongovernmental organization (NGO) workers, and researchers.

9   As part of the central government's efforts to assist economic development in China's western peripheral regions, experts and teachers from more economically developed parts of the country often temporarily transfer to disadvantaged areas such as Gongshan for periods of up to several years.

10 All names in the book are pseudonyms unless otherwise indicated.

11 As its title suggests, James C. Scott's 1998 publication *Seeing Like a State: How Certain Schemes to Improve the Human Condition Have Failed* provides historical analysis of this dilemma.

12 We should also acknowledge that some mainland Chinese scholars have been critical of the privileging of western theories and ideas in nonwestern contexts, questioning the tendency among some Chinese intellectuals to appropriate western conceptions of modernity for their analysis (see Li Tuo cited in Davies 2007: 38).

13 See Escobar 1984–85, 1995; Esteva 1992; Sachs 1992; Hobart 1993; Everett 1997; Ferguson 2003 (1990); Sivaramakrishnan and Agrawal 2003; Rossi 2004; and Mosse 2005.

14 Officially, the ideology of the CCP is informed by Marxist, Leninist, and Mao Zedong Thought. Since 1997, Deng Xiaoping Theory also has been added.

15 The theory that human society progresses through specific stages of development was first proposed by Morgan (1985 [1877]), later appropriated by Marx and Engels, and then formalized by Stalin.

16 The Great Leap Forward campaign sought to rapidly transform China from an agrarian economy into an industrial power via the collectivization of rural labor

and the swift acceleration of industrial production. It was a disaster: agricultural output declined dramatically and tens of millions died of starvation (Dikötter 2010). Concerned that bourgeois/capitalist elements were increasingly shaping CCP policy, Mao Zedong orchestrated the Cultural Revolution to institutionalize Maoist orthodoxy, rid China of its traditional cultural values, and dislodge his political enemies. The period was characterized by widespread political, social, and economic turmoil and the purging of intellectuals and those regarded as having bourgeois leanings (MacFarquhar and Schoenhals 2006).

17 Refer to "Equivalents and Abbreviations" for information on currency conversion.

18 Yan Hairong roughly translates *suzhi*'s meaning as "the somewhat ephemeral qualities of civility, self-discipline, and modernity ... [and] a value articulation of human subjectivity" (2003a: 494).

19 The Han are China's dominant ethnic group, composing approximately 91.51 percent of the population (National Bureau of Statistics of China Online 2011: section 3.5).

20 The Qinghai-Tibet railway began operation in 2006.

21 See Harrell 1995, 2001; Heberer 2001; Mackerras 1995, 2003; and Mullaney 2011.

22 This process of classification was based upon the writings of the United States anthropologist Lewis Henry Morgan (Gladney 2004: 60). In his publication *Ancient Society,* Morgan (1985 [1877]) suggests that societies progress serially through stages of development. Essentially, they move from savagery to barbarism and eventually toward civilization.

23 This most recent official figure was recorded following the 2010 census.

24 China's ethnic minority groups vary considerably in both size and geographical dispersion. The largest, the Zhuang, number more than sixteen million and are concentrated in the west of the Guangxi Autonomous Region (see Kaup 2000). One of the smallest groups, the Dulong (Drung), number approximately six thousand and are concentrated in rugged and isolated Dulongjiang township in the west of Gongshan.

25 The ambiguity of ethnic identity is captured particularly well by Stevan Harrell in *Ways of Being Ethnic in Southwest China* (2001).

26 There are also ongoing disputes about the composition of the fifty-six ethnic/national categories.

27 As Thomas S. Mullaney (2011: 40) notes, it is inaccurate to assume that each of these four hundred groups constituted a distinct, self-aware ethnic group yearning for political recognition. Among the four hundred groups listed, ninety-two recorded populations of fewer than one hundred people. Of those ninety-two groups, twenty recorded populations of a single person (ibid.: 36). A large number of groups were listed because the census question relating to ethnicity did not provide predetermined responses—respondents were allowed to self-categorize. Mullaney concludes: "Whereas there were clearly groups for whom the census did in fact constitute a moment of politically self-aware assertion, the remainder appear instead to have been individuals who were simply improvising responses to a question they had never heard or considered before" (ibid.: 40).

28 This was not the first instance in which the CCP officially recognized China's ethnic minorities. Article 14 of the 1931 CCP constitution states that the Party "recognizes the right of self-determination of the national minorities in China, their right to complete separation from China, and to the formation of an independent

state for each minority" (cited in Gladney 2004: 11). Upon coming to power in 1949, the CCP considerably toned down its policy toward ethnic minorities, with references to secession removed (ibid.: 12).

29 Ethnic minorities were not exclusively targeted for persecution during this period: across the country, millions of Han and non-Han were killed and countless religious and cultural institutions were destroyed in the name of class struggle and the "Destruction of the Four Olds" (Old Customs, Old Culture, Old Habits, and Old Ideas) campaign.

30 In 1980, Hu Yaobang, then the general secretary of the Central Committee of the CCP, led a working group to Tibet to investigate local conditions. During the visit, Hu became acutely aware of the deleterious impacts of Chinese interventions in Tibet, precipitating an important turning point in government policy directed toward China's ethnic minorities.

31 These are the Ningxia Hui Nationality Autonomous Region, the Xinjiang Uighur Nationality Autonomous Region, the Tibet Autonomous Region, the Guangxi Zhuang Nationality Autonomous Region, and the Inner Mongolia Autonomous Region.

32 In fact, autonomous areas are subjected to greater supervision and intervention from the CCP than areas that are not designated as autonomous.

33 The constitution stipulates that the titular head of government of an autonomous area must be from the ethnic minority group to which that autonomous area was nominally bestowed. This stipulation does not apply to the party secretary, a position that outranks the titular head of government.

34 Gongshan's ethnic minority officials, from the village committee (cunweiyuanhui) up to the county government, are required to study at the local Party school.

1. LIFE AT THE PERIPHERY OF THE CHINESE PARTY-STATE

1 In post-Enlightenment Europe, an intense curiosity developed about the exotic botanical diversity of the "East." This curiosity was acted upon by the so-called plant hunters, such as Francis Kingdon Ward, George Forrest, and Joseph Francis Charles Rock, who were sponsored by government and private plant collectors to venture to the East to uncover new plant species (see Glover et al. 2011; Mueggler 2011). Many of the newly discovered specimens collected by the plant hunters eventually would be propagated and displayed in public and private gardens in Europe. However, their ventures into areas such as northwestern Yunnan, Tibet, and eastern Burma were often made for purposes that extended beyond botanical curiosity. For example, Ward's *Mystery Rivers of Tibet* (1986 [1923]) is clearly written with the protection of British interests in Burma, as well as the potential for British imperial expansion into western Yunnan, in mind (212).

2 This is an important distinction between Yunnan's main ethnic minority groups and some of the ethnic minority groups concentrated in Tibet, Xinjiang, and even Inner Mongolia (Mackerras 2003: chapter 3). For instance, in Xinjiang, the Uighur ethnic minority group have historically exhibited strong nationalistic sentiments and deeply resent the large (and ever-increasing) Han presence within their nominally autonomous region. Uighur separatist groups have carried out violent forms

of resistance as well as organized terrorist attacks against state institutions (ibid.: 49–54).

3   This name is spelled Fei Hsiao-Tung in the Wade-Giles transliteration system.

4   George Ernest Morrison, *An Australian in China* (2007 [1902]); C. P. Fitzgerald, *The Tower of Five Glories: A Study of the Min Chia of Ta Li, Yunnan* (1941); Joseph Francis Charles Rock, *The Ancient Na-Khi Kingdom of Southwest China* (1947); and Henry Rodolph Davies, *Yun-Nan: The Link between India and the Yangtze* (2010 [1909]), also provide insightful pre-Liberation accounts of social and economic conditions in Yunnan.

5   Yun = cloud(s); *nan* = south.

6   Scholar-magistrates of the imperial court who were assigned to Yunnan regarded it as a punitive posting. The journey from Beijing to Kunming took approximately four months. According to one analysis, "Unscrupulous Mandarins who had the misfortune to draw such a distant assignment usually saw to it that they made their profit in short order, with slight regard for the welfare of the helpless populace" (Cressey 1934: 373).

7   While China had had a long history of relying upon native leaders in the governance of non-Han populations living in its rugged peripheral regions, it was during the Yuan dynasty (1271–1368) that an institutional relationship began to develop between the imperial court and these native leaders. During the Ming dynasty (1368–1644), this relationship was formalized via the official establishment of *tusi* offices (Herman 2006: 136). Although the *tusi* exercised a high degree of autonomy in governing the population within their dominions, they were expected to demonstrate loyalty to the imperial authorities, particularly during times of armed conflict with hostile military forces both within and beyond China's border. In so doing, they not only provided the imperial court with a useful military buffer against foreign forces; they were also a convenient, cost-effective mechanism to govern areas where it was not economically viable to establish formal governance arrangements.

8   There had been Han migration into Yunnan prior to this period. However, it had been on a relatively small scale and was largely government organized. Between the thirteenth and sixteenth centuries, it is estimated that more than one million settlers moved to China's southwest as part of government-organized migration programs (Lee 1982: 714).

9   That said, the indigenous population, including the *tusi*, were never completely displaced from the southwest. In a process best described as acculturation, many indigenous communities successfully adapted to the changing cultural and economic environment that accompanied increased Han in-migration. They not only learned Chinese and lived side by side and intermarried with the new migrants; they also adapted to their more intensive agricultural techniques and traded with them at local markets. Still, the nature of their engagement, or acculturation, was often selective and shaped by self-interest (Giersch 2006: 216–17).

10   This region is featured in the British Broadcasting Corporation's *Wild China* documentary series (2008).

11   The Irrawaddy in Ward's account is actually the Taron River, a key tributary of the Irrawaddy. In contemporary China, the Taron is known as the Dulong River (Dulongjiang), which dissects Dulongjiang township and from which the

township draws its name. In its upper reaches, including the section that flows through northwestern Yunnan, the Yangzi is known as the River of Golden Sand (Jinshajiang).

12   Today Changputong is known as Bingzhongluo, one of the five townships that constitute Gongshan County.

13   According to one account, the name *Gaoligongshan* itself derives from the standard Chinese transliteration of a local indigenous language, and it is said to mean "Gaoli Clan Mountain" (Xu Xiake cited in Giersch 2006: 17).

14   Changputong was a standard Chinese approximation of "Tra-mu-tang," the Tibetan regional name for the area. *Tra-mu-tang* means "the flat plain on the [river] bank" (Ward 1986 [1923]: 193). It is one of the few areas in Gongshan with a substantial expanse of flat agricultural land.

15   Extracts from this report have been translated and published by Herold J. Wiens (1967 [1954]).

16   This is most likely Zhiziluo, the focus of the documentary *Ghost Town* by Zhao Dayong (2008).

17   These landslides are not caused by agricultural practices alone. Government road construction is one of the major causes of soil erosion and landslides in Nujiang, although this is rarely, if ever, noted in official accounts.

18   This figure was calculated using Nujiang's 1986 rural population figure: 365,000 people (Gao 2003: 10).

2. NATURE RESERVES AND REFORESTATION

1   As Tania Murray Li contends: "Trustees use a particular population's failure to improve (to turn nature's bounty to a profit), or to conserve (to protect nature for the common good) as rationales for their dispossession, and as the justification to assign resources to people who will make better use of them. . . . This myth is alive and well in national bureaucracies and transnational agencies promoting agricultural development and conservation" (2007: 21).

2   I employ pseudonyms for hamlet names in order to protect the identities of the people residing there.

3   Although this has provided local communities with a lucrative source of cash income, it also has created conflict over access to local resources. Furthermore, it has exposed local communities to global economic fluctuations, and the 1998 Asian financial crisis led to a dramatic decline in household income among some communities in northwestern Yunnan. Those most affected were women, for whom the mushroom trade provided an opportunity to contribute to household income (Yeh 2000: 277–78).

4   As James Harkness notes: "Institutionally, setting up forest reserves in southern China has at times facilitated resource degradation as relatively effective community management institutions (*xiangguiminyue*) are replaced by extremely weak state ownership, creating a de facto open access area and inviting over-use" (1998: 921).

5   The five central tasks are (1) "Speed up the construction of the economic base" (*Jiakuai jichu sheshi jianshe*); (2) "Earnestly strengthen the protection and construction of the ecological environment" (*Qieshi jiaqiang shengtai huanjing baohu*

he jianshe); (3) "Actively regulate the industrial structure" (*Jiji tiaozheng chanye jiegou*); (4) "Develop science and technology and education, and speed up the cultivation of human talent" (*Fazhan keji he jiaoyu, jiakuai rencai peiyang*); and (5) "Expand the limits of reform and openness" (*Jiada gaige kaifang lidu*) (China.com, August 19, 2007).

6   These damaging practices, which include cutting down forest and opening up marginal land for agriculture, were actively promoted by China's governing authorities during the Maoist era as a means to increase China's grain self-sufficiency.

7   This is not to suggest that all of the marginal agricultural land that has been nominally converted to forest via the SLCP has been on slopes greater than 25 degrees. In their investigation of the implementation of the SLCP at a site in western Sichuan, Trac et al. observe that local governing authorities converted land with an average slope of only 17 degrees, even though they reported to higher-level governing authorities that all of this converted land was on slopes greater than 25 degrees (2007: 287).

8   Hoang (2009) has made similar observations among upland communities in a northwestern frontier valley of Vietnam. He notes that following the replacement of customary rights of access to forestry resources in old-growth forests with bureaucratic management and surveillance of these resources by local governing authorities, local people who had traditionally accessed these resources feel little or no incentive to report on illegal encroachment.

9   Andreas Wilkes, personal correspondence, October 27, 2008.

10 At the time of writing, it is unclear whether the SLCP subsidies have continued beyond 2011. In the absence of other accessible income-generating opportunities for much of Dulongjiang's adult population, it is likely that they have been replaced by larger direct cash payments from local government.

11 This type of prejudice is not unique to China and can also be found in upland ethnic minority communities in Vietnam (see Hoang 2009).

12 The process of applying for permission to cut down trees for housing is as follows: Each hamlet appoints a forest protection officer to act on behalf of the County Forestry Bureau, and if a household needs to fell trees, they must first apply through the officer. The officer makes an inspection to find out how much timber the household plans to fell. Following the officer's approval, the household must then gain a stamp of approval from their village committee. After receiving approval from the committee, the household then can apply for a timber-felling permit from the township forestry station. However, if the amount of timber the household plans to fell exceeds the amount that can be approved by the forestry station, they must seek permission from the County Forestry Bureau.

3. ALL IS NOT AS IT APPEARS

1   In Singapore, Confucianism was utilized by former Prime Minister Lee Kuan Yew to justify strict authoritarian rule over a largely ethnic Chinese population.

2   As early as the Shang dynasty (1700–1100 BCE), common people could access a school system that taught them the "rituals of social life." A basic examination system was also in place to appoint officials to government office (Cleverley 1991 [1985]: 1).

3   It is important to acknowledge the significant epistemological rupture that emerged during the late Qing period, when concerns over national strength and racial deterioration intersected with emerging fields of social scientific inquiry and statistical analysis to precipitate a shift toward a more meticulous management of human life (see Dikötter 1992; Sigley 1996). The contemporary focus on population quality and the scientific management of the population represents continuity with these early interventions.

4   Statistics suggest that illiteracy elimination programs in place between 1949 and 1955 had little impact on the national literacy rate. By 1955, the national illiteracy rate still stood at 75 to 80 percent (Peterson 1994: 110–11).

5   Nevertheless, ethnicity alone is not a marker of low literacy and educational levels. In some cases, literacy rates among Han students living in ethnic minority regions have been only slightly higher than those of ethnic minority students (Postiglione 2000: 54).

6   The Gongshan Education Bureau produced this report for the celebrations marking fifty years since Gongshan had been officially recognized as a county.

7   This statement is somewhat contentious, as the Tibetans had their own written script. It is most likely meant to imply that the Dulong, Nu, and Lisu did not have their own written scripts and that the local Tibetans were illiterate in their own language. Protestant missionaries invented a written script for the Lisu language in the early twentieth century and eventually translated the New Testament into it.

8   According to Harrell, "notching sticks and tying knots" is often employed as a metaphor for classifying peripheral groups as primitive remnants of ancient societies (1995: 15). Such a simple form of recording gestures toward a "savage" mind. Even though preliterate groups may have used an array of sophisticated recording techniques, the metaphor has become a truth associated with all preliterate groups. Groups that are labeled as using these techniques are regarded as equivalent to ancient people.

9   These pseudonyms are used to protect the identities of the people residing in these hamlets.

10   According to a document provided to the author by the national Ministry of Education in Beijing, in prefectures such as Nujiang, the cost of tuition and miscellaneous fees is divided between the central (80 percent) and provincial (20 percent) governments. The central and provincial governments also cover the cost of textbooks. Living expenses are split among the provincial, prefectural, and county governments (Education, Science and Culture Office of the Yunnan Provincial Finance Department/Finance Planning Office of the Yunnan Provincial Education Department 2007: 7).

11   10 *mao* = ¥1.

4. MIGRATION FROM THE MARGINS

1   Aside from surplus rural workers traveling to cities in search of work, the mobile population also includes people from urban and rural areas who travel to other urban and rural areas to undertake various activities, including business, tourism, seeing doctors, or visiting relatives.

2   At various times, the state has organized rural-to-urban migration for specific industrialization programs. Furthermore, during the Cultural Revolution there

was a large wave of urban-to-rural migration orchestrated largely by the state. Most of these migrants were students who were sent to the countryside to "learn from the peasants." Many of them remained in the countryside throughout the Cultural Revolution.

3   It is mainly poor rural areas that export surplus rural labor. Many rural areas in coastal and interior regions have net in-migration because they have local manufacturing and other industries.

4   See Harrell 1995, 2001; Hansen 1999; Heberer 2001; Lin 2007; Barabantseva 2008; and Mullaney 2011.

5   Weber's (2007 [1976]) account of the impacts of rural-to-urban migration upon rural French society in the nineteenth century provides some striking parallels to the situation in contemporary China.

6   Pierre Bourdieu defines *habitus* as "a system of lasting, transposable dispositions" (1977: 82).

7   Murphy conducted her research in several rural counties in Jiangxi Province, southeast China. Despite its state of relative economic underdevelopment, Jiangxi is in close proximity to China's prosperous coastal provinces and has been a major rural migrant-sending area since the beginning of the reform era.

8   During the first two decades of the reform era, rural-to-urban migration was generally less common among the ethnic minority population. This situation changed dramatically during the 2000s, and by 2010 it was estimated that 10 percent of the ethnic minority population (over 12 million people) were engaging in outward migration for work (*China Daily*, November 18, 2010a).

9   In 2008, a one-way bus ticket to Liuku, the prefectural seat, was approximately 55 yuan. A bus ticket from Liuku to Kunming, the provincial capital, was approximately 110 yuan. A train ticket from Kunming to a major migrant-receiving area on China's coast was another several hundred yuan.

10 The author undertook this survey in Ali and Menke hamlets between December 18 and 24, 2006.

11 This social engineering agenda is not unique to Nujiang and can be found in many other poor rural areas involved in labor export (see Murphy 2002; Yan 2003a).

12 This document was provided by the Gongshan County Labor Bureau.

13 These findings reflect Murphy's study of returning rural migrants in Jiangxi (2002: 88–123).

14 Evidence of inbuilt discrimination against ethnic minority groups was also witnessed by Heberer (2001: 223) in Liangshan Prefecture, in neighboring Sichuan. Liangshan is one of China's poorest and least economically developed areas. The Nuosu (part of the ethnic conglomeration officially categorized as Yi) are the main ethnic group in this area. Heberer notes that although industrial colonization and development were taking place in Liangshan, it provided limited benefit for the local ethnic minority population. According to Heberer, colonizing industrialists chose to employ outside labor rather than members of the local ethnic minority population, who were considered to be unsuitable for the work being undertaken. Nonetheless, discrimination is not necessarily one-way in Liangshan. Subsequent research undertaken by Heberer (2007) revealed that Han entrepreneurs engaging in business activities in Liangshan felt themselves to be at a disadvantage vis-à-vis Nuosu entrepreneurs, mainly because it was more difficult for Han entrepreneurs to create and maintain relationships with officials in the local Nuosu-dominated government administration.

CONCLUSION

1   The documentary *Ghost Town* by Zhao Dayong (2008) vividly captures the per-
     severance of Lisu and Nu identity and religious worship despite six decades of
     CCP rule, while also highlighting the social dislocation associated with recent
     modernization. The documentary was filmed in Fugong, the county directly south
     of Gongshan.

GLOSSARY OF CHINESE TERMS

Beijing Xibu Gaoji Zhiye Xueyuan 北京西部高级职业学院
Biandi sawang, zhongdian laoyu 遍地撒网, 重点捞鱼
bu fang xin 不放心

chengcai 成材
chengzhen hukou 城镇户口
chongxin renshi shehui 重新认识社会
Chuzhong Zige 初中资格
cunweiyuanhui 村委员会

dagongmei 打工妹
daidong xiangzhen qiye 带动乡镇企业
di shengchanli 低生产力
di suzhi 低素质
donggua shu 冬瓜树
Dulongjiang 独龙江

fangyan 方言
Fazhan keji he jiaoyu, jiakuai rencai peiyang
发展科技和教育, 加快人才培养

gaige kaifang 改革开放
gaokao 高考
Gaoligongshan 高黎贡山
Gaoligongshan Guojia Ji Ziran Baohu Qu 高黎贡山国家级自然保护区
gao suzhi 高素质
gao suzhi de laodongzhe 高素质的劳动者
gongban 公办
Gongshan Dulongzu Nuzu Zizhixian 贡山独龙族怒族自治县
Gongshan Dulongzu Nuzu zizhixian zhi 贡山独龙族怒族自治县志
Gongshan Xian gongmin wenming shouce 贡山县公民文明手册
Gongshan Xian Nongye Ju 贡山县农业局
Gongshan Xian Renshi Laodong Ju 贡山县人事劳动局
Gongshan Xinwen 贡山新闻
Gongxue Fupin Xingdong 工学扶贫行动
guanbi shi 关闭式
Guojia Chengren Xueli de Biye Zhengshu 国家承认学历的毕业证书
Guojia Zhiye Zige Zhengshu 国家职业资格证书

hetong 合同
hukou 户口

Jiada gaige kaifang lidu 加大改革开放力度
Jiakuai jichu sheshi jianshe 加快基础设施建设
jiang 江
Jianshe Shehuizhuyi Xin Nongcun 建设社会主义新农村
Jiating Lianchan Chengbao Zeren Zhi 家庭联产承包责任制
jieshao xin 介绍信
Jiji tiaozheng chanye jiegou 积极调整产业结构
jin 斤
jingji naozi 经济脑子
Jinshajiang 金沙江
jizhong banxue 集中办学
Juece zhe shuo 决策者说
junxian zhidu 郡县制度

keju 科举
kelian 可怜

kemu jishi, jiesheng jishu 刻木记事, 结绳计数
kexue fazhan guan 科学发展观
kuaxiang shuchu 垮乡输出

Lancang 澜沧
laowu shuchu 劳务输出
liang mian yi bu 两免一补
limao 礼貌
lingyongqian 零用钱
Lishu 栗树
liudong renkou 流动人口
luohou 落后

mao 毛
minban 民办
minzu 民族
minzu ban 民族班
Minzu Shibie 民族识别

nan 南
nongcun laodongli zhuanyi 农村劳动力转移
Nongcun Yiwu Jiaoyu Jingfei Baozhang Xin Jizhi
　　农村义务教育经费保障新机制
nu 怒
Nujiang 怒江
Nujiang bao 怒江报
Nujiang Lisuzu Zizhizhou 怒江傈僳族自治州
Nujiang Lisuzu zizhizhou gaikuang 怒江傈僳族自治州概况
Nujiang wenti 怒江问题
Nujiang Zhou Laodong He Shehui Baozhang Ju
　　怒江州劳动和社会保障局

peiyang 培养
peiyang chiku naidong jingshen 培养吃苦耐动精神
peiyang minzu ganbu 培养民族干部
pianren 骗人
Pinde yu shenghuo 品德与生活

Ping'an Lu 平安路
pinkun shanqu xian 贫困山区县
piqi 脾气
puji jiunian yiwu jiaoyu 普及九年义务教育

qianghua shichang guannian 强化市场观念
Qieshi jiaqiang shengtai huanjing baohu he jianshe
    切实加强生态环境保护和建设
Quanguo Nongcun Yiwu Jiaoyu Jingfei Baozhang Jizhi Gaige Lingdao
    Xiaozu Bangongshi
    全国农村义务教育经费保障机制改革领导小组办公室

ren de suzhi 人的素质
renkou suzhi 人口素质
Ren zai na ge difang, xin bu zai na ge difang
    人在那个地方, 心不在那个地方

san ge luohou 三个落后
sanqi 三七
saomang 扫盲
saomangban 扫盲班
shan 山
Shan qing shui xiu, min feng chun pu 山青水秀, 民风纯朴
shaoshu 少数
shaoshu minzu 少数民族
shao yao duo gei 少要多给
shehui zonghe daxue 社会综合大学
shengchanli 生产力
shengnei shuchu 省内输出
shengwai shuchu 省外输出
shimianwa 石棉瓦
Shuchu yi ren, tuopin yi hu, shuchu yi pi, daidong yi fang
    输出一人, 脱贫一户, 输出一批, 带动一方
shuli xin de zeye yishi 树立新的择业意识
suzhi 素质

tai luohou 太落后

Tianran Lin Ziyuan Baohu Gongcheng 天然林资源保护工程

tiaozheng, gaige, zhengdun, tigao 调整, 改革, 整顿, 提高

tongyi de duo minzu guojia 统一的多民族国家

Tui Geng Huan Lin Huan Cao Gongcheng 退耕还林还草工程

tuijian jiuye 推荐就业

tushan 秃杉

tusi 土司

wenhua 文化

wenmang 文盲

Wo hen zhengjie 我很整洁

xian 县

xiang 乡

xiangguiminyue 乡规民约

xiangjun 香菌

xianjin de jieji jiqi zhengdang de zhengque zhiyin
    先进的阶级及其政党的正确指引

Xiaoxuesheng guoqing shi zhidao 小学生国情十知道

Xibu Da Kaifa 西部大开发

Xingzheng Weiyuan 行政委员

yamen 衙门

Yi lin wei zhu, lin liang bing ju, quanmian fazhan
    以林为主, 林粮并举, 全面发展

Yi lin wei zhu, lin, liang, mu, yao quanmian fazhan
    以林为主, 林, 粮, 牧, 药全面发展

yishi yixiao 一师一校

yiwu 义务

youhui zhengce 优惠政策

yun 云

Yunnan 云南

zheli hai keyi 这里还可以

zhen 镇

zhihou 滞后

zhiju 治局

Zhiye Chuzhong Zige 职业初中资格

zhiye xuexiao 职业学校

zhize 职责

Zhongguo jiaoyu bao 中国教育报

zhuanke biye 专科毕业

zige kaifa de yi ge xiangmu 资格开发的一个项目

BIBLIOGRAPHY

Anagnost, Ann. 1997a. "Children and National Transcendence in China." In *Constructing China: The Interaction of Culture and Economics,* edited by Kenneth G. Lieberthal, Shuen-fu Lin, and Ernest P. Young. Ann Arbor: Center for Chinese Studies, University of Michigan, 195–222.

————. 1997b. *National Past-Times: Narrative, Representation, and Power in Modern China.* Durham, NC, and London: Duke University Press.

————. 2004. "The Corporeal Politics of Quality (Suzhi)." *Public Culture* 16 (2): 189–208.

Anonymous. 2006. "Erlinglingliu nian Nujiang zhou laodong shuchu shishi fang'an: Taolun gao" (2006 Nujiang Prefecture labor export implementation scheme: Draft discussion paper). (This document was provided to the author by the Gongshan County Labor Bureau.)

Bakken, Børge. 2000. *The Exemplary Society: Human Improvement, Social Control, and the Dangers of Modernity in China.* Oxford: Oxford University Press.

Barabantseva, Elena. 2008. "From the Language of Class to the Rhetoric of Development: Discourses of 'Nationality' and 'Ethnicity' in China." *Journal of Contemporary China* 17 (56): 565–89.

Berman, Marshall. 1982. *All That Is Solid Melts into Air: The Experience of Modernity.* New York: Simon and Schuster.

Blum, Susan D. 2001. *Portraits of Primitives.* Lanham, MD: Rowman and Littlefield.

Bourdieu, Pierre. 1977. *Outline of Theory and Practice.* Cambridge: Cambridge University Press.

British Broadcasting Corporation (BBC). 2008. *Wild China.*

Brown, Philip H., and Kevin Xu. 2010. "Hydropower Development and Resettlement Policy on China's Nu River." *Journal of Contemporary China* 19 (66): 777–97.

Center for Biodiversity and Indigenous Knowledge (CBIK). 2006. *Consultations on Agro-Biodiversity Loss and Conservation in the Dulongjiang Valley, Yunnan, China.* Kunming: Center for Biodiversity and Indigenous Knowledge. (This report was submitted to the Convention on Biodiversity Office of the State Environment Protection Agency in August 2006. Report provided to author by Andreas Wilkes.)

Central Government of the People's Republic of China. 2004. *Constitution.* http://english.gov.cn/2005-08/05/content_20813.htm. Accessed October 11, 2008.

Chan, Christina Y., and Stevan Harrell. 2009. "School Consolidation in Rural Sichuan: Quality Versus Equality." In *Affirmative Action in China and the U.S.: A Dialogue on Inequality and Minority Education,* edited by Minglang Zhou and Ann Maxwell Hill. New York: Palgrave Macmillan, 143–64.

Cheng Li. 1996. "Surplus Rural Laborers and Internal Migration in China: Current Status and Future Prospects." *Asian Survey* 36 (11): 1122–45.

Chen Shaojuan, ed. 2005. *Pinde yu shenghuo* (Moral character and life). Beijing: Renmin Jiaoyu Chubanshe.

Chen Xiang. 2006. "Guojia qidong 'Nujiang wenti' yanjiu" (The nation kick-starts an investigation of the "Nujiang issue"). *Zhongguo minzu bao* (China nationality news). May 16. http://iea.cass.cn/jianbao/F002572.doc. Accessed November 27, 2008.

Chen Zhili. 2006. "Chen Zhili: Li tui Nongcun Yiwu Jiaoyu Jingfei Baozhang Jizhi gaige" (Chen Zhili strongly advances the Rural Compulsory Education Assured Funding Mechanism reform). *Zhongguo jiaoyu bao* (China education news). November 30. www.edu.cn/edu_liter_5272/20061130/t20061130_207446.shtml. Accessed November 15, 2007.

China.com. 2007. "Quyu jingji" (Regional economy). August 19. www.china.com.cn/aboutchina/txt/2007-08/19/content_8709882.htm. Accessed December 7, 2007.

China Daily. 2010a. "Minister Prepares to Solve Ethnic Challenges." November 18. www.china.org.cn/china/2010-11/18/content_21368898.htm. Accessed July 30, 2010.

———. 2010b. "Ethnic Minorities Remain Besieged by Poverty." December 23.

www.china.org.cn/china/2010-12/23/content_21599493.htm. Accessed January 7, 2010.

———. 2011. "Nujiang Hydro Project Back on Agenda." February 1. www.china daily.com.cn/business/2011-02/01/content_11952362.htm. Accessed May 14, 2011.

China Nujiang Gorge Network. 2011. "Gongshan gaikuang" (Gongshan overview). www.nujiang.cn/zhouqing/xianxiang/gsx/201002/t20100203_1498 .html. Accessed April 24, 2011.

Cleverley, John. 1991. *The Schooling of China: Tradition and Modernity in Chinese Education.* North Sydney, Australia: Allen and Unwin. Originally published 1985.

Cressey, George Babcock. 1934. *China's Geographic Foundations: A Survey of the Land and Its People.* New York and London: McGraw-Hill.

Daniels, Christian. 1994. "Environmental Degradation, Forest Protection and Ethno-History in Yunnan (1): The Uprising by Swidden Agriculturalists in 1821." *Chinese Environmental History Newsletter* 1 (2): n.p.

Davies, Gloria. 2007. *Worrying about China: The Language of Chinese Critical Inquiry.* Cambridge, MA, and London: Harvard University Press.

Davies, Henry Rodolph. 2010. *Yun-Nan: The Link between India and the Yangtze.* Cambridge: Cambridge University Press. Originally published 1909.

Dean, Mitchell. 1999. *Governmentality: Power and Rule in Modern Society.* London, Thousand Oaks, CA, and New Delhi: Sage Publications.

Digital Countryside—Building the New Countryside Information Network. 2008. "Gongshan xian Tui Geng Huan Lin Gongcheng wancheng qingkuang" (The completion of the Sloping Land Conversion Program in Gongshan County). www.ynszxc.gov.cn/szxc/CountyModel/ShowDocument.aspx?Did=1525 &DepartmentId=1525&id=2523373. Accessed May 29, 2011.

Dikötter, Frank. 1992. *The Discourse of Race in Modern China.* London: Hurst & Company.

———. 2010. *Mao's Great Famine: The History of China's Most Devastating Catastrophe, 1958–1962.* New York: Walker & Co.

Dilger, Bernhard. 1984. "The Education of Minorities." *Comparative Education* 20 (1): 155–64.

Dirlik, Arif. 2006. "Global Modernity, Spatial Reconfigurations, and Global Health: Perspectives from the People's Republic of China." *boundary 2* 33 (1): 99–122.

Economist. 2000. "Asia: Go West, Young Han." 357 (8202): 29–30.

Economist (online). 2011. "Comparing Chinese Provinces with Countries." www .economist.com/content/chinese_equivalents. Accessed April 23, 2011.

Education, Science and Culture Office of the Yunnan Provincial Finance Depart-
ment/Finance Planning Office of the Yunnan Provincial Education Department. 2007. *Yunnan sheng: Nongcun Yiwu Jiaoyu Jingfei Baozhang Jizhi gaige
cailiao huibian* (Yunnan Province: Rural Compulsory Education Assured
Funding Mechanism reform compilation). Kunming: Yunnan sheng Caizheng
Ting Jiao Ke Wen Chu/Yunnan sheng Jiaoyu Ting Ji Cai Chu.

Elvin, Mark. 2004. *The Retreat of the Elephants: An Environmental History of
China.* New Haven, CT: Yale University Press.

Escobar, Arturo. 1984–85. "Discourse and Power in Development: Michel Foucault and the Relevance of His Work to the Third World." *Alternatives X* (Winter 1984–85): 377–400.

———. 1995. *Encountering Development: The Making and Unmaking of the Third
World.* Princeton, NJ: Princeton University Press.

Esteva, Gustavo. 1992. "Development." In *The Development Dictionary: A Guide
to Knowledge as Power,* edited by Wolfgang Sachs. London and New Jersey:
Zen Books, 6–25.

Everett, Margaret. 1997. "The Ghost in the Machine: Agency in 'Poststructural'
Critiques of Development." *Anthropological Quarterly* 70 (3): 137–51.

Fei Hsiao-Tung and Chang Chih-I. 1949. *Earthbound China: A Study of Rural
Economy in Yunnan.* London: Routledge and Kegan Paul. Originally published 1948.

Ferguson, James. 2003. *The Anti-Politics Machine: "Development," Depoliticiza-
tion, and Bureaucratic Power in Lesotho.* Minneapolis: University of Minne-
sota Press. Originally published 1990.

Fitzgerald, C. P. 1941. *The Tower of Five Glories: A Study of the Min Chia of Ta Li,
Yunnan.* London: Cresset Press.

Foreign Affairs Office of the People's Government of the Nujiang Lisu Nationality Autonomous Prefecture. 2006. "Nujiang Lisuzu zizhizhou jianjie" (A brief
introduction to the Nujiang Lisu Nationality Autonomous Prefecture). www
.yfao.gov.cn/show.aspx?id=211. Accessed November 27, 2008.

Forrest, George. 1908. "Journey on Upper Salwin, October–December, 1905."
Geographical Journal 32 (3): 239–66.

Foucault, Michel. 1978. *The History of Sexuality. Vol. I: An Introduction.* New
York: Pantheon Books.

———. 1991. "Governmentality." In *The Foucault Effect: Studies in Governmentality,* edited by Graham Burchell, Colin Gordon, and Peter Miller. Hemel
Hempstead: Harvester Wheatsheaf, 87–104.

Gaetano, Arianne M. 2004. "Filial Daughters, Modern Women: Migrant Domes-
tic Workers in Post-Mao Beijing." In *On the Move: Women in Rural-to-Urban*

Migration in Contemporary China, edited by Arianne M. Gaetano and Tamara
Jacka. New York: Columbia University Press, 41–79.

Gaetano, Arianne M., and Tamara Jacka, eds. 2004. *On the Move: Women in
Rural-to-Urban Migration in Contemporary China*. New York: Columbia University Press.

Gao Yingxin. 2003. *Shandi nonggeng minzu shengtai jingji yanjiu* (Study on eco-
economy of mountainous ethnic groups). Kunming: Yunnan Keji Chubanshe.

Giddens, Anthony. 1990. *The Consequences of Modernity*. Cambridge: Polity
Press.

Giddens, Anthony, and Christopher Pierson. 1998. *Conversations with Anthony
Giddens: Making Sense of Modernity*. Stanford, CA: Stanford University Press.

Giersch, C. Pat. 2001. "'A Motley Throng': Social Change on Southwest China's
Early Modern Frontier, 1700–1880." *Journal of Asian Studies* 60 (1): 67–94.

———. 2006. *Asian Borderlands: The Transformation of Qing China's Yunnan
Frontier*. Cambridge, MA, and London: Harvard University Press.

Gillogly, Kathleen A. 2006. "Transformations of Lisu Social Structure under
Opium Control and Watershed Conservation in Northern Thailand." PhD
diss., University of Michigan. http://manao.manoa.hawaii.edu/38/1/gillogly_
dissertation.pdf. Accessed February 6, 2009.

Gladney, Dru C. 1998. *Ethnic Identity in China: The Making of a Muslim Minority
Nationality*. Fort Worth, TX: Harcourt Brace College Publishers.

———. 2004. *Dislocating China: Reflections on Muslims, Minorities, and Other
Subaltern Subjects*. Chicago: University of Chicago Press.

Glover, Denise M., Stevan Harrell, Charles F. McKhann, and Margaret Byrne
Swain, eds. 2011. *Explorers and Scientists in China's Borderlands, 1880–1950*.
Seattle: University of Washington Press.

Gongshan Agricultural Bureau. 2009. "Gongshan xian nongmin gong waichu
wugong qingkuang" (The situation regarding Gongshan County's migrant
workers). www.ynf.gov.cn/zmb/newsview.aspx?id=854725. Accessed August
30, 2011.

Gongshan Dulongzu Nuzu zizhixian zhi (Annals of the Gongshan Dulong and Nu
Nationalities Autonomous County). 2006. Beijing: Minzu Chubanshe.

Gongshan Education Bureau (GEB). 2006. "Lijing wushi nian jianxin zhujiu
wushi nian huihuang" (Fifty years of hard work sets the foundation for fifty
more brilliant years). Gongshan: Gongshan Jiaoyu Bu.

Gongshan Government Office/Gongshan Bureau of Statistics. 2005. *2005 nian
Gongshan Dulongzu Nuzu zizhixian: Lingdao ganbu jingji gongzuo shouce*
(2005 Gongshan Dulong and Nu Nationalities Autonomous County: Eco-

nomic work handbook for leaders and officials). Gongshan: Gongshan Renmin Zhengfu Bangongshi/Gongshan Tongji Ju.

Gongshan News. 2007. *Gongshan dianshi tai* (Gongshan television station).
Broadcast January 2007.

Gongshan Xian gongmin wenming shouce (Gongshan County Citizens' Civilized
Handbook). 2006.

Goodman, David S. G. 2004. "The Campaign to 'Open Up the West': National,
Provincial-Level and Local Perspectives." *China Quarterly* 178: 317–34.

———, ed. 2008. *The New Rich in China: Future Rulers, Present Lives.* London
and New York: Routledge.

Greenhalgh, Susan, and Edwin A. Winckler. 2005. *Governing China's Population: From Leninist to Neoliberal Biopolitics.* Stanford, CA: Stanford University
Press.

Gros, Stéphane. 1996. "Terres de Confins, Terres de Colonisation. Essai sur les
Marches Sino-Tibétaines du Yunnan à Travers L'implantation de la Mission du
Tibet" (Lands at the fringes, lands of colonization. Essay on the Sino-Tibetan
borderlands of Yunnan through the history of the establishment of the Tibet
Mission). *Péninsule* 33 (2): 147–211.

———. 2001. "Ritual and Politics: Missionary Encounters with Local Culture
in Northwest Yunnan." Conference paper presented at Association for Asian
Studies Annual Meeting, Chicago, March 22–25. http://victoria.linguistlist.
org/~lapolla/rda/acpapers.dir/AASpaper.pdf. Accessed March 25, 2012. Cited
with permission.

Gupta, Akhil. 1995. "Blurred Boundaries: The Discourse of Corruption, the Culture of Politics, and the Imagined State." *American Ethnologist* 22 (2): 375–402.

Hansen, Mette Halskov. 1999. *Lessons in Being Chinese: Minority Education and
Ethnic Identity in Southwest China.* Seattle: University of Washington Press.

Harkness, James. 1998. "Recent Trends in Forestry and Conservation of Biodiversity in China." *China Quarterly* 156: 911–34.

Harrell, Stevan. 1995. "Introduction: Civilizing Projects and the Reaction to
Them." In *Cultural Encounters on China's Ethnic Frontiers,* edited by Stevan
Harrell. Seattle and London: University of Washington Press, 3–36.

———. 2001. *Ways of Being Ethnic in Southwest China.* Seattle and London: University of Washington Press.

———. 2007. "L'état, C'est Nous, or We Have Met the Oppressor and He Is Us:
The Predicament of Minority Cadres in the PRC." In *The Chinese State at the
Borders,* edited by Diana Lary. Toronto: University of British Columbia Press,
221–39.

Heberer, Thomas. 1989. *China and Its National Minorities: Autonomy or Assimilation?* Armonk and London: M. E. Sharpe.

————. 2001. "Nationalities Conflict and Ethnicity in the People's Republic of China, with Special Reference to the Yi in the Liangshan Yi Autonomous Prefecture." In *Perspectives on the Yi of Southwest China,* edited by Stevan Harrell. Berkeley: University of California Press, 214–37.

————. 2007. *Doing Business in Rural China: Liangshan's New Ethnic Entrepreneurs.* Seattle and London: University of Washington Press.

He Daguang. 2006. "Zhonggong Nujiang zhou wei guanyu zhiding Nujiang zhou Guomin Jingji he Shehui Fazhan di Shiyi ge Wu Nian Guihua de jianyi" (The CCP Committee of Nujiang Prefecture sets down Nujiang Prefecture's 11th Five Year Plan for Economic and Social Development). *Nujiang bao* (Nujiang news). January 24. www.nj.yn.gov.cn/nj/72905321797910528/20060124/16084 _1.html. Accessed November 24, 2008.

Henck, Amanda C. 2010. "Spatial and Temporal Patterns of Erosion in Western China and Tibet." PhD diss., University of Washington. http://earthweb.ess .washington.edu/ess-ew/about/sa-ew/gs-phd-dissert/yr.2010/henck_amanda/ henck_amanda_phd-2010.pdf. Accessed May 14, 2011.

Herman, John E. 1997. "Empire in the Southwest: Early Qing Reforms to the Native Chieftain System." *Journal of Asian Studies* 56 (1): 47–74.

————. 2006. "The Cant of Conquest: Tusi Offices and China's Political Incorporation of the Southwest Frontier." In *Empire at the Margins: Culture, Ethnicity, and Frontier in Early Modern China,* edited by Pamela Kyle Crossley, Helen F. Siu, and Donald S. Sutton. Berkeley: University of California Press, 135–68.

He Shizhong. 2007. "Yunnan sheng Nongye Ting gaodu zhongshi Nujiang zhou nongye he nongcun jingji fazhan wenti" (The Yunnan Provincial Agricultural Bureau pays close attention to the challenges to agriculture and rural economic development in Nujiang Prefecture). Zhou Nongye Ju Zhongzhi Ye Ke (Nujiang Prefecture Agricultural Bureau). www.njagri.gov.cn/readinfo.asp?B1 =223. Accessed November 27, 2008.

Hindess, Barry. 2001. "The Liberal Government of Unfreedom." *Alternatives: Global, Local, Political* 26 (2): 93–111.

Ho, Joanne. 2004. "Pockets of Poverty in a Fast-Growing Economy: Quantifying Market Shares in Rural Southwest China." Honors thesis, University of Washington.

Hoang, Cam. 2009. "Forest Thieves? The Politics of Forest Resources in a Northwestern Frontier Valley of Vietnam." PhD diss., University of Washington.

Hobart, Mark. 1993. "Introduction: The Growth of Ignorance?" In *An Anthro-*

pological Critique of Development: The Growth of Ignorance, edited by Mark Hobart. New York and London: Routledge, 1–30.

Hoffman, Lisa. 2006. "Autonomous Choices and Patriotic Professionalism: On Governmentality in Late-Socialist China." *Economy and Society* 35 (4): 550–70.

Information Office of the State Council of the People's Republic of China. 2005. *Government Whitepaper: Regional Autonomy for Ethnic Minorities in China.* Beijing: Information Office of the State Council of the People's Republic of China. www.china.org.cn/e-white/20050301/index.htm. Accessed October 14, 2008.

International Union for Conservation of Nature (IUCN). n.d. *World Heritage Nomination—IUCN Technical Evaluation: Three Parallel Rivers of Yunnan Protected Areas (China) ID No 1083.* http://whc.unesco.org/archive/advisory_body_evaluation/1083.pdf. Accessed December 21, 2007.

Jacka, Tamara. 2009. "Cultivating Citizens: Suzhi (Quality) Discourse in the PRC." *Positions: East Asia Cultures Critique* 17 (3): 523–35.

Jeffreys, Elaine, ed. 2009. *China's Governmentalities: Governing Change, Changing Government.* London and New York: Routledge.

Kaup, Katherine Palmer. 2000. *Creating the Zhuang: Ethnic Politics in China.* Boulder, CO, and London: Lynne Rienner.

Kipnis, Andrew. 2006a. "Suzhi: A Keyword Approach." *China Quarterly* 186: 295–313.

———. 2006b. "School Consolidation in Rural China." *Development Bulletin* 70: 123–25.

———. 2007. "Neoliberalism Reified: *Suzhi* Discourse and Tropes of Neoliberalism in the People's Republic of China." *Journal of the Royal Anthropological Institute (N.S.)* 13: 383–400.

———. 2011. *Governing Educational Desire: Culture, Politics, and Schooling in China.* Chicago: University of Chicago Press.

Lai, Harry Hongyi. 2002. "China's Western Development Program: Its Rationale, Implementation, and Prospects." *Modern China* 28 (4): 432–66.

Lee, James. 1982. "Food Supply and Population Growth in Southwest China, 1250–1850." *Journal of Asian Studies* 41 (4): 711–46.

Lee Ching Kwan. 1998. *Gender and the South China Miracle: Two Worlds of Factory Women.* Berkeley: University of California Press.

Lei Guang. 2001. "Reconstituting the Rural-Urban Divide: Peasant Migration and the Rise of Orderly Migration in Contemporary China." *Journal of Contemporary China* 10 (28): 471–93.

———. 2005. "The State Connection in China's Rural-urban Migration." *International Migration Review* 39 (2): 354–80.

Li, Tania Murray. 2007. *The Will to Improve: Governmentality, Development, and the Practice of Politics.* Durham, NC, and London: Duke University Press.

Li Dezhu. 2003. "Li Dezhu zai Quanguo Di Wu Ci Minzu Jiaoyu Gongzuo Huiyi shang zongjie de jianghua" (Li Dezhu's summary speech at the 5th National Minority Education Work Conference). Zhonghua Renmin Gongheguo Jiaoyu Bu (Ministry of Education of the People's Republic of China). www.moe.edu .cn/edoas/website18/12/info12112.htm. Accessed June 10, 2008.

Lin Yi. 2007. "Ethnicization through Schooling: The Mainstream Discursive Repertoires of Ethnic Minorities." *China Quarterly* 192: 933–48.

Lopoukhine, Nikita, and Ramasamy Jayakumar. 2006. *Report of a Joint Reactive Monitoring Mission to the Three Parallel Rivers of Yunnan Protected Areas, China, from 5 to 15 April 2006.* International Union for Conservation of Nature/ United Nations Educational, Scientific and Cultural Organization. http://whc .unesco.org/archive/2006/mis1083-2006.pdf. Accessed October 25, 2008.

MacFarquhar, Roderick, and Michael Schoenhals. 2006. *Mao's Last Revolution.* Cambridge, MA, and London: Belknap Press of Harvard University Press.

Mackerras, Colin. 1995. *China's Minority Cultures: Identities and Integration since 1912.* New York: St. Martin's Press.

———. 2003. *China's Ethnic Minorities and Globalisation.* New York and London: RoutledgeCurzon.

Magee, Darrin. 2006. "Powershed Politics: Yunnan Hydropower under Great Western Development." *China Quarterly* 185: 23–41.

Mallee, Hein. 2001. "China's New Forest Policies." In *Zhongguo Yunnan sheng Tianran Lin Ziyuan Baohu yu Tui Geng Huan Lin Huan Cao Gongcheng shequ diaoyan baogao* (A community investigation report into the Natural Forest Protection Plan and Sloping Land Conversion Program in Yunnan Province), edited by Zhao Junchen, Xu Jianchu, and Qi Kang. Kunming: Yunnan Keji Chubanshe, 6–12.

Mao Tse-tung. 1966. *Quotations from Chairman Mao Tse-tung.* Peking: Foreign Language Press. The quote cited in chapter 3 of this book was first published in 1958.

McBeath, Gerald A., and Tse-Kang Leng. 2006. *Governance of Biodiversity Conservation in China and Taiwan.* Edward Elgar: Cheltenham and Northampton.

Ministry of Education of the People's Republic of China. 1995. *Education Law of the People's Republic of China.* www.moe.edu.cn/english/laws_e.htm. Accessed July 31, 2008.

———. 2002. "Guowuyuan guanyu shenhua gaige jiakuai fazhan minzu jiaoyu de jueding" (Resolution of deepening reform and speeding up development of nationality education). www.moe.edu.cn/edoas/website18/89/info1089.htm. Accessed June 10, 2008.

Monteil, Amandine, and Benoît Vermander. n.d. "Yi Migrant Workers Survey." Unpublished research article. Cited with permission.

Morgan, Lewis Henry. 1985. *Ancient Society*. Tuscon: University of Arizona Press. Originally published 1877.

Morrison, George Ernest. 2007. *An Australian in China*. Charleston, SC: Biblio-Bazaar. Originally published 1902.

Mosse, David. 2005. *Cultivating Development: An Ethnography of Aid Policy and Practice*. London and Ann Arbor: Pluto Press.

Mueggler, Erik. 2011. *The Paper Road: Archive and Experience in the Botanical Exploration of West China and Tibet*. Berkeley: University of California Press.

Mullaney, Thomas S. 2011. *Coming to Terms with the Nation: Ethnic Classification in Modern China*. Berkeley: University of California Press.

Murphy, Rachel. 2002. *How Migrant Labor Is Changing Rural China*. Cambridge: Cambridge University Press.

———. 2004. "Turning Peasants into Modern Chinese Citizens: 'Population Quality' Discourse, Demographic Transition and Primary Education." *China Quarterly* 177: 1–20.

Murray, Geoffrey, and Ian G. Cook. 2002. *Green China: Seeking Ecological Alternatives*. London and New York: Routledge.

National Bureau of Statistics of China. 2004. *China Statistical Yearbook 2004*. Beijing: China Statistics Press.

National Bureau of Statistics of China Online. 2006. *China Statistical Yearbook 2006*. www.stats.gov.cn/tjsj/ndsj/2006/indexeh.htm. Accessed October 10, 2007.

———. 2009. *China Statistical Yearbook 2009*. www.stats.gov.cn/tjsj/ndsj/2009/indexeh.htm. Accessed April 23, 2011.

———. 2011. *China Statistical Yearbook 2011*. www.stats.gov.cn/tjsj/ndsj/2011/indexeh.htm. Accessed October 8, 2012.

National Compulsory Education Fee Reform Leading Office. n.d. "Gongzuo jieshao" (Work introduction). www.qgbzb.cee.edu.cn/show_news.jsp?id=903. Accessed November 13, 2008.

Naughton, Barry. 2007. *The Chinese Economy: Transitions and Growth*. Cambridge, MA, and London: MIT Press.

Nujiang Lisuzu zizhizhou gaikuang (Nujiang Lisu Nationality Autonomous Prefecture Survey). 1986. Kunming: Yunnan Minzu Chubanshe.

Nujiang News. 2005. "Gongshan xian quanmian jiakuai jiaoyu gaige bu cu fazhan" (Gongshan County fully speeds up educational reform efforts to advance development). November 16. www.nujiang.gov.cn/nj/72340168526266368/2005 1129/6553.html. Accessed March 20, 2008.

Nujiang Prefecture Labor and Social Guarantee Bureau. 2008. "Nujiang zhou Laodong he Shehui Baozhang Ju jiaqiang laowu shuchu cujin nongmin zeng-shou" (Gongshan County Labor and Social Guarantee Bureau—strengthen labor export—accelerate the growth of farmer incomes). www.ynnjl.gov.cn/ readinfo.aspx?B1=1108. Accessed November 27, 2008.

Peterson, Glen. 1994. "State Literacy Ideologies and the Transformation of Rural China." *Australian Journal of Chinese Affairs* 32: 95–120.

Postiglione, Gerard A. 2000. "National Minority Regions: Studying School Discontinuation." In *The Ethnographic Eye: Interpretive Studies of Education in China*, edited by Judith Liu, Heidi A. Ross, and Donald P. Kelly. New York and London: Falmer Press, 51–71.

———. 2006. "Schooling and Inequality in China." In *Education and Social Change in China: Inequality in a Market Economy*, edited by Gerard A. Postiglione. New York: M. E. Sharpe, 3–24.

Pun Ngai. 2005. *Made in China: Women Factory Workers in a Global Workplace.* Durham, NC: Duke University Press; Hong Kong: Hong Kong University Press.

Ridley, Charles P., Paul H. B. Godwin, and Dennis J. Doolin. 1971. *The Making of a Model Citizen in Communist China.* Stanford, CA: Hoover Institution Press.

Rock, Joseph Francis Charles. 1947. *The Ancient Na-Khi Kingdom of Southwest China.* Cambridge, MA: Harvard University Press.

Rose, Archibald, and J. Coggin Brown. 1910. "Lisu (Yawyin) Tribes of the Burma-China Frontier." *Memoirs of the Asiatic Society of Bengal* III (4): 249–77.

Rossi, Benedetta. 2004. "Revisiting Foucauldian Approaches: Power Dynamics in Development Discourse." *Journal of Development Studies* 40 (6): 1–29.

Sachs, Wolfgang, ed. 1992. *The Development Dictionary: A Guide to Knowledge as Power.* London and New Jersey: Zen Books.

Sautman, Barry. 1999. "Expanding Access to Higher Education for China's National Minorities: Policies for Preferential Admissions." In *China's National Minority Education: Culture, Schooling and Development*, edited by Gerard A. Postiglione. New York and London: Falmer Press, 173–210.

Schuster, Brenda L. 2009. "Gaps in the Silk Road: An Analysis of Population Health Disparities in the Xinjiang Uyghur Autonomous Region of China." *China Quarterly* 198: 433–41.

Scott, James C. 1998. *Seeing Like a State: How Certain Schemes to Improve the Human Condition Have Failed.* New Haven, CT, and London: Yale University Press.

Shapiro, Judith. 2001. *Mao's War against Nature: Politics and the Environment in Revolutionary China*. Cambridge: Cambridge University Press.

Shen Shicai, Andreas Wilkes, Qian Jie, Yin Lun, Ren Jian, and Zhang Fudou. 2010. "Agrobiodiversity and Biocultural Heritage in the Dulong Valley, China." *Mountain Research and Development* 30 (3): 205–11.

Sigley, Gary. 1996. "Governing Chinese Bodies: The Significance of Studies in the Concept of Governmentality for the Analysis of Government in China." *Economy and Society* 25 (4): 457–82.

———. 2004. "Liberal Despotism: Population Planning, Subjectivity, and Government in Contemporary China." *Alternatives* 29: 557–75.

———. 2006. "Chinese Governmentalities: Government, Governance and the Socialist Market Economy." *Economy and Society* 35 (4): 487–508.

Sivaramakrishnan, K., and Arun Agrawal. 2003. "Regional Modernities in Stories and Practices of Development." In *Regional Modernities: The Cultural Politics of Development in India*, edited by K. Sivaramakrishnan and Arun Agrawal. New Delhi: Oxford University Press, 1–61.

Smil, Vaclav. 1984. *The Bad Earth: Environmental Degradation in China*. Armonk, NY: M. E. Sharpe.

Solinger, Dorothy J. 1999. *Contesting Citizenship in Urban China: Peasant Migrants, the State, and the Logic of the Market*. Berkeley: University of California Press.

Stalin, Joseph. 1940. *Dialectical and Historical Materialism*. New York: International Publishers.

Sun Changmin. 2000. "The Floating Population and Internal Migration in China." In *The Changing Population of China*, edited by Peng Xizhe and Guo Zhigang. Oxford: Blackwell Publishers, 179–91.

Sun Hongkai and Liu Guangkun. 2009. *A Grammar of Anong: Language Death under Intense Contact*. Translated, annotated, and supplemented by Li Fengxiang, Ela Thurgood, and Graham Thurgood. Leiden: Brill. Originally published in Chinese in 2005.

Teng Xing and Wang Jun, eds. 2001. *20 shiji Zhongguo shaoshu minzu yu jiaoyu: Lilun, zhengce yu shijian* (Chinese ethnic minorities and education in the twentieth century: Theory, policy and practice). Beijing: Minzu Chubanshe.

Thøgersen, Stig. 2002. *A County of Culture: Twentieth-Century China Seen from the Village Schools of Zouping, Shandong*. Ann Arbor: University of Michigan Press.

Trac, Christine Jane, Stevan Harrell, Thomas M. Hinckley, and Amanda C. Henck. 2007. "Reforestation Programs in Southwest China: Reported Success,

Observed Failure, and the Reasons Why." *Journal of Mountain Science* 4 (4): 275–92.

Uchida, Emi, Xu Jintao, and Scott Rozelle. 2005. "Grain for Green: Cost-Effectiveness and Sustainability of China's Conservation Set-Aside Program." *Land Economics* 81 (2): 247–64.

United Nations Educational, Scientific and Cultural Organization (UNESCO). 2007. "World Heritage." http://whc.unesco.org/en/about/. Accessed December 6, 2007.

United Nations Environment Programme/World Conservation Monitoring Centre (UNEP/WCMC). 2003. "Parallel Rivers of Yunnan Protected Areas." *Protected Areas and World Heritage.* www.unep-wcmc.org/sites/wh/Three_Parallel.html. Accessed October 26, 2008.

Wang Rong. 2008. "Reform of the Rural Compulsory Education Assured Funding Mechanism: Policy Design Perspective." *Chinese Education and Society* 41 (1): 9–16.

Wang Ying, Liu Liu, Gu Yunwei, and Cheng Qiping. 2006. "Pinkun Nujiang shengtai zainan de genyuan" (The reasons behind impoverished Nujiang's environmental catastrophe). *Yunnan ribao wang* (Yunnan daily online). January 13. www.yndaily.com/html/20060113/news_88_851627.html. Accessed December 11, 2007.

Ward, F. Kingdon. 1923. "From the Yangtze to the Irrawaddy." *Geographical Journal* 62 (1): 6–18.

————. 1986. *Mystery Rivers of Tibet.* London: Cadogan Books. Originally published 1923.

Watts, Jonathan. 2010. *When a Billion Chinese Jump: How China Will Save Mankind—Or Destroy It.* London: Faber and Faber.

Weber, Eugen. 2007. *Peasants into Frenchmen: The Modernization of Rural France, 1870–1914.* Stanford, CA: Stanford University Press. Originally published 1976.

Weyerhaeuser, Horst, Andreas Wilkes, and Fredrich Kahrl. 2005. "Local Impacts and Responses to Regional Forest Conservation and Rehabilitation Programs in China's Northwest Yunnan Province." *Agricultural Systems* 85: 234–53.

Wiens, Herold J. 1967. *Han Chinese Expansion in South China.* Hamden: Shoe String Press. Originally published 1954 under the title *China's March Toward the Tropics.*

Wilkes, Andreas. 2000. "Environmental Ideologies: Ways of Talking about Nature & People in Gongshan County, Nujiang, China." In *Links between Culture and Biodiversity—Proceedings of the Cultures and Biodiversity Congress, Kunming 2000,* edited by Xu Jianchu. Kunming: Yunnan Science and Technology Press, 41–50.

————. 2005a. "Center for Biodiversity and Indigenous Knowledge Community Livelihoods Program Working Paper 12: Forest Resource Governance in an Agro-Pastoralist Community in Northwest Yunnan: 'Institutional Bricolage' as a Way of Understanding the Role of Village Autonomy in Resource Management." Kunming: Center for Biodiversity and Indigenous Knowledge.

————. 2005b. "Ethnic Minorities, Environment and Development in Yunnan: The Institutional Contexts of Biocultural Knowledge Production in Southwest China." PhD diss., University of Kent at Canterbury.

Wilkes, Andreas, and Shen Shicai. 2007. "Is Biocultural Heritage a Right? A Tale of Conflicting Conservation, Development, and Biocultural Priorities in Dulongjiang, China." *Policy Matters* 15: 76–83. http://cmsdata.iucn.org/down loads/pm15_section_2.pdf. Accessed December 16, 2012.

Wilkes, Andreas, and Yang Xuefei. 2000a. "'Zala' she: Cunmin zenme he ziran ziyuan shenghuo zai yiqi (xie gei 'Zala' cunmin de yi fen baogao)" ("Zala" community: How do villagers and natural resources coexist? [A report for the villagers of "Zala"]). Cited with permission.

————. 2000b. "'Zala' zirancun shengwu duoyang xing yingxiang yinsu fenxi zuizhong baogao" (Final report on the analysis of factors affecting biodiversity in "Zala" natural village). Cited with permission.

World Bank. 2009. *From Poor Areas to Poor People: China's Evolving Poverty Reduction Agenda—An Assessment of Poverty and Inequality in China.* Vol. 1. Beijing: World Bank. www.worldbank.org/research/2009/03/10444409/china-poor-areas-poor-people-chinas-evolving-poverty-reduction-agenda-assess ment-poverty-inequality-china-vol-1-2-main-report. Accessed October 10, 2011.

Wu Meng and Wang Liang. 1995. *Xiaoxuesheng guoqing shi zhidao* (The ten things primary school children should know about national conditions). Yunnan: Zhongguo Shaonian Ertong Chubanshe.

Xiao Jianwen. 2005. "Yunnan sheng Shengwu Duoyang Xing yu Chuantong Zhi-shi Yanjiu Hui: Shequ Shengji Bu Yanjiu Baogao 24—Dulongjiang Tui Geng Huan Lin dui nongye shengwu duoyang xing de yingxiang: Chubu diaocha jieguo" (Center for Biodiversity and Indigenous Knowledge: Community Livelihood Report 24—Preliminary survey of the impact of the Sloped Land Conversion on agro-biodiversity in Dulongjiang town). www.cbik.ac.cn/Files/DownLoad/CBIKWP24CHIN.pdf. Accessed December 20, 2007.

Xinhuanet. 2006. "Gongshan linye cangsang jubian wushi nian—Gongshan Dulongzu Nuzu zizhixian linye shiye 50 nian huihang chengjiu" (50 years of dramatic forestry change in Gongshan—Gongshan Dulong and Nu Nation-alities Autonomous County's 50 years of brilliant achievements in forestry).

September 26. www.yn.xinhuanet.com/live/2006-09/26/content_8136820 .htm. Accessed December 10, 2007.

Xinhua News Agency. 2011. "China's 'Floating Population' Exceeds 221 Mln." March 1. www.china.org.cn/china/2011-03/01/content_22025827.htm. Accessed October 22, 2011.

Xue Lan Rong and Shi Tianjian. 2001. "Inequality in Chinese Education." *Journal of Contemporary China* 10 (26): 107–24.

Xue Ye and Wang Yongchen. 2007. "Highly Controversial Hydropower Development in Western China." In *The China Environment Yearbook (2005): Crisis and Breakthrough of China's Environment*, edited by Liang Congjie and Yang Dongping. Leiden and Boston: Brill, 63–88.

Xu Jialu. 2006. "Xu Jialu: Yiwu jiaoyu jinru mianfei shidai" (Xu Jialu: compulsory education enters a free of charge era). Interview, CCTV.com. *Juece zhe shuo* (Policymakers speak). http://news.cctv.com/education/20060811/104987. shtml. Accessed November 13, 2008.

Xu Jianchu and David R. Melick. 2007. "Rethinking the Effectiveness of Public Protected Areas in Southwestern China." *Conservation Biology* 21 (2): 318–28.

Xu Jianchu and Andreas Wilkes. 2004. "Biodiversity Impact Analysis in Northwest Yunnan, Southwest China." *Biodiversity and Conservation* 13 (5): 959–83.

Xu Zhigang, M. T. Bennet, Ran Tao, and Xu Jintao. 2004. "China's Sloping Land Conversion Programme Four Years On: Current Situation and Pending Issues." *International Forestry Review* 6 (3–4): 317–26.

Yang Dongping. 2007. "China's Environmental Protection at the Crossroads." In *The China Environment Yearbook (2005): Crisis and Breakthrough of China's Environment*, edited by Liang Congjie and Yang Dongping. Leiden and Boston: Brill, xxi–lix.

Yang Yuhua. 2006. "Laowu shuchu chengwei wo zhou nongmin zengshou de xin liangdian" (Labor export becomes a bright new platform for increasing the income of the prefecture's rural population). *Nujiang bao* (Nujiang news). October 26. www.nujiang.gov.cn/nj/72340168526266368/20061026/77616 .html. Accessed March 17, 2008.

———. 2007. "Puladi xiang laowu shuchu gongzuo chengxiao tuchu" (Puladi township's labor export work results break through). *Nujiang bao* (Nujiang news). April 2. www.nujiang.gov.cn/nj/72340168526266368/20070402/116371. html. Accessed March 17, 2008.

Yang Yunhui. 2007. "Dulong cun de 'pu jiu' zhi lu: Jiaoyu zenyang fuchi dou buguo fen" (The path toward "nine-year compulsory education" in Dulongjiang: There can never be too much support for education). *Zhongguo jiaoyu*

bao (China education news). July 9. www.edu.cn/ji_jiao_news_279/20070709/
t20070709_241828.shtml. Accessed April 16, 2008.

Yan Hairong. 2003a. "Neoliberal Governmentality and Neohumanism: Organizing Suzhi/Value Flow through Labor Recruitment Networks." *Cultural
Anthropology* 18 (4): 493–523.

———. 2003b. "Spectralization of the Rural: Reinterpreting the Labor Mobility of Rural Young Women in Post-Mao China." *American Ethnologist* 30 (4):
578–96.

Yardley, Jim. 2004. "Dam Building Threatens China's 'Grand Canyon.'" *New York
Times*. March 10. www.nytimes.com/2004/03/10/international/asia/10RIVE
.html. Accessed February 12, 2005.

Yeh, Emily T. 2000. "Forest Claims, Conflicts and Commodification: The Political Ecology of Tibetan Mushroom-Harvesting Villages in Yunnan Province,
China." *China Quarterly* 161: 264–78.

Yunnan Daily Online. 2007. "Gongshan Dulongzu Nuzu zizhixian Xianwei Shuji
Zhu Yuhua: Baohu huanjing cu ke chixu fazhan" (Gongshan Dulong and Nu
Nationalities Autonomous County Party Secretary Zhu Yuhua: Protect the
environment to sustain development). January 23. www.yndaily.com/html/
20070123/news_92_173665.html. Accessed December 10, 2007.

Yunnan Representative Office of the China Work-Study Agency. n.d. *Gongxue
fupin xingdong* (Work-study poverty alleviation program). Kunming: Zhongguo Gongxue She Yunnan Daibiao Chu.

Zhang Huijun, Chen Tiejun, and He Runpei. 1997. *Nujiang xiagu jingji* (The
Nujiang gorge economy). Kunming: Yunnan Renmin Chubanshe.

Zhang Peichang, Shao Guofan, Zhao Guang, Dennis C. Le Master, George R.
Parker, John B. Dunning Jr., and Li Qinglin. 2000. "China's Forest Policy for
the 21st Century." *Science* 288 (5474): 2135–36.

Zhang Tiedao and Zhao Minxia. 2006. "Universalizing Nine-Year Compulsory
Education for Poverty Reduction in Rural China." *International Review of
Education* 52: 261–86.

Zhao Dayong. 2008. *Ghost Town.* Hong Kong: Lantern Films.

INDEX

communication infrastructure,
168–69
compulsory education for rural
China, free nine-year *(puji jiunian
yiwu jiaoyu),* 121–23
Compulsory Education Law of 1986,
115–16
compulsory education policy in
Gongshan, free nine-year:
implementation and enforcement
of, 110–11, 141–56
Confucianism, 112
Confucius, 112
conservation and economic growth,
development dilemma of balancing, 74–77
conservation programs, 26–27, 72–73;
impact in Nujiang and Gongshan,
80–86. *See also* Gaoligongshan
National-Level Nature Reserve;
Natural Forest Protection
Program; Sloping Land Conversion Program
consolidation of schools. *See* school
structure and its consolidation
Cultural Revolution, 32, 33, 115,
193n16, 198n2

dams, 13, 44, 74, 81–85, 108–9, 161
deforestation, 75, 78. *See also* logging
Deng Xiaoping, 20
Derung. *See* Dulong (Drung/Derung)
people
development, 19; scientific concept
of, 22. *See also* modernity and
development
development agendas, 6–7; objective
of, 6
development dilemma of balancing

conservation and economic
growth, 74–77. *See also* conservation programs
developmental state, Chinese, 19–23;
China as "developing," vii–viii;
"Open Up the West" and "Build
a New Socialist Countryside"
campaigns/policies, 24–26, 76, 122,
186; unequal development, 23–24.
See also conservation programs;
ethnic minorities
dietary practices, 96, 131
disembedded/disembedding, 17, 70,
187
donggua shu, 92, 102f
Dongguan, 5, 159, 160
Drung. *See* Dulong (Drung/Derung)
people
Dulong (Drung/Derung) people, 4,
29, 56, 60, 118–19; attitudes toward
and characterizations of, 62, 71;
class divisions, 60, 156; dietary
practices, 96; education, 143,
144, 172–73; religious rituals, 96;
slavery and, 53, 55; Tibet and, 53, 55
Dulongjiang: agriculture and labor
market, 4–5, 94–97, 145, 159, 160,
174; demographics, 4–5; development, 32; economics, 3, 57, 65,
95, 96, 145, 160, 173; geography,
48, 49f, 51, 52f, 56; overview, 4;
SLCP and, 94–97; Tibet and, 55;
transportation, vii, 3, 4, 51, 52f, 159,
160 *(see also* Dulongjiang Road)
Dulongjiang Road, 4, 4f, 33, 52f, 87,
159, 169

ecological forests, 79; defined, 79
economic forests, 79, 92; defined, 79

economically marginalized communities, the mobile population's
impacts on, 179; increased
competition for locals, 179–80;
new opportunities for the right
skills and resources, 180–82
education, 99–100, 105, 106, 157–58,
168; and China in historical
context, 112–13; ethnic minority,
116–18; history of education in
Gongshan, 118–21; "population
quality" and, 110, 112, 115, 122,
134, 138, 144, 161, 172; during
reform era, 115–16, 157–58. *See also*
illiteracy: efforts to eliminate;
school dropouts
education reform, 110–11; hidden
curricula, 134, 136–38, 141; special
nationality classes and, 156–57;
Two Basics, 115, 121–23. *See also*
compulsory education policy
in Gongshan; education; school
structure and its consolidation
education system under CCP rule, 110,
111, 113–15
electricity, 90, 98, 128. *See also*
hydroelectricity
Enlightenment, 15–16
Environmental Impact Assessment, 82
environmental protection. *See*
conservation and economic
growth; conservation programs
Ethnic Classification Project (Minzu
Shibie), 30–31
ethnic diversity, 9
ethnic minorities: "population
quality" of, 23, 43, 64, 112, 164, 173,
175, 188
ethnic minorities *(shaoshu minzu)*,

11, 12; assimilation of, 32;
contemporary representations of,
35; defined, 28–29; development
and, 27–32 (*see also* integration
of ethnic minorities); education,
116–18; stereotypes, characterizations, and attitudes toward, 62,
71, 172, 199n14. *See also* Han
migration and "colonization";
specific topics
ethnic minority regions: autonomy,
affirmative action, and economic
development of, 32–35

farmers' markets. *See* markets, local
Fei Xiaotong, 43–45
fixed labor system, 162, 163
forest reserves, 27. *See also* nature
reserves
forests, 75; ecological, 79; economic,
79, 92. *See also* logging; nontimber
forest products; Sloping Land
Conversion Program
Forrest, George, 55, 194n1
Foucault, Michel, 16–17, 187. *See also*
governmentality
Fugong County, 8f, 48, 54–57, 67, 89,
143, 169, 200n1

gaige kaifang (era of "reform and
opening up"). *See* reform era
Gao Yingxin, 65–68
Gaoligongshan National-Level Nature
Reserve (Gaoligongshan Guojia
Ji Ziran Baohu Qu), 9, 11, 72–74,
83–87
Giddens, Anthony, 17, 187
*Gongshan County Citizens' Civilized
Handbook,* 62

114–15, 117, 120, 121, 123, 170–71,
173f, 198n4
illiteracy rates, 9, 37, 113, 116, 117, 120,
156, 168, 169, 198nn4-5
infant mortality, 36
integration of ethnic minorities, 26,
27, 34, 46, 70. *See also* Chinese
Communist Party: strategies to
integrate ethnic minorities into
Chinese Party-state and industrial
economy; education; ethnic
minorities; Han migration and
"colonization"; migration for work
International Union for Conservation
of Nature (IUCN), 83–85

Jiang Zemin, 25
Jie Yi, 81

labor export programs, 5, 169–74, 171f
labor market, 163. *See also* Dulongjiang: agriculture and labor market;
migration for work
labor system, fixed, 162, 163
law on nine-year compulsory education. *See* Compulsory Education
Law of 1986
life expectancy, 36–37
Lisu language, 154
Lisu people, 9, 53–54, 56–57, 98,
118–19. *See also* Gongshan High
School: dropouts from
literacy. *See* illiteracy
Litton, G., 55
logging, 74, 78, 100, 104–7
logging ban, 77–78, 87, 98, 100, 101,
105, 179. *See also* Zala hamlet

Manzi Primary School, 125–26

Mao Zedong, 113–15, 192–93n16
Maoist period, 20, 32–33, 75. *See also*
Cultural Revolution
market economy, 18–21, 26, 75, 86, 93,
124, 160; Gongshan and, 6, 11–12,
34, 37, 42, 47, 60, 70, 190; labor
export programs and, 171–72;
Nujiang and, 69; transition from
socialist command economy
to, 111, 157. *See also* Chinese
Communist Party: strategies to
integrate ethnic minorities into
Chinese Party-state and industrial
economy; migration for work
markets, local, 179–80
Menke hamlet, 120, 121
Menke people, 185–87
migrant-sending areas, impacts of
rural-to-urban migration on,
165–66
migrants, China's rural, 161–66, 181f
migration for work, outward, 65,
159–61; in Gongshan, 70, 72,
166–76, 182–83; the mobile population and its impacts on economically marginalized communities,
179–82; new gateways, 168–75; old
barriers, 166–68; stories behind,
175–79. *See also* labor export
programs; migrants
minzu, 28–29, 31. *See also* ethnic
minorities
missionaries, 58–59
mobile population, 162, 165, 198n1;
impacts on economically marginalized communities, 179–82. *See
also* migrants
modernity: experience of, 5–6; history
and meanings of the term, 15–16,

reform era *(gaige kaifang)*, 5, 191n2.
See also education: during reform
era
religion, 58–59, 96, 112
Rose, Archibald, 41

Safe Path (Pingan Lu) project, 185–86
Salween River. *See* Nu River
satellite television, 140f, 141
school dropouts: campaign to
return, 150–51; from Gongshan
High School, 145–56; reasons for
dropping out, 143–45, 149–50;
special vocational schools for, 142,
152–56. *See also* vocational schools
for dropouts
school structure and its consolidation,
123–27; problems associated with
consolidation, 129–34; reasons
for the consolidation, 127–29;
and student care, 130–34. *See also*
education reform
schooling: transition to, 129–30. *See
also* education
Shanghai, 138
Shenzhen, 138
Shi Lishan, 81–82
slavery, 53, 54
Sloping Land Conversion Program
(SLCP), 27, 79–80; Dulongjiang
and, 94–97; in Gongshan, 47,
92–108
socioeconomic inequality. *See*
developmental state; economically marginalized communities;
ethnic minorities; Han migration
and "colonization": and inequality
between ethnic minorities and
Han

Stalin, Joseph, 20
suzhi (quality), 22–23; defined, 22,
193n18; raising, 153, 161, 164. *See
also* "human quality"; "population
quality"

Talaka hamlet, 97–104, 99f; households, 104–8
taxation, 54, 57
teachers, 120. *See also* education;
school dropouts; school structure
and its consolidation
television, satellite, 140f, 141
*Ten Things Primary School Children
Should Know about National
Conditions, The* (Wu and Wang),
137, 137f
Three Parallel Rivers UNESCO World
Heritage Area, 51–52, 83–85
Tibet, 42, 48, 53–55, 57; Dulong
and, 53, 55; Gongshan and,
53, 55; government control
and surveillance of, 24; Han
population in, 25, 36; "Open
Up the West" and "Build a New
Socialist Countryside" campaigns/
policies and, 24, 25; Qinghai-Tibet
railway, 25, 33; railway in, 33; and
social and economic integration,
24–26
Tibet Mission, 58–59
transport infrastructure, 168–69
tusi (native officials), 45, 46, 53, 54,
58–60, 195n7
Two Basics. *See* education reform

UNESCO (United Nations Educational, Scientific and Cultural
Organization), 51–52, 83–85